A HISTORY OF MONTANA IN 101 PLACES

A HISTORY OF MONTANA IN 101 PLACES

Sites and Stories from the MONTANA HISTORICAL SOCIETY

ELLEN BAUMLER, CHRISTINE BROWN,
MARTHA KOHL, AND KIRBY LAMBERT
PHOTOGRAPHS BY TOM FERRIS

MONTANA HISTORICAL SOCIETY PRESS
HELENA

Front cover photograph: Tom Ferris

All photographs by Tom Ferris except where noted

Cover and book design by Luke Duran

Printed in Canada.

Distributed by Farcountry Press, 2750 Broadwater Avenue, Helena, MT 59602

(800) 821-3874

ISBN 978-0-9721522-0-4 (paper)
ISBN 978-1-7370960-9-2 (hardcover)

Library of Congress Cataloging-in-Publication Data available on request

This book was made possible
in part by generous financial support
from the Pomeroy Foundation.

This book is dedicated to the memory of
Ellen Baumler (1949–2023),
whose spirit lives on in the stories
she told and the places she loved.

CONTENTS

Sweet Grass Hills
Simpson
Bank
Shelby
Chester
Havre
Chinook
Harlem
Box Elder
Malta
Bears Paw Mtns.
Glasgow
Fort Benton
Great Falls
Upper Missouri River Breaks NM
Belt
Roy
Stanford
Jordan
Lewistown
Winnett
Moore
M O N T A N A
White Sulphur Springs
Harlowton
Sumatra
Townsend
Roundup
Ryegate
Hysham
Pompeys Pillar NM
Manhattan
Belgrade
Big Timber
Billings
Colstrip
Bozeman
Livingston
Laurel
Columbus
Hardin
Pictograph Cave NHL
Chief Plenty Coups NHL
Little Bighorn Battlefield
Granite Peak 12799 (3901)
Red Lodge
Bridger
Gardiner
Silver Gate

AUTHOR'S NOTE

By Christine Brown

Following the release and popularity of the book *A History of Montana in 101 Objects* in 2020, I began recruiting authors to start work on the next volume. I loved the way the *Objects* book made Montana history so accessible and relevant through the varied stories found in the Montana Historical Society's (MTHS) museum collections. But as much as I loved that volume, I wanted to explore more and share how Montana's historic places provide a vivid, sometimes even more tangible, connection to history. Luckily, my colleagues Kirby Lambert and Martha Kohl and recently retired MTHS historian Ellen Baumler agreed to the challenge.

Kirby's thirty-five years of experience as a historian, author, and historic-photo wrangler and Ellen's, Martha's, and my seventy-plus years of combined experience researching and writing about historic Montana places proved invaluable. Martha and Ellen alone had written thousands of stories about historic sites for the MTHS's National Register of Historic Places sign program. The sign texts provided a starting point for the many essays in the book and helped us craft our first far-too-large list of sites, which initially included 250 of our favorite places.

To cut that roster by more than half, we first limited our choices to those properties that were already listed, determined eligible, or eminently eligible for listing in the National Register of Historic Places, which typically requires a property to be at least fifty years old. We made a few exceptions in our last chapter, which covers the period from 1946 to the present, because we wanted to include properties that reflected more recent developments.

We further winnowed the list by limiting the number of places in one geographical region. From there, we kept or eliminated sites by thinking thematically. We wanted to include those places that represent broad patterns of human occupation from ancient

Residents and employees of the Montana State Orphanage in Twin Bridges posed for this uncredited 1896 photograph outside of the "the Castle," the facility's first dormitory. The orphanage, which opened in 1895 and operated until the mid-1970s, was one of the many storied places that the authors were unable to fit into the book.
951-328, MTHS PHOTOGRAPH ARCHIVES

times to the present. Within those boundaries, we narrowed our choices to include examples of sites influenced by industry, government, architectural style, cultural traditions, building methods and materials, technological change, and economic shifts.

Even with those criteria in mind, we still exceeded our target of 101 places. So that several significant sites could remain, readers will notice that we slyly created group essays that include three to five places, each of which represents a certain type of place (for instance, churches or houses). Even then, we had to make hard choices. Which Indigenous places? Which Lewis and Clark sites? Through it all, we kept in mind that while so much of Montana's past is worth celebrating, other aspects of it are truly tragic; and in many cases it is the buried story, not its present-day appearance, that makes a site noteworthy.

Some folks will be disappointed that their favorite historic Montana site isn't in the book. We're disappointed too, but we hope that our work will pique your interest in Montana's historic places and the stories they can tell. We also hope we have spurred others to craft National Register nominations, pursue preservation projects, and visit the remarkable history in our backyard.

ACKNOWLEDGMENTS

The authors wish to express their heartfelt gratitude to the countless individuals and organizations, past and present, that have played a role in preserving Montana's historic places—both the ones included in this book and the untold others that could have been. For invaluable assistance provided in this endeavor, the authors are indebted to:

Tom Ferris for traveling the entire state, hiking miles in the rain, bushwhacking, and getting up before dawn

Pete Brown, John Boughton, Jessica Bush, and Kate Hampton of the Montana State Historic Preservation Office

Patricia Davis, Heather Hultman, and Jeff Malcomson with the MTHS Photograph Archives

Aaron Rau and Kendra Newhall of the MTHS Museum

Jeff Bartos, Diana Di Stefano, editor Cody Ewert, and designer Luke Duran of the MTHS Publications Program

Proofreader Ann Seifert and indexer Fred Brown

MTHS Interns Natalie Bahou, Jules Boughton, and Ella Rowland

Steve Aaberg, Rich Aarstad, Jon Axline, Whisper Camel-Means, Daniel Gardiner, Dick Gibson, Troy Hallsell, Melissa Hibbard, Colleen Hill, Rebecca Kohl, Kevin Kooistra, Steve Lozar, Laura Marsh, Dale Martin, members of the MTHS Tribal Stakeholder Group, Mary Murphy, Fred Quivik, and Lori Smoker, subject matter experts who generously contributed their knowledge

Butte-Silver Bow Archives; Cascade County Historical Society, Great Falls; Gates of the Mountains Boat Tours, Helena; and the Western Heritage Center, Billings

Tony Bynum, Craig Davidson, Cheryl Hill, Judy Hoy, David Richards, Scott Smoker, and Geoff Wyatt for additional photography

GLOSSARY OF TRIBAL NAMES

Throughout this book, we use the names that Indigenous nations call themselves rather than the names by which the US government and most non-tribal members have historically known them. Note that there are multiple ways to spell the names that Montana's tribal nations call themselves. One reason for this variation is the multiple ways non-Indian explorers, historians, government officials, and others have documented tribal names. Tribes have also maintained their histories and cultures orally, instead of in writing. We have chosen spellings recommended to us by members of the Montana Historical Society's Tribal Stakeholder Group (TSG), all of whom were appointed by their various tribal councils. For those tribal nations outside of Montana, who don't have representatives on the TSG, we have used the spellings listed on their tribal government websites.

Below is a list of tribal names in the nation's own language, the common name, and a pronunciation guide that uses the following symbols.

A as in father: *ah*
A as in day: *ay*
E as in she: *ee*
E as in bed: *eh*
I as in in: *ill*
I as in ice: *ai*
O as in no: *oh*
Oo as in you: *oo*
U as in up: *uh*

To hear native speakers pronounce many of these names, visit **MontanaTribes.Org**

Name the Nation Calls Itself	Common Name	Pronunciation
Aaniiihnen	Gros Ventre/White Clay	Ah-ah-nee-nin
Anishinaabe	Chippewa or Ojibwe	N-ishn-ah-beh
Apsáalooke	Crow	Ahp-sah-loo-guh
Dakota	Sioux (part of the Oceti Sakowin Confederacy)	Dah-koh-tah
Diné	Navaho/Navajo	Dee-nay
Haudenosaunee	Iroquois	Hoh-den-uh-shoh-nee
Hinono'ei	Arapaho	Ahn-nah-neh-nay
Hiráaca	Hidatsa	Hee-rah-ts-a
Ksanka	Kootenai (band in Montana)	K-sahn-kah
Ktunaxa	Kootenai (entire group)	K-tuh-nah-hah
Lakota	Sioux (part of the Oceti Sakowin Confederacy)	Lah-koh-tah
Métis	Métis	May-tee
Nakoda	Assiniboine	Nah-koh-dah
Newe	Shoshone and Bannock	Neh-way
Neyiowahk	Cree	Neh-hehn-oh-wahg
Nimiipuu	Nez Perce	Nee-mee-poo
Niitsiitopii	Blackfeet	Nee-see-toh-pee
Piikuni	Southern Piegan/Blackfeet	Pee-kuh-nee
Ql̓ispé	Pend d'Oreille	Kah-lee-speh
Sahnish	Arikara	Sah-neesh
Séliš	Salish	Selish
Tsétsėhéstȧhese naa Suhtaio	Northern Cheyenne	Tsi-tsi-sahs nah Suh-tai-yoh

While visiting his uncle near the Bear Paw Mountains, Pete Brown found that this rickety windmill was perfect for risk-taking and a photo op. He also found that the state's landscapes and historic buildings made the past tangible and relevant. COURTESY OF MIKE LEY

INTRODUCTION: NOT JUST STORIES

By Pete Brown, Montana State Historic Preservation Officer

My introduction to Montana's historic places came as an eighteen-year-old in 1990, when I traveled to visit my uncle, Mike Ley, who had moved from Indiana to the Bear Paw Mountains—known as the Bears Paw Mountains on maps, but not by locals—in the mid-1970s. He came first as a Catholic volunteer at Fort Belknap Indian Reservation, where he coached basketball, drove the school bus, and was known for cobbling together a two-person snow sled using a discarded loveseat bolted to an overturned car hood that he pulled with a chain mounted to his pickup. When St. Mary's at Rocky Boy Indian Reservation needed a new church, Mike moved there to help cut trees and used his construction background to serve as crew leader for the log-built church. He ultimately went to seminary school and became a priest, spending time in Rocky Boy, Big Sandy, and Lewistown.

While most people might cross paths with the parish priest on Sundays, Mike integrated with the community through hunting. A priest as outgoing as he was never had to ask twice for access to a parishioner's land, and he had an open invitation to join hunting parties at Rocky Boy and Fort Belknap. Mike was highly regarded by these folks and welcomed into their homes, invited to cattle brandings, sweat lodge ceremonies, and the Sun Dance. His connections opened some real doors during my visit.

As the lone member of our family who had ventured to the West, away from the evermore densely developed—"toxic," as he called it—East, Mike was eager to give his teenage nephew the grand tour of this corner of Montana where, relative to most everywhere else in the late twentieth-century United States, change came slowly.

As a teenager, my world was one of cable TV, convenience stores, skateboarding, and the social politics of high school. My mom was a secretary and my dad a salesman for the Dixie corporation. Like many suburbanites, my family's culture was rooted in the moment and had little to do with a historic connection to people and place. We had a few passed-down family stories, but nothing that informed my sense of purpose or identity. I know more about Benjamin Franklin than I do about my ancestors. My people arrived in the United States from across Europe, assimilated into the new country, and rode the general patterns of the last two hundred years, from agrarian and rural lives, to industrial and urban, to white collar and suburban. The family farm, with its walnut tree-lined lane has long been a parking lot, and I haven't lived within 150 miles of it since 1976.

In the heyday of malls and highway bypasses circumventing downtowns, historic commercial districts across the country were disenfranchised and bore the desperate look of fading midcentury façade makeovers. The historic places I was most likely to experience were compartmentalized attractions, living history encounters with guys in tricorne hats shooting blanks, old-time main street reconstructions in the museum basement, or a pioneer's cabin relocated to the town park. These places all presented discrete slices of community history, as if history had no throughline to the present.

Thus, when I boarded a plane for Great Falls, I was dwelling on the one thing everyone knows about Montana: its big sky. I certainly wasn't thinking about homesteading's legacy, colonization, or enduring Native American traditions. Leave it to Uncle Mike to throw the tourism brochure out the window. No brochure would lead a visitor to where we were going.

Now there's reenacted "living history" in a museum sense and then there's living history, which is what Uncle Mike showed me. An early stop on our adventure was the Osterman Ranch, thirty miles south of Big Sandy. Herman and Elizabeth Osterman proved up on their Eagle Creek homestead in 1899, the year their first son Henry was born. To cultivate the semiarid land and support their sheep, the Ostermans dug ditches to divert the creek as it wound south from the Bear Paws to the Missouri River. Changes came over the century, but like introducing ditches, they made choices that allowed them to support the ranch and the family.

Ninety-one years later, Uncle Mike and I sat with Henry in the log house where he was born. We peppered the wool-clad Montana archetype with questions about life on Eagle Creek over the last century. He appreciated the rarity of his audience as much as we appreciated his tales. He regaled us with stories about surviving yellow fever, dowsing for ground water, and sharing his telephone, the area's first, with neighbors. Pointing to jars on a shelf, he underscored his claims of his good marksmanship and a lifelong battle against rattlesnakes. Each of the multiple jars was loaded with rattles. "Take one," he said, smiling at me, and I did.

Heading south from the Osterman Ranch, past golden rolls of hay in stubble fields, we crossed the Missouri at Stafford Ferry, a barge tethered to a cable that was run by a tractor engine. We passed an oncoming truck near Lone Tree Bench. We exchanged waves to its driver, entered his cloud of dust, and he ours. Uncle Mike shouted to me over the road noise, "Lone Tree Bench, where do you think Osterman got his logs to build that house? Had to be the Bear Paws, and they're twenty miles away." Bombing down the dirt road in relative comfort, knowing there was lunch in Winifred, I imagined the Ostermans carving out their place in a world where the weather and topography set the terms. It must have been better than what they left in Germany, or a case of keep going or starve, or both. Skidding all those logs . . . and the rattlesnakes.

The next day, after hiking up Mount Baldy in the Bear Paws, experiencing the stark quiet of a windless day above tree line, we grilled venison and planned an antelope hunt with Mike's old Fort Belknap friend Matt. Without a hunting license or experience, I was along for the ride. Within an hour, and without breaking a sweat, Uncle Mike and Matt each fired single shots, dropped two antelopes, and showed me how to gut the still-warm carcasses. Game hunting to put food on the table made sense to me, but I had no frame of reference for what Matt was doing when he placed two fresh Marlboros on the gut piles and paused in reflection.

Cigarettes were the absolute boogeyman in my family, emblems of teen degeneracy and the cause of tar-clogged lungs in old age. "Cigarettes?" I said involuntarily, and Matt smiled at the novelty of my question. Many Native peoples, he explained, considered tobacco sacred and tradition required that you leave an offering when you take something. It never occurred to me that tobacco could grow in Montana and was sacred, not profane. Matt's grateful, tangible gesture had no parallel to giving thanks in my world. It was integral to his hunt—equal to the tools he used to obtain meat and so unlike the reflexive thank yous I uttered every day.

On the moonless drive home, Uncle Mike's stories made up for the absence of visuals. "An old-timer once told me how much the lightbulb changed their lives." he said. "People stayed up later and socialized more. Just flip a switch and it's on, no fuel." He then told me about the importance that stories of all kinds have for Native people—practical, spiritual, humorous—and how he once traded a truckload of firewood for a story from an old-

Although Mike Ley, standing at far right, knew nothing about how to coach basketball, he led the St. Paul's Mission basketball team to second in their division.
COURTESY OF SANFORD SIEGEL

timer: "If he thought less of me, he wouldn't have offered the trade. Money is impersonal, every dollar looks the same, you could find one blowing down the street, but there's more to a story. He gave me something not open to just anyone. It's not just a story, it was something that he passed on to me."

Stories would have been important in the Ostermans' lives too. Henry had some colorful ones. If for nothing other than practical reasons, Henry's father would have told his eldest son stories about what he had observed and learned through success and failure on the ranch, things that his son would need to know to keep the operation going. There was no manual on running sheep and cows on Eagle Creek.

When I returned home to the suburbs, where all vistas had been closed off by development, things felt constrained, and I missed Montana. My stories about Montana didn't quite land with people who'd never escaped their immediate situation. I ate the jar of canned antelope Uncle Mike sent with me. It tasted truly awful, but not eating it would have betrayed all I had just experienced and would have represented a backslide into suburbia.

After that first visit, I returned to Montana every chance I got, staying as long as I could during different seasons, and having similar experiences with Uncle Mike: bringing fresh-shot duck for the soup at a sweat lodge ceremony; drinking burned coffee with Rusty Sparks after hunting on his land; doing odd jobs at Giles Gregoire's ranch, then eating up his tales of ranch accidents over lunch. This was living!

My time in Montana taught me that much of the state's history is still tangible and immediate and that traditions endure here. Like any living thing, cultures survive in the environment from which they have grown but can be upset when a variable is introduced. As a self-conscious outsider, I had a reverence for the Montana people and places I had come to know. I decided that if I ever moved to Montana, I would pursue something compatible with what had so impressed me at age eighteen. That led me to study historic preservation and then to a career at the Montana State Historic Preservation Office (SHPO).

Since 2002, I have worked on projects with people from towns ranging from Ekalaka to Libby and Hamilton to Wibaux. These preservation projects recognize that buildings are best preserved through use. The property owners make reasonable changes that benefit their business or residence and meet the building's historical character on its terms. The renewal of these places maintains the connection between Montana's past and present.

Positively influencing the state as it changes includes preserving what has characterized our streets and landscapes for decades, or in some cases millennia. Preservation is never a given and is never a passive pursuit. It not only requires physical repairs to a place but also involves influencing civic decisions that pertain to that place's historical integrity. Sometimes direct action might mean minimal intervention, to retain a place's honest patina or to avoid drawing attention to something that could be loved to death.

The place we call Montana has changed with each phase of development. Ice age glaciers carved valleys that served as the first peoples' travel corridors. These corridors later became stage routes, then rail lines, and in some cases, highways. Native peoples' land base shrank drastically, and the bison many relied on were hunted close to extinction. New settlers came, and soon log buildings and hide lodges gave way to wood-framed, steel, and masonry buildings, some of which rose, fell, and were replaced as economies boomed, went bust, and rebounded.

The places in this book reflect the diversity of people and their activities across thousands of years, millions of acres, and countless allegiances, ethnicities, and traditions. They reflect our inherent traits of mobility, adaptability, resourcefulness, and a will to pass something on. Uncle Mike, whether he was aware that he gave me a history lesson or not, passed on to me an awareness of Montana's singularity, still-relevant history, and the tradition carried on by its places and people. I always liked William Faulkner's statement that "the past is never dead. It's not even past." The throughline connecting people and places, then and now, endures through preservation.

Above: A weathered cattle gate stands in front of this view of the Bear Paw Mountains in north-central Montana.
COURTESY OF SANFORD SIEGEL

Opposite page: During his initial visit to Montana in 1990, the author snapped this photograph of a lonesome homestead-era outbuilding still with its wood roof intact, the only shelter for miles.
COURTESY OF PETE BROWN

CHAPTER ONE

BEFORE MONTANA

From time immemorial, people have called the place now known as Montana home. While many tribal nations have origin stories that place their people here from the beginning of time, the oldest physical evidence of human habitation dates to approximately thirteen thousand years ago. The Séliš (Salish) people tell stories about giant mammals and a great flood, and indeed, such mammals lived during the last ice age, fifteen thousand to thirteen thousand years ago, when cataclysmic floodwaters repeatedly burst through the ice dam that had created Glacial Lake Missoula.

Indigenous people adapted as the region's environment changed over millennia. Technology, hunting methods, foodways, and cultures all evolved as the region became warmer and drier eight thousand years ago and then cooler and wetter fifteen hundred years ago. Every Indigenous nation had, and still has, its own language and culture, and the people of this region traveled seasonally, returning each year to sites where they mined rocks for tools; gathered for trade and ceremony; harvested trees and other plants for lodge poles, travois, medicine, and food; set controlled burns to shape habitat; and hunted animals for their meat and hides. Bison, especially, became a species so intertwined with lifeways of the Plains tribes that, according to Lakota (Sioux) activist and spiritual leader John Fire Lame Deer, "it was hard to say where the animals ended and the human began." Tribes also participated in a trade network that extended from the Pacific Ocean to the confluence of the Missouri and Mississippi Rivers and from the Arctic to present-day Mexico. Their early presence remains evident in archaeological sites, including stone circles, buffalo jump drive lines, scarred trees, pictographs, and petroglyphs.

Prior to the arrival of Euro-Americans, most of Montana's First Peoples relied heavily on bison for both their physical and spiritual well-being.

ELK HEAD (AANIIIHNEN), *ELK HEAD KILLS A BUFFALO—HORSE STOLEN FROM THE WHITES*, GRAPHITE ON PAPER, CA. 1884. X1937.01.03, MTHS MUSEUM, GIFT OF MRS. W. E. SANDERS

Members of the Lewis and Clark Expedition had several close encounters with grizzlies, which they frequently referred to as white bears. This painting depicts the Corps of Discovery traveling up the Missouri River, unaware that they were being carefully observed by these "most tremendious looking anamal[s]." ROBERT F. MORGAN, *WHITE BEARS AND WHITE CLIFFS*, OIL ON CANVAS, 1988. 1988.103.01, MTHS MUSEUM

A dramatic transformation occurred after Europeans arrived on the continent. Diseases from across the Atlantic traveled along traditional trade routes long before Europeans themselves arrived in the region, and epidemics decimated Native families in the 1700s. The arrival of horses, from the south, and firearms, from the north, also brought about dramatic changes. Guns initially shifted the balance of power toward northern nations like the Piikuni (Blackfeet). Horses—used for transport, hunting, gift-giving, and ceremony—quickly became an essential part of every tribal culture in the region.

Although European trade goods—from metal arrowheads to Venetian glass beads—arrived in the 1700s, members of the Lewis and Clark Expedition were the first documented Euro-Americans to travel across the region in 1805 and 1806. During their transcontinental voyage, they

Established in 1829 on what is now the North Dakota/Montana border and strategically situated approximately two miles from the confluence of the Missouri and Yellowstone Rivers, Fort Union played a key role in the development of Montana's fur trade.
KARL BODMER, *FORT UNION ON THE MISSOURI*, LITHOGRAPH, 1839–1900. 1983.63.37, MTHS MUSEUM

spent more time in present-day Montana than any other state. Here, the captains encountered and recorded thirty-one plant species and thirty-two animal, fish, and bird species that were new to them. It was also in Montana that they realized they had failed in their primary mission—to find the mythical Northwest Passage, a water route to the Pacific that would facilitate trade with the Far East.

Fur trappers and traders arrived quickly on the heels of Lewis and Clark, so quickly, in fact, that the captains met eleven different trapping parties heading upriver on their return voyage to St. Louis. Plentiful and lush beaver pelts lured international corporations, connecting the region—and its Native nations—to international markets. Between 1808 and 1865, fur companies established dozens of trading

On July 16, 1855, representatives of the Séliš (Salish), Upper Qĺispé (Pend d'Oreille), and Ktunaxa (Kootenai) tribes unintentionally ceded approximately twenty million acres of their traditional homelands to the US government by signing the Hellgate Treaty at Council Grove near present-day Missoula. The Prussian-born American artist Gustav Sohon painted this depiction of the meeting in this contemporary painting.

GUSTAV SOHON, *COUNCIL IN BITTERROOT VALLEY*, WATERCOLOR ON PAPER, JULY 1855. 1918.114.34, WASHINGTON STATE HISTORICAL SOCIETY, TACOMA

posts at strategic points along major waterways. The largest were Fort Union, situated at the confluence of the Missouri and Yellowstone Rivers, and Fort Benton, the last navigable port on the Missouri River. At these posts, both Indian and non-Indian trappers traded furs and hides for imported goods: traps and cooking pots; axes, hatchets, and metal knives; wool blankets and cotton cloth; and sugar, tobacco, coffee, flour, and liquor. Beaver pelts traveled east on steamboats, and then companies often shipped them overseas, where European manufacturers used their waterproof underfur to make felt for top hats. In the 1830s, however, European hatmakers began using silk instead of beaver felt, and fur traders shifted their attention to bison hides, which were transformed into everything from carriage coats to machine belts. Hide hunters ultimately pushed bison to near extinction, sending the Indian nations who relied on the buffalo, both physically and spiritually, into crisis.

Compared to later Euro-American migrants, fur trappers and traders integrated relatively seamlessly into Native cultures even as the trade itself—the region's first extractive industry—reconfigured tribal lifeways and economies. Most of the non-Natives involved in the fur trade never intended to stay in the region long term. By the 1850s, however, more radical changes loomed. In 1855, the US government sent Isaac Stevens, governor of Washington Territory, to negotiate a series of treaties that defined tribal territories and secured permission for the US government to build roads and railroads and for settlers to cross Native lands. Misunderstanding, miscommunication, and mistranslation plagued these proceedings. In general, tribal leaders left the proceedings believing that they had agreed to allow roads to cross their land, and perhaps to share their land with a few settlers, in return for compensation. However, the US government insisted that by signing these treaties, Native nations had ceded all territory outside of specifically defined reservations.

And so it was in the mid-1850s that the region stood on the cusp of change. Catholic missionaries had arrived, steamboat traffic on the Missouri River increased, and more people traveled along newly established overland routes, including a trickle of gold prospectors searching for the next big strike. *—MK*

1. First Peoples Buffalo Jump

Ulm | 47°29′23″N 111°31′45″W

Before acquiring horses in the 1700s, Indigenous peoples living on the Northern Plains hunted in groups, on foot. They took advantage of the terrain around them—including areas they turned into "buffalo jumps"—to help them harvest the bison on which they depended for survival. Communal bison hunting required tremendous sophistication and a deep understanding of bison behavior and plains topography. Although sites varied considerably, the ideal location for a large-scale communal hunt had nearby water and good grazing to attract a bison herd. It also had places for hunters to hide as they lured the animals into a gradually constricting landscape, across terrain that slanted slightly uphill or downhill to conceal the jump. Jumps did not require a high cliff, only a steep bank or "drop-fall."

It took many days to encourage the grazing bison to move through converging drive lines—a path marked by cairns—toward the jump. According to archaeologist Carl Davis, when they were finally close enough to the jump's edge, "band members quickly closed on the herd, shouting, waving robes, and creating enough commotion to start a stampede." Sometimes "brave young men disguised in bison calf robes . . . raced aside and ahead of the stampeding herd, leading it to the very edge of the cliff." Once the bison tumbled from the cliff, dozens of hunters waiting below killed the wounded animals.

After the hunt, the community worked together to haul the meat, hides, and marrow bones to a processing site. They ate some of the meat right away, but cut most of it into thin strips, which they then air- or smoke-dried on pole racks. Portions of the preserved meat were made into pemmican by pounding it together with berries, fat, and bone marrow. The meat not only nourished the hunters and their families but was also an important commodity in the trade between the Northern Plains hunters and the Indigenous farming villages downriver along the Missouri.

One of the oldest and most intact bison jumps in North America, First Peoples Buffalo Jump has all the attributes of a good communal kill site. Over fourteen hundred rock cairns that form forty-seven stone alignments still stand, some of which constitute mile-long drive lines. Other constructions include low rock walls, possibly designed to trip bison and increase the impact of their fall.

Four bone middens, beds filled with bones, reflect the tens of thousands of bison slaughtered and processed here. Tipi rings still mark twenty-two campsites, where families lived for weeks as they gathered not just to hunt but for family reunions, weddings, and religious rituals. The site's ceremonial significance is reflected in its pictographs, petroglyphs, and a large stone circle thought to have been used for ceremonies.

The jump remained in continuous use until around 1700, when the arrival of smallpox and horses transformed life on the Northern Plains. In the late nineteenth century, the site became a sandstone quarry. From 1945 to 1947, the Frost Fertilizer Company mined the middens for phosphorus-rich bones. Pressure from archaeologists and preservationists stopped the mining. Now a state park, First Peoples remains important to members of Native nations who continue to visit the property for "sacred and celebratory ceremonies." Its national significance has also been recognized by the US government, which designated First Peoples Buffalo Jump as a National Historic Landmark in 2015. —*MK*

2. Pictograph Cave

Billings | 45°44′15″N 108°25′53″W

NATURAL FORCES OF WIND and water carved the Eagle Sandstone cliff creating Pictograph, Middle, and Ghost Caves. These three caves comprise Pictograph Cave National Historic Landmark. The caves are exceptional for the rare preservation of perishable items and for their stunning art. The site is equally significant to the Treasure State's archaeological history, offering a window into the lives of Montana's early hunter-gatherers.

Generations of semi-nomadic people used and inhabited the three caves for thousands of years. In Pictograph Cave—the deepest of the three—early inhabitants painted over one hundred images on the walls. The earliest depicts a turtle and is more than two thousand years old. More recent paintings include flintlock rifles and riders on horseback. European-imported guns and horses made their way to the Northern Plains through the tribal nations' vast trade networks after the 1750s.

The earliest painters used black pigment. Later artists used red ochre, sometimes covering older drawings. The Apsáalooke (Crow) nation has resided in the region since at least 1700, and their ancestors may have created some of the more recent pictographs. The Apsáalooke people knew the caves by the name Alahpaláaxawaalaatuua, which means "where there is spirit writing." Local settlers in the early 1900s, perhaps aware of this moniker, knew them as the "Indian Ghost Caves." Forebears of other tribes most certainly left their marks, but the paintings' origins and meanings are enigmatic. Lakota lore tells of a giant who came from above and sat on the cliff. The next day, pictures filled the caves.

The site offers ample evidence of the extensive Indigenous trade network that existed before contact with Euro-Americans. Examples include the fragment of a 1,370-year-old coiled basket, which resembles those made in the Great Basin, and a thong necklace strung with Pacific shell beads. The more than thirty thousand artifacts found in the caves include pottery fragments; plant remains; jewelry; and stone, bone, and wood tools. The site also yielded the remains of nine people who lived during the pre-contact era.

Archaeological excavation of the caves began in 1936, at the dawn of Montana archaeology. The Works Progress Administration, a New Deal program aimed at boosting employment during the Great Depression, funded the excavation. Amateur archaeologist Oscar Lewis served as project foreman under Melville Sayre, a Montana School of Mines (now Montana Technological University) English professor. In 1941, professional archaeologist William Mulloy took charge of the excavation. Known as the grandfather of Montana archaeology, Mulloy published the first cultural chronology of the region in 1958, basing his work on hundreds of projectile points from the Pictograph Cave site.

The National Park Service designated Pictograph, Middle, and Ghost Caves as Pictograph Cave National Historic Landmark in 1964, and Montana added the site to its state park system in 1969. *—EB*

Left: The oldest drawings that adorn the walls of Pictograph Cave document the presence of humans in the area at least two thousand years ago. More recent renderings, like this one showing firearms, indicate that the caves remained significant to Indigenous peoples well after contact with Euro-Americans.

Right: This photographic postcard from roughly 1940 offers a vertical view of Pictograph Caves State Park, then known as Indian Caves.

BPL.2017.07.53, MTHS PHOTOGRAPH ARCHIVES

3. Sleeping Buffalo Rock

Phillips County | LOCATION UNDISCLOSED

A windswept ridge overlooking the Cree Crossing on the Milk River was the original resting place of this ancient, weather-worn effigy, a gray granite boulder resembling the leader of a herd of reclining buffalo. Incised markings, made in the distant past, define its horns, eyes, backbone, and ribs. Since late prehistoric times, Indigenous peoples of the Northern Plains have revered the Sleeping Buffalo Rock.

Oral traditions reveal that the Sleeping Buffalo was well known to the Anishinaabe (Chippewa), Neyiowahk (Cree), Lakota, Nakoda (Assiniboine), Aaniiihnen (Gros Ventre), Piikuni, Apsáalooke, and Tsétsėhéstȧhese naa Suhtaio (Northern Cheyenne) peoples. The buffalo—a courageous and powerful animal—was central to the lifeways of the people of the Northern Plains and critical to their survival, providing them food, blankets, and tools. As the people moved with the seasons, the trail to the Cree Crossing where the Milk River narrows was known to several tribes. While each group had its own distinctive culture and beliefs, they shared a worldview intertwining the sacred and secular. All embraced the Sleeping Buffalo Rock as a powerful object endowed with great spiritual energy.

Many stories about the Sleeping Buffalo Rock have been passed down from generation to generation. Some tell how the "herd" had the power to fool buffalo-hunting parties, while others attest to its medicinal strength. Nakoda elder Leslie Fourstar, for example, professes that after he invoked the power of the Sleeping Buffalo to revive his stillborn daughter, she eventually began to breathe and went on to live a full life.

The late Bill Tallbull, Tsétsėhéstȧhese naa Suhtaio cultural and spiritual leader, explained that animal and human spirits move underground or into stones for protection or survival. Tallbull believed the Sleeping Buffalo Rock was part of a larger sacred arrangement. The ground below the boulder may have originated as a buffalo wallow, and he contended that the rock's healing power lay in the wallow.

In 1932, the separation of the Sleeping Buffalo Rock from its original ridgetop perch left a gaping void. This was a painful event for many Native people. According to Tallbull, removing the Sleeping Buffalo was "like taking the altar from the church." Relocated to City Park in Malta, locals claimed the Sleeping Buffalo was restless; stories tell of its changing position and nighttime bellowing. After a second move, the Sleeping Buffalo came to rest aside Highway 2 west of Saco in 1967. In 1987, a smaller object known as the Medicine Rock, incised with hoofprints and symbols and equally venerated, was placed with the Sleeping Buffalo.

These two timeless objects continue to figure prominently in traditional ceremonies; however, the rocks frequently suffered vandalism and disrespect in their roadside location. In 2024, tribal historic preservation officers from the Fort Belknap, Blackfeet, and Fort Peck reservations and officials from the Montana Department of Transportation, Bureau of Land Management, and Montana State Historic Preservation Office worked together to develop a plan to move the stones closer to their original home near Cree Crossing. As one Anishinaabe Neyiowahk elder explained, "These rocks are sacred, just like our old people." They provide a cultural link to ancestral peoples of the high plains and the time when, as Tallbull put it, "The power of the prairie was the buffalo." *—EB*

Photographer Judy Hoy snapped this photograph of Sleeping Buffalo Rock in 1969, two years after it came to rest along Highway 2 between Saco and Malta.
COURTESY OF JUDY HOY

4. Kootenai Falls

Lincoln County | 48°27′20″N 115°45′48″W

The Kootenai River journeys southward from British Columbia into northwest Montana where, in Lincoln County, it bends west, then northwest, flowing through the Idaho panhandle before returning to Canada and, ultimately, joining the Columbia River. Kootenai Falls, located between Libby and Troy, is among the 485-mile-long waterway's most spectacular features. Here, as the river rushes over stair-stepped beds of hard quartzite, it drops ninety feet down a series of cascades, making it the largest undammed waterfall in Montana.

The river and the falls bear the name of the region's original inhabitants, who call themselves Ktunaxa (Kootenai). Prior to contact with Euro-Americans, the Ktunaxa led a semi-nomadic life carefully intertwined with nature and centered along the numerous waterways that create the Kootenai River drainage, an area replete with ample rainfall and abundant wildlife.

According to Séliš-Ktunaxa historian Steve Lozar, Kootenai Falls sits at the geographic and emotional center of Ktunaxa country; everything radiated from the falls, which were a point of connection for the seven smaller bands that constituted the Ktunaxa people. During warm months, members of the Ksanka (Standing Arrow) band of the Ktunaxa—whose descendants now live on the Flathead Reservation—camped and fished near the falls. These summer camps provided an opportunity for families to meet up, for young people to court, and for elders to pass down skills and plan the next year's travels.

CRAIG DAVIDSON PHOTOGRAPH

Although their language was (and remains) unique—an "isolate" unrelated to other Indigenous languages—the Ktunaxa shared cultural traits with both Northern Plains peoples living to the east and northern plateau tribes living farther west. Like plains tribes they periodically ventured across the Rocky Mountains to hunt buffalo and lived primarily in tipis made of hide. They also constructed unique portable summer lodges from tule, or bulrush. Like their plateau neighbors, they built bark and dugout canoes, participated in communal fishing, and made baskets, bird traps, and fish weirs from the bark and roots of cedars and pines. Like both groups, the Ktunaxa relied on their expert knowledge of native plants to supply food and medicine.

The Ktunaxa acquired horses and some manufactured goods through intertribal trade during the mid-eighteenth century, but it was the fur trade that first brought them into direct contact with non-Indians beginning in the 1790s. According to historian Cynthia J. Manning, "The Kootenai Indians exhibited an immediate willingness to trap for whites." Early fur trader Ross Cox affirmed that the Ktunaxa "appear to be perfectly aware that beaver was the only object that induced us to visit their country; and they accordingly exerted themselves to procure it, not, as some of them candidly declared, for our purposes, but for the purpose of obtaining fire-arms, spears &c., to enable them to meet their old enemies the Black-feet on more equal terms."

Euro-American missionaries followed the fur trappers, arriving in Ktunaxa territory in the 1840s. It was the US government, however, that ultimately forced the removal of the Ktunaxa from their traditional homelands. The Hellgate Treaty of 1855 established the Flathead Reservation. The Ksanka people eventually relocated there along with the Séliš and Ql̓ispé (Pend d'Oreilles), leaving behind the place that, according to Ktunaxa belief, had been their home since the beginning of time. Today, members of the Ktunaxa Nation also live on a small reservation in Idaho and several reserves in British Columbia. *—KL*

5. Medicine Rocks State Park

Carter County | 46°02′40″N 104°28′17″W

Like the landscape itself, physical remnants of Montana's past are often layered and nuanced. At first glance, the appeal of Medicine Rocks State Park as a geologic wonder appears paramount, but closer examination reveals a unique historic record carved in stone by earlier generations of visitors.

Traveling through southeastern Montana in 1883, young rancher and future US president Theodore Roosevelt was struck by the rock formations, calling the area "as fantastically beautiful a place as I have ever seen." Still known today in large part for their otherworldly beauty, Medicine Rocks' eroded formations began millions of years ago as sand deposits when this now-arid region was an estuary bordering a saltwater sea. Over time, the waters receded, leaving porous sandstone exposed to the forces of nature. Wind, rain, snow, and ice eroded the softer elements, creating stone outcroppings marked by holes, caves, columns, arches, and spires.

Long before Roosevelt or any other Euro-Americans arrived in the area, the Apsáalooke, Lakota, and Tsétsėhéstȧhese naa Suhtaio peoples, among others, began leaving their marks on these sandstone formations. Petroglyphs carved into the soft stone during the late pre-contact period depict shield-bearing warriors, "V-necked" humans, and animals, including deer or elk. Later images document Indigenous peoples encountering Euro-Americans and acquiring horses. While these extant petroglyphs are indeed significant, many more have undoubtedly been lost to the ravages of time or covered by subsequent additions.

By far the greatest number of the park's inscriptions document the region's settlement by non-Indians. The two earliest dates carved into the stone are 1803 and 1824. While these dates seem suspiciously early, these engravings could be authentic given the presence of explorers and fur trappers in the region. The founding of Ekalaka in 1885, the establishment of cattle ranches during the later decades of the nineteenth century, and the coming of homesteaders in the twentieth century exponentially increased settlement of the surrounding countryside. Engravings from this period most commonly include the names or initials of visitors, often accompanied by the date of their visit.

In addition, as archaeologist Tim Urbaniak wrote, "The inscriptions further define the tapestry of the American experience through text and symbols representative of associated groups that include the Masons, specific ranch brands, the Civilian Conservation Corps, military service, and the 4-H. At Medicine Rocks State Park, the history of our nation is literally written upon the landscape that all past generations have found so special."

While Indigenous peoples valued the Medicine Rocks, at least in part, as a highly spiritual place, non-Indians visited primarily for camping, picnicking, and sightseeing. With the failure of area homesteads during the Great Depression, the land reverted to county control and, in 1957, Carter County commissioners gave Medicine Rocks to the state. The park was listed on the National Register of Historic Places in 2017. Three years later, it joined Glacier National Park as Montana's second officially designated International Dark Sky Sanctuary. *—KL*

This unidentified group of tourists posed in front of the Medicine Rocks sometime around 1919.
LOT 048 MERO, MTHS PHOTOGRAPH ARCHIVES

Henry Jensen's 1928 depiction of a three-masted schooner Is one of thousands of inscriptions left by early sightseers as a record of their visit to Medicine Rocks.

6. Lewis and Clark National Historic Landmarks

Montana's vast, varied landscape lay before the members of the Lewis and Clark Expedition in 1805 and 1806. Their findings and challenges, recorded in their journals, illustrate Montana's role in one of America's greatest epics. The expedition spent more time in Montana than any other place. Three of Montana's seven Lewis and Clark–related National Historic Landmarks represent turning points in their journey.

In 1912, painter Edgar S. Paxson crafted this depiction of the Corps of Discovery's arrival at the confluence of the Missouri River near present-day Three Forks.
EDGAR S. PAXSON, *LEWIS AND CLARK AT THREE FORKS*, OIL ON CANVAS, 1912. X1912.07.01, MONTANA STATE CAPITOL ART COLLECTION, MTHS

GEOFF WYATT PHOTOGRAPH

Three Forks of the Missouri

Gallatin County | 45°55′15″N 111°29′53″W

On July 27, 1805, Meriwether Lewis climbed the limestone cliff overlooking the Three Forks of the Missouri. Noting the lofty mountains and sweeping plains, Lewis realized that the panorama below him represented "an essential point in the geography" of the West.

Along major intertribal trade and travel routes, the headwaters was a confluence of people as well as rivers, where generations of Native peoples—and later, early trappers—gathered. This strategic location was also a place of fierce conflict. A Hiráaca (Hidatsa) raiding party had captured Sacagawea there five years before, and in 1808, expedition members John Colter and John Potts returned to the confluence to trap beaver. The Piikuni, determined to keep the Americans out of their territory, killed Potts; Colter barely survived. In 1810, a group of Piikuni struck again, killing George Drouillard.

Unconcerned that Native people already had names for these waterways, Lewis and Clark named the rivers Jefferson, Madison, and Gallatin after key players in the Louisiana Purchase: President Thomas Jefferson, Secretary of State James Madison, and Treasury Secretary Albert Gallatin. Today, Headwaters State Park, opened to the public in 1951, contains 532 acres of land encompassing the area where the rivers meet.

Travelers' Rest State Park

Lolo | 46°44′20″N 114°04′50″W

On the banks of Lolo Creek at the eastern end of the Lolo Trail, a two-hundred-mile pathway that the Lewis and Clark Expedition took across the Bitterroot Mountains, Travelers' Rest National Historic Landmark is a cultural crossroads where the Séliš, Ql̓ispé, Nimiipuu (Nez Perce), and others camped centuries before the Corps of Discovery ventured west. The area has changed little since the intrepid explorers rested there on their way to the Pacific from September 9 to 11, 1805, before beginning their arduous trek across the Bitterroots. It was here that they first encountered the Séliš, who proved crucial to their success.

Homeward bound the following summer, the Corps again camped at Travelers' Rest from June 30 to July 3, 1806, where three very ill men took liberal doses of mercury-laced Dr. Rush's pills. In 2002, archaeologists unearthed a mercury-tainted trench latrine, fire hearths, and lead used in the repair and manufacture of firearms. Travelers' Rest is the only Montana site where physical evidence documents a campsite associated with Lewis and Clark. A state park since 2001, it is significant not only for its archaeological footprint but also as a landscape where diverse events, people, and cultures converged.

Pompeys Pillar

Yellowstone County | 45°59′43″N 108°00′21″W

Captain William Clark's signature and the date July 25, 1806, inscribed on Pompeys Pillar are the only known physical marks that the explorers left on Montana's landscape.

While traveling down the Yellowstone River on the Expedition's return trip from the Pacific, Clark stopped to climb a spectacular sandstone formation rising two hundred feet above the plain. He named the tower after Sacagawea's eighteen-month-old son, Jean Baptiste Charbonneau, whom Clark had nicknamed "Pomp." Clark's signature and the date, etched in the soft sandstone, is the only physical evidence of Lewis and Clark in Montana other than the traces of mercury found at Travelers' Rest.

The pillar, situated at a natural river crossing just over thirty miles northeast of present-day Billings, was a favored campsite of the Apsáalooke and other groups. Ancient petroglyphs depicting animals, shields, and other signs provide evidence of the many Native people, including Newe (Shoshone), Lakota, Tsétsėhéstȧhese naa Suhtaio, Hinono'ei (Arapaho), Piikuni, and Séliš, among others, who camped, traded, and traveled here. Others who later carved their names into the rock include the captain of the steamboat *Josephine* in 1875 and US infantrymen commanded by Colonel John Gibbon in 1876. Considered a sacred site, the Apsáalooke call it Iishpíialawaache, "where the mountain lion sits." Pompeys Pillar became a National Historic Landmark in 1965 and a National Monument in 2001. *—EB*

7. Fort Connah

Lake County | 47°24′20″N 114°05′14″W

With rugged mountains forming a majestic backdrop, the British Hudson's Bay Company established a trading post on a small rise in the Mission Valley in 1846. It was the powerful company's last post built within the boundaries of the United States and represents the British effort to stave off competition from American fur traders west of the Continental Divide. Because the fort was under construction, it escaped scrutiny when the 1846 Oregon Treaty established US ownership of land below the forty-ninth parallel.

Fort Connah was an important trading post for tribes on either side of the Rocky Mountains. Furs were the main commodity, but buffalo meat, pemmican, saddle blankets, rawhide, and rope were other key trade items, as the Hudson's Bay Company could not obtain them at its posts farther west. The Hudson's Bay Company defied American law and operated Fort Connah in the twilight of the fur trade era until encroaching settlement forced its closure in 1871.

Angus McDonald (1816–1889) took charge as post agent in 1847, naming it Fort Connen after the River Conon valley in his native Scotland. The name evolved through Native American usage to Fort Connah. In 1852, Angus returned to Fort Colvile, Washington Territory, to become chief trader of the district. McDonald's son Duncan, who was born at Fort Connah, served as its last agent from 1867 to 1871. Angus later acquired the property and died there in 1889. He and his wife Catherine—of French, Haudenosaunee (Iroquois), and Nimiipuu descent—had twelve children. They and some of their many descendants are buried in the nearby McDonald family cemetery. The McDonalds are still regarded as vital to the development of the region, and their association with the fort lends the site significance.

The fort complex originally included a wooden bastion, several storerooms, a dwelling, and a corral. The single remaining building, built in 1846 or 1847, likely first functioned as one of the storerooms. Its builders created the walls by sliding

An undated photograph credited to Rollin H. McKay captures the exterior of Fort Connah as it appeared in the early twentieth century.
947-203, MTHS PHOTOGRAPH ARCHIVES

squared and end-notched horizontal logs down a channeled-out vertical log post, creating a fine example of French Canadian "piece-sur-piece" construction. The method originated in Denmark and spread to northern France before French fur traders brought it to North America in the mid-1700s; it allowed builders to construct walls of any width using short or long tree trunks. This structure can be identified as the only channeled log building in an 1866 sketch of the fort by Danish-born artist Peter Peterson Tofft.

Fort Connah's storeroom building is among Montana's few physical reminders of the fur trade era and likely the state's oldest surviving building. The site is under the care of the Fort Connah Restoration Society. *—EB*

The interior of Fort Connah's only remaining original structure showcases the builder's French Canadian "piece-sur-piece" construction.

8. Judith Landing

Fergus/Chouteau County | 47°43′58″N 109°40′34″W

Few Montana places encompass as much varied history as the Judith Landing Historic District, a vast, undeveloped, fifteen-square-mile area at the confluence of the Missouri and Judith Rivers in central Montana. For millennia, Native peoples used this wide landing spot as a seasonal campground and burial site. While camped here in May 1805, Captains Meriwether Lewis and William Clark named the Judith River after Clark's future wife. They also noted evidence of more than a hundred fire rings and, downriver, a recent bison jump kill site. Many other early nineteenth-century explorers, fur traders, and naturalists noted evidence of Indigenous occupation, but it was not until the late twentieth century that archaeologists formally documented a history of Indian use.

Explorers and fur traders after Lewis and Clark also noted (and likely collected) fossils at Judith Landing. In 1855, young paleontologist Ferdinand Hayden collected the teeth and bones of ankylosaurs, crocodiles, hadrosaurs, and ceratopsian and theropod dinosaurs. His findings, published by respected Smithsonian naturalist Joseph Leidy in 1856, were the first skeletal dinosaur remains officially documented in North America. Hayden's dinosaur discoveries sparked intense interest in North American paleontological research that has never waned.

Judith Landing also marks the site of two momentous tribal councils. In mid-September 1846, during a grand council arranged by prominent Jesuit missionary Pierre Jean de Smet, the Piikuni and several western tribes agreed to end their rivalry.

A second peace council in mid-October 1855, led by Washington territorial governor Isaac Stevens, brought together approximately 3,500 tribal members representing the Piikuni, Aaniiihnen, Séliš, Upper Ql̓ispé, Ktunaxa, Nimiipuu, and Neyiowahk nations. Here, they signed the Lame Bull Treaty, which established the boundaries of a communal hunting ground, created the first Blackfeet Agency at Fort Benton, and essentially paved the way for non-Indian settlement across the plains.

The 1860s brought "woodhawks" to the area to cut firewood to fuel steamboat travel. The resulting tree stumps are still visible, along with remnants of Camp Cooke (1866–1870), the first US military camp built in Montana. In 1867, Fort Benton merchant Thomas C. Power opened a trading post close to Camp Cooke. Power, with partner James Wells, bought Camp Cooke in 1870 and rechristened it Fort Clagett. A decade later, Wells moved the post east of the Judith to a more advantageous river crossing, opened a post office, and began ranching. In 1882, he built a large stone store/warehouse at the river's edge, and Judith Landing blossomed into a small supply town for area ranchers.

Businessman and rancher Gilman R. Norris took charge of the post in 1884 and, with Power, started the Judith Mercantile and Cattle Co., also known as the PN Ranch. Norris's elegant 1901 ranch house still reflects the high status of the PN as one of the most prosperous ranches in the region and marks many layers of history on this stretch of the river. *—CWB*

Council Island (below) marks the spot of two early tribal council meetings. The ruins of the store that T. C. Power built in 1882 (left), meanwhile, reminds visitors of Judith Landing's former significance as a supply town for local ranchers.

CHAPTER TWO

NEWCOMERS TO AN OLD LAND 1864–1882

Euro-American colonization increasingly affected the Native nations that lived, hunted, and traveled in the Northern Great Plains and Rocky Mountains by the mid-nineteenth century. Alcohol tore at their social fabric, and smallpox, carried upriver on an American Fur Company steamboat in 1837, devastated the Piikuni (Blackfeet). Christianity, introduced to the region through the fur trade, gained traction with the arrival of Jesuit missionaries to the Bitterroot Valley in 1840. However, it was gold that truly transformed the country. Before the discovery of gold, Euro-Americans were visitors to what was, essentially, a foreign land. Once gold strikes in southwest Montana lured thousands of newcomers to the region, the US government created Montana Territory, and the newcomers did all they could to replicate the social conditions of the states.

The new arrivals imported huge quantities of manufactured goods, built permanent settlements, tore up the landscape, and attracted large-scale capital investment. Concentrated in mineral-rich gulches in the southwest portion of the territory, gold towns lured eager young men willing to perform long hours of backbreaking labor in pursuit of fortune. Unsurprisingly, 80 percent of the newcomers were men and 70 percent were under the age of forty-six. Despite relative uniformity in age and gender, they were a diverse lot. Many were immigrants: 10 percent were Chinese or Chinese American and 9 percent were Irish. In all, 39 percent were born outside of the United States, which was almost double the percentage of the foreign-born population of New York City and 2.5 times greater than number of the immigrants making up the national population.

Montana's gold rush towns grew quickly from clusters of ramshackle tents and cabins to platted settlements built of milled lumber, brick, and stone. Many early businesses disguised their gable roofs with false fronts to make their frontier buildings appear larger and more sophisticated. Despite these attempts to project architectural permanence, towns lasted only as long as their inhabitants could make a profit either by mining gold or by "mining the miners." Every successful camp boasted boarding houses, restaurants, mercantiles, bowling alleys, saloons, barbershops, brothels, and other businesses to tempt young miners to part with their gold dust.

Montana Territory's instant towns required connections to the outside world to export the gold that was their raison d'être. Transporting gold was dangerous, as it required travel over long distances across unpoliced routes. In response to a wave of highway robberies, miners and merchants organized a vigilante force, which combated the territory's lawlessness by brutally and effectively tak-

As evidenced by these "diggings" at Dana's Bar on the Missouri River near Helena, photographed around 1875 by Edgar H. Train, extracting gold from bedrock required tremendous effort and arduous labor. Mining left scars on the landscape that are often still visible today.
LOT 026 B3F15.03, MTHS PHOTOGRAPH ARCHIVES

ing extralegal action, hanging dozens of suspected outlaws in 1864. According to historian Frederick Allen, even after the creation of a rudimentary judicial system, "random lynchings continued in Montana Territory throughout the 1860s."

Equally, since there was almost no manufacturing in the territory, residents needed to import almost everything they used: tools, hardware, and heavy equipment; liquor, canned fruit, sugar, coffee, and tobacco; boots and blankets; coal oil and kerosene lanterns. Fort Benton prospered and grew in the 1860s as thousands of tons of cargo made its way up the Missouri River on steamboats. Wagons then hauled the freight from Fort Benton and other river landings to the gold camps, as well as north from the railhead in Corrine, Utah, and, briefly, over the Bozeman Trail.

In 1865, after heavy snowstorms disrupted deliveries to Virginia City, a flour shortage prompted miners to go door to door confiscating flour for redistribution. The "flour riots" underscored the market for locally produced commodities. Soon, many emigrants were finding greater success as farmers and ranchers than they ever had as miners. Their growing farms and cattle operations competed with tribal nations for land and resources, and when conflicts occurred, settlers demanded government protection.

Military forts soon dotted the landscape. The US Army established Montana's first fort, Camp Cooke, in 1866 to protect freight traffic on the Missouri River. It was soon followed by Fort C. F. Smith (1866), constructed on the Bighorn River to protect Bozeman Trail travelers; Fort Shaw (1866–1867), established to police the Mullan Road; and

Right: As the head of navigation on the Missouri River, Fort Benton played a crucial role in Montana's early supply chain. After steamboats unloaded their cargo on the Fort Benton levee, freighters redistributed supplies across the region by mule- or ox-drawn wagons. This photograph, taken around 1878 by W. E. Hook Sr., gives a sense of the vast quantities of goods that passed through this place during Montana's early territorial period.
HOOK STEREOGRAPH COLLECTION, MTHS PHOTOGRAPH ARCHIVES

Opposite page: As indicated by the dark plumes of smoke billowing from the stacks of the *Rosebud*, which D. F. Barry photographed as it traveled up the Missouri River in 1886, steamboats consumed an enormous amount of firewood. It was not unusual for larger steamboats traveling upriver to stop twice a day to take on new supplies of locally cut fuel.
955-147, MTHS PHOTOGRAPH ARCHIVES

ROSE BUD

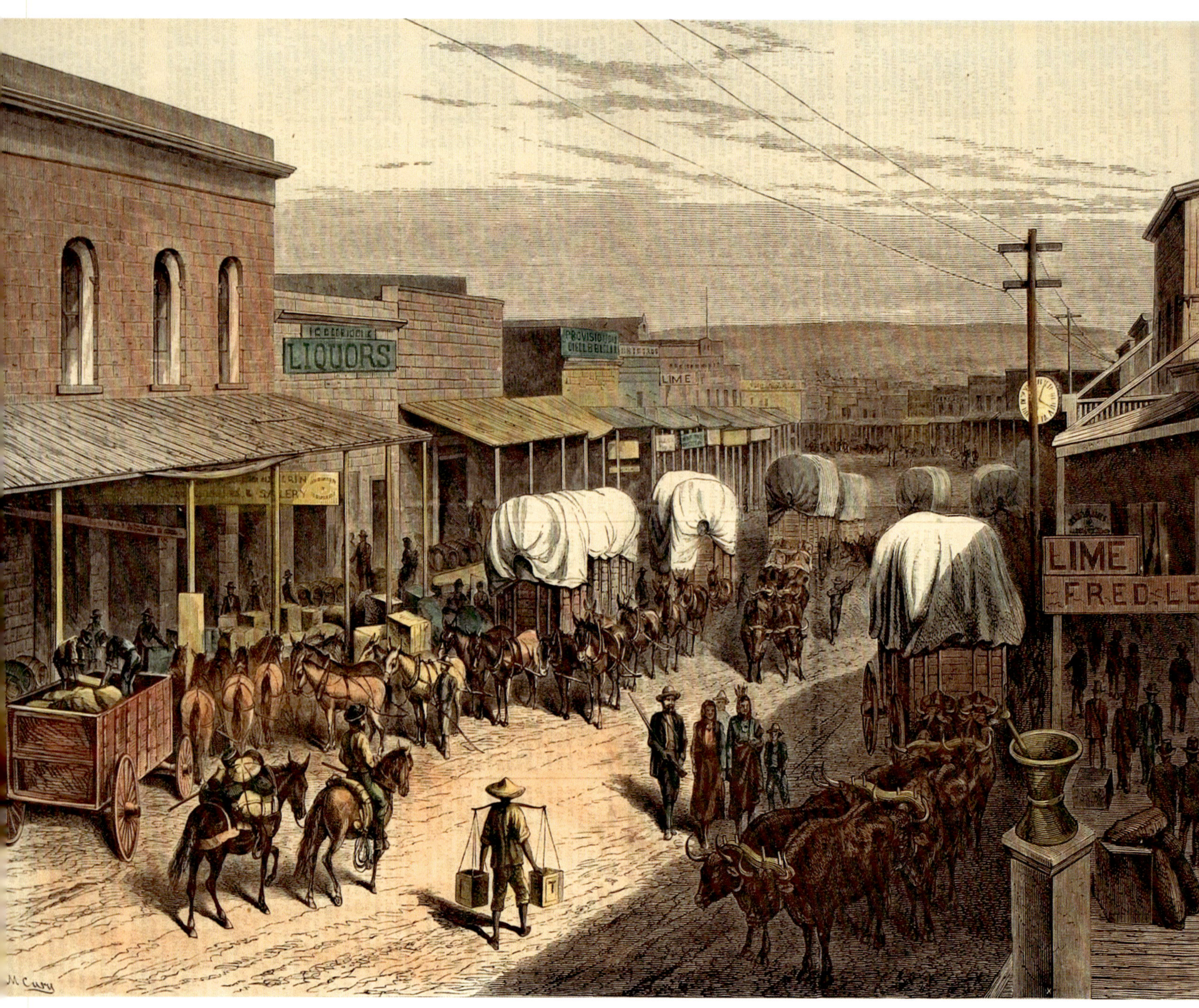

Founded in 1864, Helena was among the thriving camps that sprang up overnight in southwest Montana as the search for gold drew men from all parts of the globe. A decade after its founding, Wiliam de la Montagne Cary depicted white settlers, American Indians, and a Chinese merchant navigating a bustling street in the future capital city. While Helena continued to grow, many other formerly booming camps became ghost towns as soon as the riches played out.

WILLIAM DE LA MONTAGNE CARY, *WAGON TRAINS AT HELENA, MONTANA*, LITHOGRAPH, 1874. X1939.05.01, MTHS MUSEUM

Fort Ellis (1867), also positioned on the Bozeman Trail. Ultimately, the US government built sixteen military outposts prior to statehood, four of which were added in 1877 as a direct response to Lieutenant Colonel George Armstrong Custer's defeat at the Battle of Little Bighorn—known by many Native participants as the Battle of Greasy Grass—the previous year.

These forts provided additional markets for agricultural goods and the soldiers to enforce Indian removal, which opened additional land for farmers and ranchers. Still, development necessarily remained limited as long as supplies had to be imported via steamboat and ox-drawn wagon, gold and silver had to be exported via stagecoach or boat, and cattle had to be trailed overland to distant consumers. Euro-Americans determined to extract wealth from—and to build permanent homes in—the territory knew that growth and prosperity would depend on a massive investment in infrastructure: railroads. *—MK*

A contingent of soldiers at Fort Keogh, wearing voluminous bison-fur coats, stands in formation in this 1882 L. A. Huffman photograph. The largest fort in the territory—housing 1,500 soldiers and their families—Fort Keogh was established in 1876 in the wake of the Seventh Cavalry's defeat at the Battle of the Little Bighorn. Built on the south bank of the Yellowstone River near present-day Miles City, the fort was named after Captain Myles Keogh, who died in that battle.
981-363, MTHS PHOTOGRAPH ARCHIVES

9. St. Mary's Mission

Stevensville | 46°30′29″N 114°5′43″W

Jesuit priests and lay brothers established St. Mary's Mission in the Bitterroot Valley in 1841, answering Séliš (Salish) and Nimiipuu (Nez Perce) pleas for the "powerful medicine" of the Catholic faith. It was the first Catholic mission in the Northwest. After nearly a decade, conflicts between the missionaries and the Séliš arose when the Jesuits began to teach Catholicism to the enemy Piikuni, forcing the mission to close. John Owen purchased the property and built Fort Owen nearby. The Jesuits returned in 1866 to reestablish ties and build a new mission. The present-day historic district includes St. Mary's chapel, Father Ravalli's pharmacy, Chief Victor's house, two cemeteries, and several ancient apple trees. Its vernacular log architecture illustrates Montana's earliest building techniques and artistic adaptations to primitive conditions, while its varied landscape uniquely reflects spiritual and cultural impacts and the consequences of westward expansion on Native peoples.

An architect, artist, and physician, Father Anthony Ravalli, S.J., designed St. Mary's chapel in 1866. The multitalented priest, who was also the architect of Idaho's famed Cataldo Mission, ingeniously adapted European ecclesiastical architecture to the remote frontier. Built in three sections of hewn logs joined with pegs and chinked with clay, the building includes the original chapel and study/living quarters. The third section, a kitchen, has been reconstructed. Gabled rooflines and the finished corners of half-dovetail logs define each section. Lay brother William Claessens, S.J., was the builder. In 1879, he expanded the chapel, adding the front façade, loft, and belltower according to Father Ravalli's plans. Ravalli also designed and built the elaborate altar and all the interior furnishings, including a near life-sized effigy of St. Ignatius and statue of the Blessed Mary. Having no access to manufactured supplies, Ravalli fashioned his own tools and paint, crafting his paint brushes from the tail hair of his favorite cat.

In his ca. 1841 drawing *St. Mary's among the Flatheads*, Fr. Nicholas Point captured the wide-ranging efforts to build the original mission, which the Jesuits occupied until 1850.

PIERRE JEAN DE SMET PAPERS (CAGE 537), FOLDER 14, BOX 7, MANUSCRIPTS, ARCHIVES, AND SPECIAL COLLECTIONS, WASHINGTON STATE UNIVERSITY LIBRARIES, PULLMAN

Brother Claessens also built Father Ravalli's two-story log pharmacy with a bedroom, hospital room, and ample shelves for his medicinal concoctions. Ravalli settled there permanently in 1868 and dispensed his remedies, caring for the health of local and regional Indians and whites. When his store of European pharmaceuticals was depleted, he manufactured his own, learning about local plants from the Séliš. He also cultivated an herb garden and planted an apple orchard. Two gnarled trees survive as living evidence of the agriculture practiced at the mission and the harbinger of the apple boom that would later bring settlers by the hundreds to the Bitterroot Valley.

John Owen built a simple cottage for influential Séliš leader Chief Victor in 1862 before the returning Jesuits reestablished the mission. Hewn log walls chinked with clay, half-dovetailed ends forming neat corners, and a gable roof

are consistent with the style of the buildings at Fort Owen. Victor and his home served as a bridge between the Native and white worlds, symbolizing the Séliš people's difficult transition from semi-nomadic lifeways to subsistence farming.

Two cemeteries, Catholic and Séliš, sit side by side yet distinctly separate. Father Ravalli's gravesite and memorial obelisk dominate among the Catholic tombstones, which span from the nineteenth century to the present. In stark contrast, smooth, unmarked ground defines the Indian burial ground where Bitterroot Séliš were interred from 1866 to 1891.

St. Mary's closed in 1891 when the US government forced the impoverished Séliš to leave their beloved Bitterroot Valley for the Flathead Reservation. An influx of homesteaders prompted the creation of St. Mary's Parish in 1910, and the old mission church reopened. In 1911, the Séliš returned to St. Mary's for the first time since 1891 to celebrate their Bitterroot heritage. They maintain this tradition. *—EB*

10. Bannack

Beaverhead County | 45°09′40″N 112°59′44″W

When a lucky gold strike on Grasshopper Creek in July 1862 brought hopeful miners over the Continental Divide, Bannack, Montana's first boomtown, sprang to life. The town's boom-and-bust history encompasses periods of both prosperous resource extraction and economic depression. Its built environment spans from the 1860s to the mid-twentieth century.

Some three thousand residents, housed in tents and makeshift buildings, crowded around the diggings by the spring of 1863. The rough, primitive gold camp saw six vigilante hangings, including that of its infamous sheriff, Henry Plummer, who built Montana's first jail. The sod-roofed log jail is Bannack's oldest surviving building.

Bannack was briefly designated capital of the new Montana Territory in 1864, but a gold strike at Alder Gulch soon drew most of the town's population to Virginia City. Quartz mining continued in the surrounding hills, and Bannack rebounded in the 1870s, serving as the Beaverhead County seat until it moved to Dillon in 1881. The town's Masonic Lodge Hall, original Beaverhead County courthouse (now the Hotel Meade), and Methodist church building all open onto Main Street and reflect this prosperous period.

Above: Masonic Lodge Hall
Left: The Hotel Meade, once the county courthouse, stands on the far right next to two historic storefronts.

Many of Montana's first prominent citizens were Freemasons, and the fraternal order was a driving force in the early and controversial attempts to establish law and order in the territory. In 1874, Bannack Masons built a hall to serve as both a meeting place and a school. Although the Masons used the hall only briefly, the school served Bannack's children for seventy years.

Bannack's Masonic Lodge Hall not only represents the town's 1870s resurgence but also exemplifies town-phase architecture on the western frontier. The balloon-frame walls covered with beveled siding feature Greek Revival–style pilasters at the corners and entry. These are adaptations of the brick and stone ornamentation found on high-style buildings in urban centers far from remote southwestern Montana. Building materials, however, were in short supply. A bread kneading board, brought west and donated by a generous housewife, was carved with the Masonic emblem and lodge numbers and installed at the gable's peak.

Loren Olds designed the 1876 Classical Revival–style courthouse. This near replica of the Madison County courthouse, which Olds also designed, is Bannack's only brick building and the only one drawn up by an architect. In August 1877, it sheltered frightened residents who took refuge fearing attack from advancing Nimiipuu people amid their desperate flight from the US Army, but no attack came to pass. In 1890, the Meade family converted the former courthouse into a hotel.

Bannack citizens banded together to complete the modest Methodist church after the Nimiipuu panic interrupted its construction. Beveled siding covers the studs, while a Gothic arch over the vestibule is the only ornamentation. William Wesley "Brother Van" Orsdel, Montana's famous itinerant preacher, delivered the first sermon at the church on August 19, 1877.

Bannack's landscape bears the scars of changing technologies, from placer mining and Montana's first hard rock quartz claims to later hydraulicking and dredging. The community endured fluctuating fortunes until World War II, when most residents had moved on. In 1954, the State of Montana acquired most of the town and it became a state park. In 1961, Bannack earned designation as a National Historic Landmark. *—EB*

11. Virginia City

Madison County | 45°17′46″N 111°56′13″W

The spectacular gold deposit discovered in Alder Gulch on May 26, 1863, led to the rapid growth of this colorful and legendary gold camp town. Virginia City became one of the most ethnically diverse places in the American West as thousands of fortune-seekers rushed to the diggings. By 1864, Alder Gulch boasted an estimated ten thousand residents. With the creation of Montana Territory that year, Virginia City soon became the territorial capital, the seat of Madison County, and Montana's first transportation, financial, and social hub. Its prominence was short-lived, as the placer mines soon played out and the population followed new gold discoveries. The proposed route of the Northern Pacific Railroad (known as the Northern Pacific Railway after 1893) bypassed Alder Gulch in the 1870s, further diminishing Virginia City's importance. Today, simple log cabins converted to commercial use recall the frenzied gold rush; several stone business blocks attest to brief stability; and the 1876 architect-designed Madison County courthouse recalls a final burst of optimism. These structures make up a stunning architectural chronology.

Of the estimated one-thousand buildings that once crowded Virginia City, some 250 survivors include more than fifty first-generation buildings that reflect the rapid transition from gold camp to town. Many of the first miners' cabins of V-notched logs were soon repurposed for commercial use. Within weeks, as sawmills produced the first lumber, false fronts and planed siding covered the street-facing façade of the Goldberg/McGovern Store (1863) and the cabins along Wallace Street. Decorative pilasters and classical ornamentation in wood echoed familiar stone and brick features found in much

The members of Virginia City's Masonic Lodge No. 1 parade down Wallace Street in this ca. 1866 photograph.
956-284, MTHS PHOTOGRAPH ARCHIVES

larger cities. Like the Goldberg Store, most storefronts featured French doors with small panes of glass—freighted in at a dollar apiece—in lieu of larger display windows. The Goldberg interior is typical of frontier decorating: wallpapered muslin stretched smooth over log mimics refined plaster walls.

The Kiskadden Stone Block (1863, pictured at left) and Content's Corner (1864) were among the first stone buildings and attest to the town's early stability. Both include rubblestone construction, originally covered in stucco, scored to imitate cut stone. Illusory refinements like scored stucco, false fronts, and wallpapered muslin provided a sense of civilized security on the remote frontier. The Kiskadden Block, converted to a livery in 1870, includes an impressive false front. The Gothic windows of Content's Corner—built just a year later—reflect the maturation of the town's architecture.

The territorial capital moved to Helena in 1875, but plans for a county courthouse went forward. Self-taught architect Loren B. Olds designed the Italianate-style building, still in use today, which features a second-story balcony, roof brackets, and a cupola. Inside, a graceful curving staircase mirrors the one in the Beaverhead County courthouse at Bannack, also designed by Olds. Virginia City's courthouse and several other brick buildings constructed later represent the town's post–gold rush history and its final stage of growth.

During the 1890s through the 1930s, dredging crews boarded in Virginia City and supported its few businesses. In 1942, amid World War II, the federal government declared gold mining a nonessential industry, shutting down the town's economy. As the town teetered on abandonment in 1944, Great Falls legislator Charles Bovey and his wife Sue began purchasing and stabilizing some of the fragile buildings. Through the Boveys' efforts and those of their son Ford, the town earned National Historic Landmark status as one of the most intact gold rush–era towns in the West. The State of Montana purchased the Bovey properties in 1997, and the town remains under mixed private and state ownership. Virginia City's layered history uniquely interprets the boom and bust of the gold rushes and the fleeting glory that brought so many to the West. *—EB*

12. Fort Benton

Chouteau County | 47°49′44″N 110°39′21″W

Founded in 1846 as the fur trade transitioned from beaver pelts to buffalo robes, Fort Benton served as a trading post, military fort, and center for the distribution of Indian annuities. It was also the head of navigation on the Missouri River, meaning it was as far upriver as large ships could travel. The first steamboat arrived at the fort in 1860. Montana's earliest gold discoveries followed soon thereafter, making Fort Benton the "Gateway to the West" and the region's unchallenged freighting and transportation hub. Millions of dollars in gold dust and more than eight hundred thousand buffalo robes left the levee bound for St. Louis. Workers unloaded everything from grand pianos to mining equipment from steamboats before reloading these objects onto ox-drawn wagon trains bound for remote mining camps.

When placer mining regions went bust in the late 1860s, Fort Benton merchants found new markets along the Whoop-Up Trail. The first Canadian-bound trade goods included illegal whiskey; later, more respectable merchandise reached settlers and the Northwest Mounted Police. "Merchant princes" I. G. Baker, Thomas C. Power, John Murphy and Samuel Neel, and Charles and William Conrad developed the territory's largest banking and mercantile operations.

Steamboat-era commercial buildings line the historic riverfront section of town that makes up the Fort Benton National Historic Landmark. Most were constructed of locally manufactured brick, and their architectural features include cornices with corbelling, other intricate masonry, and striking arched door and window openings. The I. G. Baker home, the Murphy, Neel & Co. mercantile, and the Grand Union Hotel especially recall this heady period.

I. G. Baker and his brother George founded their mercantile business in 1866. Baker built a two-room adobe home the following year. Remodels in 1869 and 1876 added two additional rooms, a wood shingle gable roof, overhanging eaves, and horizontal wood siding. Montana Territory's acting governor Thomas F. Meagher enjoyed his last meal in the home before his mysterious drowning in 1867. The house is now a museum.

The Murphy, Neel & Co. mercantile, like several other major business houses in Fort Benton, maintained a huge, varied inventory. Constructed in 1881 at a cost of $15,000, the impressive brick store

Originally built of contrasting red and cream brick, Fort Benton's Grand Union Hotel, seen here ca. 1882, stood out among the town's earlier buildings.

83-0143, ARCHIVES AND SPECIAL COLLECTIONS, MANSFIELD LIBRARY, UNIVERSITY OF MONTANA

The Grand Union's façade has changed little since the hotel opened in 1882.

and warehouse features distinctive brick corbelling and seven gracefully arched doors with double sash windows that allowed sunlight to illuminate rows of shelves packed with merchandise.

The Grand Union Hotel, designed by Thomas Tweedy and built by Frank Coombs in 1881–1882, reflects Fort Benton's brief reign as the "Chicago of the Plains." Overlooking the busy levee, the hotel afforded a bird's-eye view of the diverse goods that crossed the docks. Weary river travelers found its forty-five rooms and suites a luxurious refuge before setting out for remote destinations.

Built of local red brick and a contrasting cream-colored brick (now painted maroon and brown), the Grand Union's intricate masonry patterns and gracefully curved double-hung windows with projecting brick heads and keystones brought urbanity to Fort Benton. Financed by local stockholders at a cost of $50,000, the hotel opened in 1882. Its interior furnishings added an unprecedented $150,000 to the project's cost. Accom-

modations included a saloon, a fine dining room, a saddle room for cowboys to store their gear in winter, and a hidden room to safeguard gold awaiting shipment downriver. A separate ladies' entrance—meant to steer respectable women away from rooms adjoining saloons—led to elegant parlors. Each of the spacious guest rooms had black walnut, marble-topped furnishings. The handsome black walnut staircase still dominates the lobby. After being fully restored and reopened in the late 1990s following several years of inactivity, it is Montana's oldest operating hotel.

Fort Benton's levee saw two hundred thousand pounds of cargo and forty thousand passengers cross its docks, but the glory days of steamboat travel and trade ended abruptly. Transcontinental railroads reached Montana in the early 1880s, and by 1887, rail travel took over and steamboats became a thing of the past. Despite its relatively short period of prominence, Fort Benton's historic buildings offer visitors unique insight into this pivotal chapter of Montana history. *—EB*

In 1866, noted Montana pioneer Granville Stuart traveled up the Missouri from St. Louis aboard the steamer *W. B. Dance*, a journey that took eight weeks. He sketched this scene following his arrival in Fort Benton on June 8. The adobe-walled fort can be seen in the lower right foreground, while three steamboats are docked upriver along the levee.

FORT BENTON, LOOKING WEST, (UP THE RIVER) FROM LOOKOUT HILL, CHOUTEAU CO. MONTANA, INK WASH ON PAPER, JUN. 9, 1866. X1968.43.01 I, MTHS MUSEUM

13. Reed and Bowles Trading Post

Fergus County | 47°12′11″N 109°38′29″W

Reed and Bowles Trading Post highlights the stories of unsavory territorial characters and reflects central Montana's transition away from its early day-trading economy to a rural ranching community.

For thousands of years several Northern Plains tribes frequented the Judith Basin on seasonal hunting and trading trips. By the mid-1860s, the US military began campaigns against Indigenous peoples in Montana Territory that aimed to restrict them to increasingly reduced land bases in order to open more territory for mineral extraction, transportation, and agriculture.

In 1873, negotiations for an anticipated reservation for the Apsáalooke (Crow) people in the Judith Basin drew the attention of Bozeman merchant and rancher Nelson Story and former trader Charles W. Hoffman. That November, Story and Hoffman hired Peter Koch to "build, stock and manage" Fort Sherman (sometimes called Fort Story), a trading post at the confluence of Big Spring Creek and Little Casino Creek, north of present-day Lewistown.

When the plan for a reservation in the Judith Basin failed, Story and Hoffman sold the post to T. L. Dawes in 1874. Dawes then sold the post to nefarious traders Alonzo Reed and John Bowles in 1875. They dismantled the post, hauled it a mile and a half down Big Spring Creek, and reassembled it along the Carroll Trail, a new wagon road that linked the steamboat landing at Carroll on the Missouri River with the territorial capital at Helena. Hunter Charles Alston Messiter, who visited in 1878, described four or five small log cabins surrounded by a square stockade with large entrance gates. He also noted, "The whole place was very untidy and dirty."

Historic archaeology plays an important role in uncovering details from the past, especially in the absence of written records. In 2023, excavations at the Reed and Bowles Trading Post unearthed a pit forge with a tuyere (blower/bellows) visible in the lower left corner of this photograph.

From 1875 to 1880, Reed and Bowles provisioned freighters and travelers along the trail and conducted an illegal trade in liquor and firearms with passing Indian bands. Stories abound of Reed and Bowles's drunken sprees, underhanded business practices, and murderous reprisals. One visitor reported that Reed shot various men for small transgressions and buried them across the creek. Another story recounts Bowles selling the bones of Long Horse, his Apsáalooke father-in-law, to an Irish ethnologist.

By the late 1870s, an influx of Euro-American ranchers and a small group of Métis (people of Indigenous and European heritage with a distinct culture and language) settled in the Judith Basin. In 1879, Métis trader Francis A. Janeaux established a trading post farther east of Reed and Bowles, and the settlement evolved over the next decade to become the community of Lewistown. As the center of trade shifted, Reed and Bowles dissolved their business. Bowles stayed at the post until selling it in 1883. Reed established a homestead, trading post, and post office at the south edge of Janeaux's settlement. The post office still stands.

Though the Reed and Bowles Trading Post quickly faded from prominence after 1880, its early significance has not been forgotten. Locals have maintained and rehabilitated the only remaining building within the original stockade. The humble side-gable roof log cabin has changed little since 1875 and remains a tangible reminder of central Montana's territorial history. *—CWB*

14. Grant-Kohrs Ranch

Deer Lodge | 46°24′30″N 112°44′22″W

John Francis "Johnny" Grant, a French-Canadian Métis, trailed the first horses and cattle over the Continental Divide to winter in the Deer Lodge Valley in 1857. He built his herds by reconditioning worn-out livestock acquired from immigrants along the Oregon Trail and then trading one healthy animal for two depleted ones. Grant, his Newe (Bannock) wife Quarra, secondary wives from other tribes, and his large extended family settled near the banks of the Clark Fork River in 1862. German butcher Conrad Kohrs purchased the ranch in 1866. He and his half-brother John Bielenberg developed Montana's stock-raising industry from this ranch and eventually grazed enormous herds on ten million acres of open range across four states and Canada. Designated a National Historic Landmark in 1960, the main house and outbuildings on what is now known as Grant-Kohrs Ranch demonstrate the evolution of large-scale stock-raising and ranching in the American West.

Johnny Grant built the center log portion of the main residence, one of the first high-style homes in Montana, in 1862. Carpenter Alexander Pambrun used the French Canadian "piece-sur-piece," or channeled log, construction technique

(also seen at Fort Connah). This method uses notched horizontal logs stacked between vertical log posts and then covered with clapboard. The vernacular Greek Revival–style dwelling featured chimneys at either end, a salt-box roof, green-painted shutters, and twenty-eight sashed windows. Grant had these materials shipped via steamboat to Fort Benton and freighted overland at great expense.

While the house was under construction, Grant built two cabins of daubed, half-dovetail logs as temporary housing. A "dogtrot," or open breezeway, connected the two cabins. These elements were later incorporated into the long, low, whitewashed building that became "Bunkhouse Row," the focal point of cowboy life. Bunkhouse Row served as a dining hall, dormitory, and gathering place for wranglers, ranch hands, and other employees. The original cabins and the central portion of the main house reflect the Grant era.

Conrad Kohrs took possession of the ranch in 1866 and married German-born Augusta Kruse in 1868. She lavishly decorated the home with handsome Victorian-era furnishings shipped from back east and Europe. Around 1890, Kohrs added a formal entry, a two-story brick addition with a Queen Anne–style porch at the back, and multiple chimneys. A conservatory at the southwest corner was the final addition in 1907. Although enlarged and somewhat altered with a complementary Greek Revival–style entryway, the front-facing view closely resembles the original 1862 façade. The home well represents the Kohrs family's financial and social prominence.

The draft horse barn and small stallion barns reflect the early 1870s period when Kohrs and Bielenberg operated the ranch. Typical of early, functional buildings, the massive, gable-roofed barn of V-notched logs sheltered purebred Belgian, Clydesdale, and Percheron working draft horses. Barns behind the main house reflect their original purpose: large-scale horse breeding. Three log barns each housed one stallion. A hayloft accessed by a ladder allowed ranch hands to feed and water the potentially dangerous animals without entering the stalls.

Kohrs focused on the business and politics of cattle ranching, serving as a territorial and state senator and president of the Montana Stockgrowers Association. Always "out in the field," Bielenberg excelled at breeding Shorthorn and Hereford cattle and Thoroughbred and draft horses.

Following the deaths of Kohrs and Bielenberg, the ranch passed to a family trust in the 1920s. Kohr's grandson, Conrad "Con" Warren, became ranch manager in 1929 and, with his wife Nellie, purchased the ranch from the trust in 1940. The couple shared a determination to preserve the remarkably intact ranch for future generations. As noted by the National Park Service (NPS), "Nell cared for their extraordinary collection of antiques and documents, while her husband concentrated on ranching in difficult times that included the Great Depression and World War II." Through the couple's efforts, the NPS opened Grant-Kohrs Ranch National Historic Site to the public in 1977. It continues to serve as a "virtual time machine to America's western cattle ranching heritage, spanning the end of the fur trade through modern, mechanized feedlot operations." —*EB*

This illustration of the Conrad Kohrs residence near Deer Lodge appeared in Michael A. Leeson's *History of Montana: 1739–1885*, published in 1885.
LOCKER 978.9 L51, MTHS RESEARCH CENTER

15. Battlefields

The years 1876 and 1877 marked a turning point in the Euro-American invasion of Indigenous homelands. Older generations of Western historians described this period as the time of the so-called Indian Wars. By 1876, the US government had already negotiated a series of treaties with Indian nations, during which tribes gave up huge swaths of land. As settlers moved into the West, the US government repeatedly demanded that tribal nations renegotiate these treaties. For example, in 1855, the Nimiipuu signed a treaty recognizing their claim to their traditional territory. In 1867, the government proposed a new treaty, ultimately signed by a minority of Nimiipuu representatives, which reduced their territory by 90 percent. Ten years later, the army sent troops to force the members of the Nimiipuu who had not signed the 1867 treaty (known as the non-treaty Nimiipuu) onto a much smaller reservation in north-central Idaho.

The Fort Laramie Treaty, signed in 1868, guaranteed the Lakota people half of what is present-day South Dakota and designated an additional sixty million acres in present-day Nebraska, Wyoming, and Montana as "unceded hunting grounds." However, after discovery of gold in the Black Hills in 1874, the United States demanded that the Lakota people relinquish the Black Hills and settle permanently on reservations.

In 1876–1877, the US military targeted the Lakota, Tsétsėhesėstȧhase naa Suhtaio (Northern Cheyenne), and Hinono'ei (Arapaho) peoples, who remained on unceded hunting grounds rather than moving to reservations. In 1877, they similarly pursuedthe non-treaty Nimiipuu. In both campaigns, the US military attacked Indian villages—homes to women, children, and elders as well as warriors. The major sites of these deadly clashes have been named National Historic Landmarks. These four sites are also historical parks, preserved as places for reflection, learning, and memory.

Granville Stuart drew this depiction of the battlefield at Big Hole in 1878, the year after US troops led by Colonel John Gibbon attacked a group of fleeing Nimiipuu at the site.

GRANVILLE STUART, *VIEW OF THE BATTLE GROUND OF BIG HOLE, LOOKING NORTH*, GRAPHITE SKETCH ON PAPER, 1878. X1968.43.17, MTHS MUSEUM COLLECTIONS

Big Hole National Battlefield/ Place of the Buffalo Calf at Salish (Country)

Beaverhead County | 45°38′15″N 113°38′37″W

In the summer of 1877, the non-treaty Nimiipuu had reluctantly agreed to move onto the Lapwai reservation in Idaho from their homeland in northeastern Oregon. But when a group of young warriors raided settlers, US troops attacked the non-treaty bands at White Bird Canyon. After pushing the soldiers back, the Nimiipuu decided to flee to escape the inevitable army response. They crossed Lolo Pass into Montana with approximately eight hundred people. Camping at the Big Hole—an area they had often visited and where they had good trade relations with white settlers—they believed they had reached temporary safety. Instead, on August 9, 1877, Colonel John Gibbon's troops began firing into their lodges at dawn. Before they could escape, between seventy and ninety Nimiipuu died, mostly women and children, as did twenty-nine US Army soldiers.

Above: The Little Bighorn Battlefield's Indian Memorial features the bronze Spirit Warrior Sculpture by Oglala Lakota artist Colleen Cutschall.
Below: The Battle of Bear Paw was the final engagement of the Nez Perce War of 1877.

Rosebud Battlefield National Historic Landmark/Where the Girl Saved Her Brother

Big Horn County | 45°13′50″N 106°59′52″W

On June 17, 1876, General George Crook's troops, along with 276 Apsáalooke and Newe (Shoshone) allies, were heading to attack a large Lakota village on the Little Bighorn River when Lakota and Tsetsėhesėstȧhase naa Suhtaio warriors intercepted them near the headwaters of Rosebud Creek. The Tsėtsėhėstȧhese naa Suhtaio named the battlefield Where the Girl Saved Her Brother. The name commemorates Buffalo Calf Road Woman, who charged into the fray to rescue her brother, Chief Comes in Sight, after his horse was shot from under him. Thirty-nine Native warriors and ten US soldiers died in the six-hour battle.

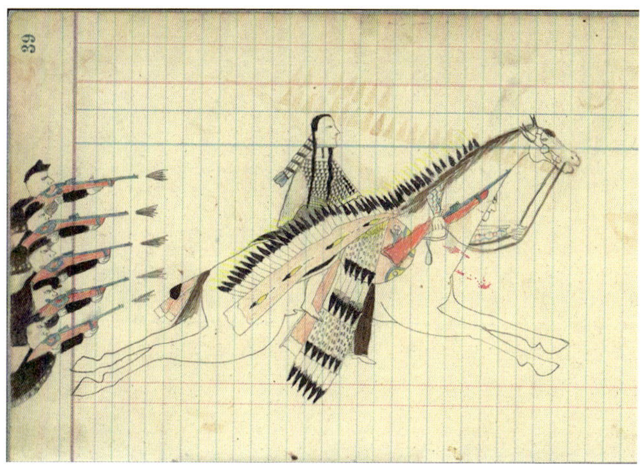

This ledger drawing depicts the moment when Buffalo Calf Road Woman rescued her brother during a battle between US soldiers and Lakota and Tsėtsėhėstȧhese naa Suhtaio warriors near Rosebud Creek.

YELLOW NOSE, UTE, *UNTITLED (BUFFALO CALF ROAD WOMAN RESCUING HER BROTHER, COMES IN SIGHT)*, GRAPHITE, COLORED PENCIL, AND INK, CA. 1889. MS 166032, BUREAU OF AMERICAN ETHNOLOGY, NATIONAL ANTHROPOLOGICAL ARCHIVES, SMITHSONIAN INSTITUTION

Little Bighorn Battlefield National Monument/ Battle of Greasy Grass

Crow Agency | 45°34′13″N 107°25′39″W

On June 25–26, 1876, 263 soldiers, including Lieutenant Colonel George Armstrong Custer, died here while fighting several thousand Lakota, Tsėtsėhėstȧhese naa Suhtaio, and Hinono'ei warriors. Approximately thirty Lakota and Tsėtsėhesėstȧhase naa Suhtaio combatants also died that day, as did several Apsáalooke and Sahnish (Arikara) people who served as US Army scouts. The loss persuaded the US military to dedicate more resources to subduing the Lakota people, and Custer's name became a rallying cry for those seeking to avenge the rout. Possibly the most famous battlefield in North America, it is now a National Park Service site and includes a military cemetery—the Seventh Cavalry Memorial, erected in 1881—and an Indian Memorial, dedicated in 2003.

Bear Paw Battlefield/Place of Many Manure Fires

Blaine County | 48°22′39″N 109°12′26″W

For most of the Nimiipuu, their 1,170-mile flight ended only forty-two miles from the "Medicine Line" (the US-Canadian border), where they would have been beyond the reach of the army. On September 30, 1877, US troops caught up with the band, capturing their herd of horses. Without the ability to counterattack or flee, the warriors defended their camp, which they called Place of Many Manure Fires because they burned dried manure there due to the scarcity of wood. October 1 brought snow to the mountains as both sides dug in. On October 5, exhausted and freezing, Chief Joseph and four hundred Nimiipuu surrendered. Handing his rifle to General Nelson A. Miles, Chief Joseph reportedly declared, "From where the sun now stands, I will fight no more forever." Approximately three hundred Nimiipuu escaped to Canada. *—MK*

16. Fort Shaw

Cascade County | 47°30′32″N 111°49′12″W

As non-Indians encroached on their traditional homelands, often breaking treaties, Indigenous peoples fought back. In response, Euro-American settlers called for protection, leading the army to build a series of military forts located at strategic points around the new territory.

Accordingly, the US government established Fort Shaw in 1867 on the south bank of the Sun River in Piikuni territory. The site was chosen to help guard gold seekers and others traveling the Mullan Road, a 624-mile military wagon route that connected Fort Benton to Fort Walla Walla, Washington. In due course, Fort Shaw also helped open the Sun River valley to settlement both by alleviating white settlers' fears and by providing a ready market for the agricultural goods they would grow. Additionally, troops stationed at Fort Shaw played roles in the period's most significant conflicts, including the horrific Marias Massacre (1870), Battle of the Little Bighorn (1876), and Battle of the Big Hole (1877).

Colonel I. V. D. Reeves designed the fort. Soldiers of the Thirteenth US Infantry harvested clay from nearby Adobe Creek to make bricks to construct the officers' quarters and post hospital as well as other major buildings no longer standing. They finished the outer walls with clapboard siding and plastered the interior walls. Sandstone for the officers' wash houses was quarried from Shaw Butte about three miles away. Lumber was either milled on-site at the post's sawmill or shipped by steamboat from St. Louis to Fort Benton and then freighted overland.

The military soon rechristened the outpost, originally named Camp Reynolds, in honor of Colonel Robert G. Shaw, a white officer killed during the Civil War while commanding the Fifty-Fourth Massachusetts Infantry—one of the first regiments of African American troops in the Union Army. Following the war, segregated African American troops were sent to the West, where, according to historian Ken Robison, they were dispatched "to the most dangerous and isolated posts, and they were called first to fight." From 1888 to 1891, the last soldiers to serve at Fort Shaw were four companies of the Twenty-Fifth Colored Infantry Regiment.

In 1891—with tribes confined to reservations a fraction of the size of their original territories—the army abandoned Fort Shaw. The following year, the federal government converted the post into an off-reservation boarding school. Forced assimilation at such Indian boarding schools wrought nearly unbearable trauma for students and their families. Nevertheless, the Fort Shaw Government Industrial School is best known for the prowess of its girls' basketball team. After two years wowing Treasure State crowds with victories over both high school and college rivals, the ten-member team (composed of girls representing a number of tribes) became a national sensation at the 1904 St. Louis World's Fair, where they were declared the undisputed "World Champions." In spite of the renown garnered by the team, the boarding school closed in 1910. The Fort Shaw community repurposed the property as a public school in 1927.

Located approximately one mile west of the post, the seven-and-a-half-acre Fort Shaw Military Cemetery was plotted and first used during the summer of 1867. Over the next fifty-three years, the burial grounds became the final resting place for many of the participants in the Fort Shaw story: soldiers, both Black and white; boarding school students; and homesteaders alike. —*KL*

Left: Government Industrial School work on projects as teachers and older students look on in this photograph taken around 1900.
947-400, MTHS PHOTOGRAPH ARCHIVES

Opposite page: Clarence E. Le Munyon photographed this group of soldiers from the Twenty-Fifth Colored Infantry Regiment standing at attention in front of the barracks building at Fort Shaw in 1890.
947-375, MTHS PHOTOGRAPH ARCHIVES

17. US Assay Office

Helena | 46°35′47″N 112°01′35″W

Much of the great wealth that once came from Montana's gold and silver mines was weighed, tested, and melted in Helena's assay office—the first official federal building constructed in Helena. Mining booms in the West in the 1850s and 1860s warranted construction of branch assay and mint buildings in San Francisco, Denver, and Boise. Likewise, the need for a federal assay office in Montana Territory was evident early in the 1870s. Although most miners used gold dust as currency, merchants, bankers, and particularly successful miners needed a safe and reliable place to deposit and exchange larger stores of gold. Without a federal assay office nearby, they were forced to take on considerable expense and risk to transport their gold to distant repositories.

In May 1874, Congress appropriated $75,000 to build this facility. US Treasury Department architect A. B. Mullet, designer of the San Francisco Mint, drew the plans, which his successor William Potter modified. Excavation began in 1875, and the building opened for business in mid-January 1877. Mullet and Potter's Italianate-style building was striking yet restrained. Reflecting the US government's confidence in the region's mining economy without appearing too lavish, the design featured stout brick walls accented by limestone string courses and unified by symmetrically placed arched windows and graceful, segmental stone lintels. Inside, a central hall divided receiving and weighing rooms on the right and melting rooms on the left. The second and third floors held offices.

Assayer Charles Rumley was the first superintendent of Helena's assay office. In late 1878, president Rutherford B. Hayes appointed Russell B. Harrison to the position. Harrison—great-grandson of William Henry Harrison (ninth president of the United States) and son of then-US senator and future US president Benjamin Harrison—served until 1885. Harrison and his family lived in the one-story assayer's quarters at the east rear of the building.

By December 1877, the Helena office brought in gold deposits equaling nearly $380,000. Banner years in 1879 and 1880 netted around $500,000 each year in gold bullion (equal to about $13.5 million in 2023 dollars). To showcase Montana's high status as a gold mining region, in 1889 Colonel Charles Broadwater commissioned the US assay office to create the world's largest gold bar. The pyramid-shaped ingot, weighing 434 pounds and valued at $100,000, was displayed in Helena at Broadwater's Montana National Bank, an exposition in Minneapolis, and the Chase National Bank in New York City.

By 1900, the Helena assay office had melted $30 million ($1.1 billion in 2023) worth of gold into bars for Uncle Sam. A 1919 Treasury Department report indicated that receipts from Helena's assay office—one of five remaining in the country at the time—were exceeded only by those of the Seattle office. Helena's facility remained open until a changing economy brought its closure in 1934. The well-preserved building now houses several apartments and stands as a symbol of Montana's national prominence as a gold mining region. —***CWB***

This 1875 sketch depicts the US Assay Office in Helena, a substantial building meant to convey security without appearing overly ornate.
LOT 4477, LIBRARY OF CONGRESS PRINTS AND PHOTOGRAPHS DIVISION

CHAPTER THREE

NEXT STOP: STATEHOOD 1883–1898

"To find mines, to plant mining communities, and to supply them," recalled Wilbur Fisk Sanders, who arrived in Bannack in 1863, "was then supposed to be the extent of the industries which would occupy . . . Montana." In later years, he looked back in amazement at Montana's transformation "from a Commonwealth of wigwams and wickiups . . . to a Commonwealth of American homes." It "seems wholly not unlike a dream," he said. "We wonder that we existed with such strange surroundings and did not appreciate . . . how suddenly and absolutely they were to pass away."

Railroads were the main engine of Montana's rapid development. The first railroad, a spur line from Corrine, Utah, entered Montana Territory in 1881. The Northern Pacific crossed Montana in 1883, completing the country's first northern transcontinental route. After successfully lobbying the US government to negotiate with tribal nations to dramatically reduce the size of reservations along Montana's northern tier, Northern Pacific's competitor, the Great Northern Railway, finished its own transcontinental rail line in 1893.

The impact of these railroads was instantaneous. In 1870, Montana Territory was home to an estimated 19,300 Indians and about the same number of non-Indians. By 1890, Montana's non-Indian population had swelled to 142,924. For members of Montana's Indigenous nations, this was the beginning of a particularly dark period. By 1883, hide-hunting, disease, and habitat destruction had almost entirely eradicated bison from the Northern Plains. More than five hundred Piikuni (Blackfeet)—approximately a quarter of the tribe—starved to death that winter. Tribal members found themselves forcibly confined to reservations, where Indian agents tried to control many aspects of their daily life, even banning religious ceremonies. Forced assimilation—or cultural genocide—took its most dangerous form in the creation of Indian boarding schools both on and off reservations. If parents refused to cooperate, tribal police seized children as young as five years old, delivering them to boarding schools where teachers stripped them of their traditional clothing and belongings and punished them for speaking Indigenous languages. More than simply providing an education, these schools sought, according to the National Native American Boarding School Healing Coalition, "the systematic destruction of Native cultures and communities."

For most non-Indians living in Montana Territory, the changes wrought by the coming of the railroad were cause for celebration. After the Northern Pacific arrived in 1883, it only took two days to travel from Helena to St. Louis, a journey that had previously taken three to four months overland and two months by steamboat. Railroads brought new settlers and facilitated access to consumer goods.

Thousands of experienced Chinese laborers—like the ones seen here working along the Yellowstone River in Custer County—were among the men who performed the grueling manual labor needed to complete Montana's first transcontinental railroad line.

F. JAY HAYNES PHOTOGRAPH, 1881. H-00711, MTHS PHOTOGRAPH ARCHIVES

Montana's cowboy artist Charles M. Russell produced this now-famous sketch to illustrate the effect of accumulated snow during the brutal winter of 1886–1887. When it was published in newspapers across the country, its impact was so great that Russell's wife and business manager Nancy later referred to it as the sketch that launched Charlie's career.

CHARLES M. RUSSELL, *WAITING FOR A CHINOOK*, WATERCOLOR ON CARDBOARD, 1887. L1953.01.01, MTHS MUSEUM COLLECTIONS, COURTESY OF THE MONTANA STOCKGROWERS ASSOCIATION

Additionally, they transformed Montana architecture, making it easy and inexpensive to transport precut and precast architectural elements, plate glass windows, high-fire brick (which was much more durable than locally manufactured brick), and stone from distant quarries.

The railroads also spurred economic development. Corporate mining interests increasingly invested in Montana Territory as shipping costs dropped for both heavy equipment and basic commodities like salt, a principal ingredient in the roasting process used to extract silver. Hauled by wagon from Utah, salt cost $120 per ton in Philipsburg in 1871. After the Northern Pacific arrived in 1883, salt prices fell to $25 per ton. Railroads were even more essential to copper mining, and Butte—home to some of the richest copper mines in the world—boomed after the first train arrived in December 1881, carrying forty passengers and 5,600 pounds of mining equipment for future copper magnate William A. Clark. By 1887, Butte was the largest copper producer in the world.

Above left: Many American Indian children were forcibly removed from their families to be placed in off-reservation boarding schools. This ledger drawing credited to boys at the Carlisle Indian Industrial School in Pennsylvania depicts one such traumatic occurrence—Major Wyman, US Indian agent at Crow Agency, and his chief of police, Boy That Grabs, taking a young girl from her mother.

UNKNOWN ARTIST, *CROW INDIAN WOMAN LEADING HER LITTLE GIRL*, GRAPHITE AND COLORED PENCIL ON PAPER, 1891. 1930.51, CHARLES H. BARSTOW COLLECTION, MONTANA STATE UNIVERSITY BILLINGS

Above right: Railroads facilitated the use of architectural elements that originated outside of Montana. This includes the Wisconsin brownstone used as trim on the Lewis and Clark County Courthouse in Helena, completed in 1887.

UNKNOWN PHOTOGRAPHER, CA. 1888–1890. 953-351, MTHS PHOTOGRAPH ARCHIVES

Railroads opened huge swaths of western Montana's forests, where loggers provided railroad ties to build the tracks, timber to shore up underground mines, and lumber to construct homes and businesses. The railroads also provided easy access to Chicago's slaughterhouses, which made eastern Montana even more attractive to stockgrowers, leading to more cattle on Montana's arid prairies than the land could support. That, combined with exceptionally heavy snowfalls and low temperatures, led to a massive livestock die-off during the winter of 1886–1887 and the end of open-range cattle grazing.

With the economy flourishing and the population booming, many Montanans chafed at their territorial status. The first bid for statehood came prematurely in 1866. In 1884, politicians met to craft a second constitution, which Montana voters quickly ratified. However, inter-party disagreements in Congress stalled Montana's addition to the Union until 1889, when, after a third constitutional convention, Montana became the forty-first state.

A vigorous battle over the location of the state capital ensued, leading contending cities to build new hotels and business blocks and invest in infrastructure and beautification projects. Helena finally emerged victorious in 1894, but other cities found consolation in the form of significant state institutions ranging from prisons and universities to the state hospital and veterans' home. Coveted for the jobs and economic stability they promised, these institutions took on additional importance after the Panic of 1893, an international economic collapse that rivaled the Great Depression. Montana particularly suffered once the US government decided to end its purchase of silver for currency. Within a few months, nearly a third of Montana workers, about twenty thousand people, lost their jobs. This economic upheaval meant that new building projects ceased almost entirely and silver mining communities became ghost towns almost overnight. Montana would not fully recover until the turn of the twentieth century. *—MK*

18. Fort Assinniboine

Hill County | 48°29′59″N 109°47′39″W

For centuries, ancestors of the Lakota and Dakota (Sioux), Piikuni, Apsáalooke (Crow), Aaniiihnen (Gros Ventre), Nakoda (Assiniboine), Anishinaabe (Chippewa), and Neyiowahk (Cree) peoples occupied and visited the vast plains of central North America where present-day Montana, Alberta, and Saskatchewan now meet. They lived on both sides of a yet-to-be-established border, moving seasonally to hunt and gather resources. Since the mid-1700s, they also maintained close economic and personal relationships with French, British, and American fur traders. Tribal members relied on traders for access to manufactured goods while traders depended on tribal members for information, food, hides, and labor. Intermarriage between Indigenous women and fur trappers and traders was common; ultimately, their offspring formed a new cultural group known as the Métis.

As more Euro-Americans entered the territory, relations between Indigenous nations and the US government became increasingly fraught. In 1876 and 1877, the US Army went to war against both the Nimiipuu (Nez Perce) and the Lakota,

and members of both tribal nations fled to Canada seeking safety. During the same era, the Canadian government sent troops to Manitoba to engage the Métis who were resisting their displacement from territory formerly controlled by the Hudson's Bay Company. In response, many Métis fled across the border into the United States.

In the aftermath of military conflicts on both sides of the border, US and Canadian military leaders conspired to further limit movement of Indigenous nations between countries, including those, like the Neyiowahk, who had historically lived and hunted buffalo on both sides of the "Medicine Line." In 1879, the US government authorized construction of Fort Assiniboine (six miles south of present-day Havre), the spelling of which was later changed to Assinniboine. The fort's location allowed the United States to monitor Native nations, control cross-border movement of people and goods, and reduce the likelihood of conflict. Put simply, Fort Assinniboine served as the first border patrol station in Montana.

Completed in 1884, the massive seven-hundred-thousand-acre military reserve rose rapidly from the plains. Five hundred Métis workers made bricks, and 350 civilians from eastern locales helped soldiers construct about one hundred buildings at a final cost of $500,000 (about $15 million in 2023 dollars). It was the largest post in the Northwest and one of the largest ever constructed in the United States. As soldiers and workers built the fort in 1881, Lakota leader Sitting Bull surrendered at Fort Buford in North Dakota, and US soldiers shifted their attention to forcibly deporting Neyiowahk and Métis people from Montana. In campaigns throughout the 1880s, Fort Assinniboine soldiers burned hundreds of homes and forced Neyiowahk and Métis people (some who were born in the United States) into Canada. During the largest operation in 1896, the all-Black Tenth Cavalry herded more than six hundred Neyiowahk people into train cars and shipped them north across the forty-ninth parallel. The army halted the forced removal of the Neyiowahk in 1898 when the Tenth Cavalry, as well as the all-Black Twenty-Fourth and Twenty-Fifth Infantries, deployed to Cuba, where they fought in the Spanish American War.

The military expanded Fort Assinniboine for use as a training facility after 1902, but changing political priorities led to its closure in 1911. The vast tract of land and buildings benefited many, including the Anishinaabe and Neyiowahk people who received 56,000 acres for Rocky Boy's Indian Reservation in 1916. Another portion became the Northern Agricultural Research Center, and a one-mile-wide corridor surrounding Beaver Creek became part of a county park. In 1933, workers used brick from the demolished barracks to construct Pershing Hall at Northern Montana College in Havre, now known as Montana State University-Northern. —***CWB***

A large crew of men and horses can be seen making mortar to construct the brick officers' quarters at Fort Assinniboine in this 1880 F. Jay Haynes photograph.

H-00386, MTHS PHOTOGRAPH ARCHIVES

19. Canyon Creek Charcoal Kilns

Beaverhead County | 45°36′20″N 112°55′53″W

Twenty-three towering, brick, beehive-shaped kilns nestled high in the East Pioneer Mountains near Canyon Creek stand as striking reminders of the area's industrial mining history. The kilns, built in 1885 for the Hecla Consolidated Mining Company (HCMC), transformed wood into charcoal, the fuel used to power the blast furnaces at its nearby Glendale smelter.

Profiting from the richness of Montana's veins of precious metal depended not only on men and mules to remove ore from the earth but also on the resource-intensive task of smelting to extract the valuable base metals from the other minerals included in the rocks. In the 1860s, mine owners shipped their ore long distances to smelters as far away as Swansea, Wales, for refining—a risky, time-consuming, and expensive process. By the 1870s, when industrial hard-rock mining (as opposed to placer mining with pans) took hold in Montana, well-capitalized mine owners began building their own smelters. Armstrong, Dahler & Co., later incorporated as HCMC, developed numerous silver mines on Lion Mountain in the 1870s. The company built its first smelter at Glendale in 1874–1875. By 1876, the smelter was cranking out three to five

This uncredited ca. 1905 photograph shows a group of workers standing outside the charcoal kilns near Glendale.
LOT 026 B6F11.04, MTHS PHOTOGRAPH ARCHIVES

tons of crude bullion each day. To maintain that pace, the smelter's insatiable furnaces consumed anywhere from 56,000 to 80,000 pounds of charcoal per day. Two stone kilns on the site turned out approximately 32,000 pounds per day, while the rest of the fuel was imported.

A fire destroyed HCMC's smelter in 1879, but the company immediately rebuilt the facility on a larger scale. Demand for fuel soared, and HCMC added a total of thirty-eight new kilns on Trapper, Sucker, and Canyon Creeks between 1882 and 1885. Contractors McLain and McCoy constructed the Canyon Creek kilns between July and December 1885. To make charcoal, company loggers denuded nearby forests and delivered trees via wood chutes to the kiln site. Woodchoppers then cut the trees into four-foot lengths for careful stacking inside the kilns. Each twenty-two-foot-tall kiln held twenty-five to thirty-five cords of wood.

It took one day to charge (load) a kiln, six to eight days to burn, two or three days to cool off, and one day to discharge (unload). The firemen lived at the site through the whole process, watching closely as white, then yellow, then blue smoke poured from the top vents. Blue smoke indicated the burn was nearly complete and the firemen could slowly seal all the vents from top to bottom, extinguishing the fire. Burning the wood slowly with just enough oxygen ensured the wood would turn to charcoal instead of ash.

By 1888, HCMC's voracious smelter furnaces were consuming about eight million pounds of charcoal per month. Most of it came from area kilns, and Italian contractors supplied the rest. After the Panic of 1893, when silver prices plummeted, operations at the HCMC slowed, and the facility closed in 1900. In the sixteen years they operated, the HCMC kilns burned an estimated eighteen square miles of forest down to 1.5 billion pounds of charcoal. *—CWB*

20. St. Peter's Mission

Cascade County | 47°18′02″N 111°55′14″W

Jesuit priests first attempted to establish a mission among the Piikuni in 1859, but troubled relations with their intended converts forestalled their efforts. After three other locations proved unsuitable, the determined clerics settled at this site in 1866, abandoned it a short time later, then returned in 1874. The following year, the missionaries built the original portion of the log chapel, which they soon expanded, nearly doubling its size. The logs were hand-hewn with half-dovetail corner notching and the interior was finished with tongue-and-groove siding. The clapboard bell tower was built as a free-standing structure and initially placed beside the church; later, it was relocated to the front of the building and incorporated as its entrance. A small churchyard lies nearby.

From the beginning, the founders of St. Peter's envisioned a school as part of their mission, but the same year that the Jesuits returned to St. Peter's the federal government relocated the southern boundary of the Blackfeet Indian Reservation sixty miles northward. The change both removed potential Piikuni students from the mission's proximity and opened the area to settlement by non-Piikuni. By the early 1880s, the Jesuits were operating a school for boys, which included the sons of white settlers as well as Métis who had relocated to the area following the 1869–1870 Red River Rebellion in Canada.

In 1884, Ursuline nuns, led by Mother Amadeus, arrived at St. Peter's to begin educating girls, and by century's end the simple mission had been transformed into an expansive boarding school for Native students. Facilities included a four-story boys' school and dormitory; a three-story girls' school, dormitory, and convent for the nuns; a three-story residence for the priests; and a variety of ancillary structures including a laundry, bakery, barn, and corral. In addition, because Ursuline education included training in music and the arts, there was also a log "opera house" used for classes, recitals, school plays, and graduations. The operation became one of the most significant communities between Helena and Great Falls.

White students continued to attend day school at the mission but were taught separately from their Indian counterparts. Indian boarding school students came to St. Peter's—most often against their will—from many different tribes. Instruction included curriculum focused on the Catholic religion and traditional academics as well as industrial arts for the boys and

Only ruins remain of Mount Angela—the monumental stone building that housed the convent and girls' school—which burned in 1918.

The log chapel at St. Peter's—as it appeared before the bell tower was moved to the front of the church—provides a backdrop for this procession of boys who likely were students at the mission. The building on the right served as a dormitory until more substantial buildings were constructed.
R. E. DECAMP PHOTOGRAPHER, UNDATED. 950-777, MTHS PHOTOGRAPH ARCHIVES

domestic arts for the girls. The school made every effort to eradicate all aspects of students' "Indianness," a factor that, combined with separation from their families, proved traumatizing for most students and devastating for traditional Native cultures. The impacts of these practices still resonate in many American Indian families and communities.

In addition to Mother Amadeus, who played an instrumental role in the Ursulines' story, not only in Montana but also in Alaska, Louis Riel and Mary Fields were two of the most notable figures who, for a time, called St. Peter's home. Riel—an influential Métis leader and folk hero hanged by the Canadian government for treason in 1895—taught at the school in 1893-1894. Fields—a liquor-drinking, gun-carrying, cigar-smoking formerly enslaved woman—worked at the mission for eight years until the bishop deemed her character too unsavory. She later became a star route mail carrier (the first African American woman to receive such a contract), delivering mail by stagecoach from Cascade to St. Peter's and earning the sobriquet "Stagecoach Mary" in the process. In an interview with *Ebony*, actor Gary Cooper—a fellow Montanan—later characterized Fields as "one of the freest souls to ever draw a breath, or a .38."

Following a period of declining support and disastrous fires, the mission closed in 1918. Today, only the small log church, silent cemetery, and scattered stone ruins belie the importance and diversity of the community once encompassed by St. Peter's Mission. *—KL*

21. Dion Buildings

Glendive | 47°6′31″N 104°42′38″W

Before railroads crisscrossed Montana, goods that could not be made locally or shipped by riverboat had to be hauled by wagons for hundreds of miles on primitive roads at considerable expense. When the Northern Pacific Railroa completed its line to Glendive in 1881, it connected Montana Territory to eastern cities and offered unlimited possibilities for shipping. Architects and builders in the West could now order prefabricated building materials. This advance is evident along Glendive's Merrill Avenue, where three buildings built for the Dion family between 1886 and 1929 trace changing tastes and architectural trends.

Left: In 1886, fire destroyed Henry Dion's original saloon and general store, seen here second and third from right in this F. Jay Haynes photograph from five years earlier. H-00570, MTHS PHOTOGRAPH ARCHIVES

Opposite page: Undeterred, Dion rebuilt a brick Romanesque Revival–style building that year (right). Eight years later, he built a mercantile annex (center), to which his sons added a second story in 1910. Dion added his namesake building in 1905 (left). Following trends prescribing sleek, modern design, his sons remodeled the 1886 and 1905 buildings in 1929.

Henry Dion (pronounced like lion) was a town founder, businessman, and rancher. In 1886, a major fire (the city's third) swept through Glendive, destroying Dion's original 1881 wood-frame saloon and general store. Determined to make the town fireproof, Dion established a brickyard to help the community rebuild. His striking Romanesque Revival–style building was the first new building completed after the fire, and it immediately boosted Glendive's status. Its expansive glass display windows, second-story windows with white limestone arches, and pyramidal column capitals (all imported by rail) brought big-city style to the prairie. Gothic and Romanesque design was at the height of fashion in the East until about 1880 but remained popular in western commercial buildings through the 1880s and later.

The building was home to Dion's general store, saloon, bank, and, after 1911, the Exchange State Bank, of which Dion was president. The Glendive Club, a social organization for businessmen, occupied the second floor. Dion sold the building to his sons Fred and Harry in 1908. Extensive remodeling in 1929 introduced a restrained classical commercial style to Glendive. Shorter display windows surrounded by sleek white limestone panels and minimal ornamentation reflected a new taste for simplicity, as well as a scarcity of funds for frivolous decoration.

The central Dion Brothers building emerged in response to two influxes of homesteaders. The first wave, arriving in the early 1890s, spurred Henry Dion to build a one-story mercantile annex, which he completed in 1894. When he sold the business to his sons in 1908, during the second wave of new settlers, they hired local architect Brynjulf Rivenes to redesign the building and add a second story in the Neoclassical Revival style, which became popular following the 1893 Columbian Exposition in Chicago, where buildings with classical columns, arches, and domes influenced architects nationwide. Rivenes's 1910 design for the expanded Dion Brothers block features multicolored bricks, a stepped parapet, bracketed cornice, and large sandstone lion heads atop the building's central brick piers.

In 1905, Henry Dion built his last business block next door to the mercantile. Bucking the architectural trends of the day, he chose to revive the Romanesque style popular in his younger years to match his original 1886 building. An investment property, the building hosted a saloon, a shoe repair business, and later a pool hall and barber shop. Under his sons' modernization plan in 1929, contractors covered the storefront with sleek, black glass panels and a glass-block transom. Nearly a century later, in 2020–2021, the building's owners used Revitalizing Montana Rural Heritage grant funds from the Montana State Historic Preservation Office to restore lost historic features to the ground-level storefronts. —*CWB*

22. Houses

House types and styles have always reflected social, economic, and technological change. In Montana, the arrival of transcontinental railroads, beginning in the 1880s, transformed residential architecture. Railroads transported mass-produced building materials, and lumber yards, conveniently located near the train yards, could supply everything from lumber and nails to mortar and glass, cabinetry, and ornate trimwork. Even as brickyards and quarries, established in many Montana towns by 1885, provided a steady flow of masonry materials, railroads could supply multi-hued brick varieties from out-of-state manufacturers.

With readily available materials came new technology. Builders dispensed with log and heavy timber framing, opting for the latest "stick" or balloon framing, which employed lightweight milled lumber, thin wood siding, and machine-made wire nails. This change offered lower- and middle-class Montanans affordable housing and provided endless options for the well-to-do to express their style and status.

Three main variations of the exuberant Victorian style—Folk Victorian, Queen Anne, and Richardsonian Romanesque—accommodated varying budgets. The Folk Victorian, which applied mass-produced ornamentation to modest, one-story cottages, became the most popular and affordable style. Owners of middle- and upper-class Queen Anne–style homes applied more of the same ornament to larger homes with gracious front porches, steeply pitched roofs, and multi-textured siding. The third, less-common style favored by wealthy homeowners was Richardsonian Romanesque. Developed by architect Henry Hobson Richardson, it emphasized massive stone walls and arched window and door openings found in Italian Renaissance architecture.

Rancher Pierre Wibaux's well-preserved house and office—located, naturally, in the eastern Montana community of Wibaux—is now a museum.

409 Alaska Street

Butte | 45°54′08″N 112°39′24″W

Shotgun houses like 409 Alaska Street in Butte's Centerville neighborhood illustrate the new generation of working-class houses built in Montana in the late 1800s. The form, which originated in West Africa, made its way to New Orleans in the early 1800s and spread across the United States by the 1890s. Small and quick to build, shotgun and hipped-roof Folk Victorian cottages replaced log buildings and tents in many early Montana towns, providing low-cost housing for workers. Architectural historians don't agree on how the shotgun house got its name, but its long narrow footprint and string of connected rooms suggests a "straight shot" from the front to the back.

William A. Clark Mansion

Butte | 45°54′08″N 112°39′24″W

In stark contrast to most of Butte's working-class homes (and many of its upper-middle-class homes), self-made multimillionaire William A. Clark spent an estimated $260,000 on the construction of his enormous and richly decorated thirty-two-room residence, built between 1884 and 1888. The price tag represented only a half-day's earnings out of Clark's $17 million-a-month income and demonstrated the astounding income inequality between Butte's elite and worker residents. The irregular architectural plan, a classic of Queen Anne styling, features porticos, arched windows, and elaborate decorative elements. The interior boasts finishing in a different wood for each room, frescoed ceilings, and Tiffany stained glass windows and chandeliers. The intricately carved staircase took four years to complete and was dismantled and displayed at the 1904 World's Fair in St. Louis.

Byron Sherman House, White Sulphur Springs (left) and 511 4th Avenue East, Kalispell (right)

Byron Sherman House

White Sulphur Springs | 46°32′43″N 110°54′14″W

Businessman Byron Sherman's imposing stone mansion, dubbed the Castle, is one of Montana's finest examples of a Romanesque-style residence and a symbol of Sherman's success. This style—most often used for commercial and civic buildings—enjoyed immense popularity among wealthy landowners throughout the 1890s. Perhaps influenced by Helena's then-new Power Block (1889) or the Hotel Bozeman (1892), Sherman designed the home himself. Constructed in 1892, its tall arched windows and doors, castellated parapets, and conical-roof tower are stylistic hallmarks that evoke memories of Medieval castles. Despite its aged character, modern innovations such as wind-powered plumbing, a coal-fired water heater, and an acetylene plant for gas lights represented first-class living. The Meagher County Historical Association has operated the Castle as a museum since 1960.

511 4th Avenue East

Kalispell | 48°14′02″N 114°20′20″W

This beautiful 1894 gable-front-and-wing residence captures the Queen Anne style. Built for John McIntosh, a successful hardware store and opera-house owner in Kalispell, and his wife, Sophie, the home displays decorative detailing usually found on larger two- and three-story residences. Embellishments include fishscale shingles, wavy clapboard, a sunray pattern, and elaborate stained glass transoms in the cutaway bay. —CWB

1888
SAYRS
BREWERY

23. Sayrs Building (Hyde Block)

Philipsburg | 46°19.937′N, 113° 17.667′W

Montana's mining history can be summarized as a tale of boom and bust. Philipsburg—a small town nestled beneath the Flint Creek Range in Granite County—illustrates how the ebb and flow of mining left its mark not only on the landscape but on the built environment as well. Today, Philipsburg is one of the state's best-preserved late nineteenth-century mining towns, and the colorful Sayrs Building is one of its most striking examples of boomtime prosperity.

Prospectors discovered silver in what is now Granite County in 1864. By the end of the decade, Philipsburg—which was platted by mining engineer Philip Deidesheimer in 1867—had already experienced its first round of boom and bust. The mid-1880s brought a revival of mining activities that, coupled with the 1887 arrival of the Drummond and Philipsburg Railroad, led to a period of unequaled prosperity. In the years that followed, miners removed silver ore valued at tens of millions of dollars from the mountains surrounding Philipsburg.

In the early 1880s, Philipsburg's main commercial thoroughfare, Broadway Street, was still lined with false-front stores and other frame buildings. The affluence brought by the silver boom allowed business owners to replace many frame structures with substantial, style-conscious brick edifices. In 1888, Joseph Hyde erected the Hyde Block at the corner of Broadway and Sansome Streets to house his First National Bank. The brightly colored Victorian building features a metal façade manufactured by Mesker Bros. Ironworks of St. Louis, Missouri. Mesker Bros. made sheet-metal façades and cast-iron storefront components that could be ordered from catalogs and shipped by rail. According to the company's records, at least five other buildings in Philipsburg were also finished with their products.

Five years later, the Panic of 1893—a national economic crisis exacerbated by a crash in the silver mining industry—forced the closure of Hyde's bank. In 1904, Hyde sold out to Frank Sayrs, whose name still graces the building. Since then, the two-story structure has been home to a variety of businesses including a tailor shop, drug stores, a recreation center, and most recently a craft brewery. Although Hyde's bank was not the only casualty of the 1893 crash, Philipsburg fared better than the neighboring community of Granite, which went from a silver mining camp with three thousand residents to a ghost town almost overnight.

The Sayrs Building's cast-iron and sheet metal façade supported enormous windows and allowed for rich ornamentation.

Silver mining did not disappear after 1893, but it never regained its pre-Panic domination of the region's economy. In the early 1890s, sapphires were discovered on the west fork of Rock Creek, about fifteen miles west of Philipsburg. Montana remains the only place in the United States where sapphires are found in any significant number. During World War I, Philipsburg became the largest domestic supplier of manganese—used for hardening iron and steel—until that too went bust in the 1920s.

Today, limited mining still occurs around Philipsburg, but the community's greatest wealth lies in its past. Fortunately, that past can be easily glimpsed with a stroll through its remarkably well-preserved historic district. *—KL*

24. Fraternity Hall and Gilliam Hall

Elkhorn | 46°16′29″N 111°56′45″W

In 1868, Swiss miner Peter Wys discovered the lucrative silver veins of the Elkhorn Mine, which would eventually yield $14 million of ore. After Wys died in 1872, Helena entrepreneur Anton M. Holter and partners developed the Elkhorn Mine. Holter sold out to an English syndicate circa 1888, and the mining camp flourished into the 1890s. At its peak, the community housed more than 2,500 residents, and three passenger trains arrived weekly on the Northern Pacific's branch line.

In 1893, the Fraternity Hall Association incorporated to build the town's architectural and social center, aptly named Fraternity Hall. The town's various fraternal organizations, including the Masons, Oddfellows, and Knights of Pythias, shared its upstairs lodge room. The popular hall was the heart of the community. Dances, traveling theatrical troupes, graduation ceremonies, prize fights, and other public gatherings bound citizens together.

Fraternity Hall's outstanding Greek Revival architecture typifies frontier aspirations of grandeur and mimics high-style buildings in urban centers elsewhere. The false front, common to mining camps across the West, was designed to make buildings appear taller and more substantial. The sophisticated, Neoclassical-style cantilevered balcony suspended above the entry is unique. The elaborate crenelated (notched) cornice at the roofline recalls elements crafted of stone or brick in more urban places, but here it was readily adapted to available wood.

Although local lore says that an argument over a dance led to a murder at Fraternity Hall, the incident actually began next door at Gilliam Hall, which was built in the 1880s. A dance held on Thanksgiving Eve in 1889 was so well attended

Ground floor interior of Gilliam Hall.

Gilliam Hall (left) and Fraternity Hall (right).

that Gilliam's dance floor could only accommodate half the crowd at one time. Manager Mat Fogarty had to limit the number of dancers on the floor, compelling them to take turns. When Thomas King refused to follow the rules, a fight ensued and escalated into a huge free-for-all at Lloyd's Saloon, one of Elkhorn's many bars. Taking their fight into the street early on Thanksgiving morning, King shot and killed Fogarty. Thomas King was hanged at Boulder for the crime in June 1890, several years before Fraternity Hall was built. His hanging was also notable as the first execution in the new state of Montana.

The Panic of 1893 hurt Montana's silver industry, and by 1897 the Elkhorn Mine had begun to play out. Although it operated off and on into the twentieth century, Elkhorn's death knell sounded when the Northern Pacific removed its tracks in 1931. Remarkably well-preserved, Fraternity Hall has endured time, neglect, and heavy snows to become one of Montana's most photographed buildings. With its companion, Gilliam Hall, the two buildings comprise Montana's smallest state park. *—EB*

25. Gleim Buildings

Missoula | 46°53′34″N 114°01′18″W

West Front Street was the heart of Missoula's emergent red-light district when Irish-born Mary Gleim entered the scene in 1888. Historic maps show frame and brick buildings labeled "female boarding"—a common euphemism for prostitution—lining both sides of the street. Gleim amassed a great deal of red-light real estate and reigned over the women who worked there. She built both 265 and 255-257 West Front Street to serve her business interests.

Highly educated, Gleim spoke many languages and was a skilled entrepreneur. Her wealthy husband, John E. Gleim of St. Louis, financed her early real estate deals. By the 1890s, Mary owned eight female boarding houses along West Front Street and tightly controlled her tenants.

Gleim added 265 West Front Street to her properties in 1893, financing its construction to add to the numerous boarding houses for women on the block. The handsome brick brothel is an excellent example of the vernacular adaptation of Romanesque architecture. It features grand, round-arched windows, attractive checkerboard banding, and rusticated granite sills. Gleim built a second female boarding house at 255-257 West Front Street between 1893 and 1902. The intricate brickwork, plate-glass storefront, and gently curved windows with wooden heads belie the building's sordid purpose. Such establishments were never exactly legal under city laws but persisted in Missoula and elsewhere in Montana, especially with the arrival of railroad construction crews from the 1880s into the 1910s.

Reputedly a smuggler of laces, diamonds, and opium, Gleim weighed in at three hundred pounds. She was frequently in court and known for her noisy outbursts. In 1893, a conviction for the attempted murder of rival Bobby Burns landed her a prison term at the state penitentiary at Deer Lodge. Future Montana governor Joseph Dixon was the prosecuting attorney. She served two years before winning a new trial, by which time the victim had died and witnesses had scattered. The case was dismissed.

"Mother Gleim," as she was also known, died intestate in 1914, leaving an estate of more than $100,000. Several cousins inherited her vast holdings, which included property in Canada and western Montana, a ranch, livestock, and interests in various companies. The heirs, however, did not know where many of her properties were located and some apparently went unclaimed. The key to a safety deposit box could not be found and, amid high drama, bank officials opened it in the presence of the heirs and their attorney only to find that the box was empty.

By the time of her death, Gleim's smaller houses had already closed due to local government crackdowns. The judge ordered all her properties boarded up, putting the district mostly out of business. The building at 255-257 West Front Street later became an automobile repair shop, and 265 housed a series of billiard parlors over several decades. These two substantial brick buildings, carefully restored, are rare surviving reminders of a once-thriving enterprise and a notorious madam. *—EB*

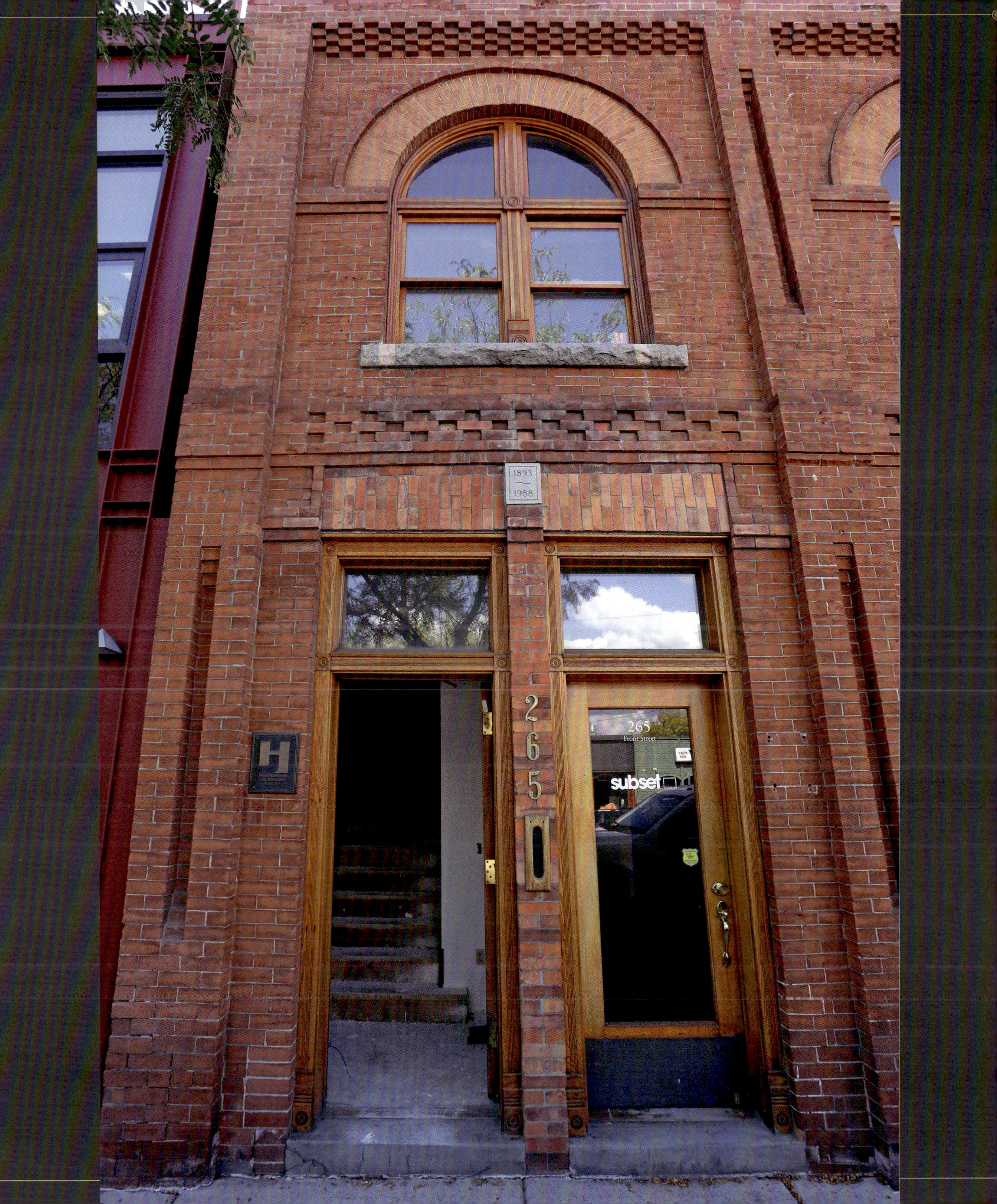
1893
1988
265
265
Front Street
subset

26. Temple Emanu-El

Helena | 46°35′24″N 112°1′54″W

A diverse and curious public gathered in 1890 for the laying of the cornerstone of the first Jewish synagogue established between St. Paul, Minnesota, and Portland, Oregon. Reflecting the intent of its congregation "to ornament the city we love," the magnificent temple was dedicated in 1891. It not only represents the crowning achievement of Helena's early, vibrant Jewish community but also is a stunning example of preservation and adaptive reuse.

Opportunity drew European Jewish immigrants from Austria, Prussia, Bavaria, and Poland to the gold camp at Last Chance Gulch, where business and religion brought them together. The Jewish community contributed a firm financial foundation to the early settlement. Jewish pioneers' ties to resources in larger cities allowed them to rebuild businesses that were destroyed in the ruinous fires that plagued the early gold camp. Helena's Jews organized and worshipped together as early as 1866, established a Hebrew Benevolent Society, kept their religious traditions, and founded the Home of Peace Cemetery in 1867.

Helena warmly accepted its Jewish citizens, and by the end of the 1870s, 20 percent of the Board of Trade (the forerunner of the Chamber of Commerce) was Jewish. Masonic lodges embraced Jews and the prestigious Montana Club counted Jews among its members. Jews were lawyers, bankers, merchants, and service providers who owned some of Helena's most beautiful homes. Despite this prosperity, the congregation was without a rabbi or a permanent place to worship.

At the end of the 1880s, Rabbi Samuel Schulmann came to Helena. His German Reform Judaism appealed to Helena's many German Jews. Rabbi Schulmann took up the cause to build a synagogue. Helena architects Frederick Heinlein and Thomas F. Matthias, who were not Jewish, drew the plans for the Romanesque and Moorish-style synagogue under the tutelage of a building committee. The building featured Romanesque arches, heavy stonework, and strong Eastern influences in the keyhole and rose windows. Twin, star-studded "onion" domes originally capped the corner towers. Multicolored stained glass softened the crimson, blue, and gold interior. The sanctuary rose to a height of thirty feet and accommodated three hundred worshippers, while removable galleries added another two hundred seats. The temple reflected the cosmopolitan aspirations of the Queen City of the Rockies, and the city's residents were duly proud of it.

Job opportunities elsewhere lured second-generation Jewish immigrants away from Montana and the congregation dwindled. In the 1930s, the State of Montana acquired the building, promising to use it for social services, and readied it for state occupancy. Changes included removal of the star-studded "onion" domes and religious symbols, including the Hebrew inscription "Gate to the Eternal" above the entry. The sanctuary was divided into two stories to accommodate offices. The building then housed the state's Social and Rehabilitative Services Department until 1976. The state sold the building to the Catholic Diocese of Helena, which used it for diocesan offices from 1981 to 2020. In 2022, the Montana Jewish Project purchased the building, returning the historic synagogue to Jewish ownership. *—EB*

Left: When the State of Montana acquired the building in the 1930s, it removed the distinctive "onion" domes that originally characterized the temple.

Opposite page: This uncredited photograph shows how Helena's Temple Emanu-El appeared around 1891.
953-239. MTHS PHOTOGRAPH ARCHIVES

27. Hotel Bozeman

Bozeman | 45°40′46″N 111°4′37″W

After Montana became a state in 1889, one of its first orders of business was to select a permanent capital. The citizens of Bozeman—eager to attain that honor—believed that constructing a first-class hotel would boost their chances. Consequently, they raised $20,000 and a group of Boston investors added $100,000 to finance a grand hostelry. Although its bid for capital proved unsuccessful, the Hotel Bozeman elevated the town's appeal and became an anchor for the east end of the Sweet Pea City's remarkable Main Street Historic District.

The building's backers chose English-born, London-educated architect George Hancock for their project. Hancock—who with his brother Walter maintained a prolific practice in Fargo, North Dakota—relocated temporarily to Bozeman. His first Montana commission was St. James Episcopal Church, completed in 1890; the Hotel Bozeman followed soon thereafter. As historian Derek Strahn remarked, the four-story building "added a taste of urban formality to what was still basically a rural community. . . . During the failed, but well-fought [capital] contest, a regional promotional magazine,

The Rockies, praised Bozeman for having 'every convenience found in eastern cities of ten times its population.' George Hancock was instrumental in helping to legitimize that claim."

Hancock designed the new, 136-room inn in a vernacular Romanesque style. The arched windows, elaborate stained glass, and five-story turreted bay contributed a dignified, stately presence to Main Street. Inside, modern amenities included steam heat, fire escapes, call bells, a formal dining room, reading room, elevator, barber shop, and ladies' parlor with its own entrance. An annex adjoining the hotel on its west side—also designed by Hancock, whose architectural detailing tied the new structure visually to the larger building—was completed in 1890. Initially, the annex housed three real estate firms, but for three-quarters of a century it was home to the *Bozeman Chronicle*.

At the time Hotel Bozeman was dedicated in March 1891, Bozeman had a population of just over two thousand, and its muddy Main Street was still unpaved. Nevertheless, the community instituted other improvements in its excitement to transform itself into a capital-worthy metropolis. In 1890, builders completed an opera house/city hall across Main Street from the hotel. The elaborate structure housed the city's administrative offices, police department and jail cells, courtroom, fire department, and library. A two-story auditorium held nine hundred seats that could be removed to accommodate dancing (although the dressing rooms with their five-and-one-half-foot tall ceilings were a source of consternation).

Electric streetlights were added along Main Street, and in 1892 an electric streetcar system was completed. The *Bozeman Avant Courier* celebrated this development by declaring "the electric streetcar has come to stay and with it increased prosperity for Bozeman and eventually the acquisition of the permanent capital."

Despite these considerable efforts, Bozeman did not win the capital fight. It did, however, continue to flourish as the economic and cultural center of the Gallatin Valley. And in 1893, it received a noteworthy consolation prize when the state legislature named it as the home of the Agricultural College of the State of Montana (now Montana State University). *—KL*

Gaily festooned participants in Bozeman's 1910 Sweat Pea Carnival parade down Main Street. The Hotel Bozeman, draped with flags and bunting, can be seen in the background.

SCHLECTEN STUDIO PHOTOGRAPH. LOT 048 BOZE, MTHS PHOTOGRAPH ARCHIVES

28. Alvin Young Ranch

Big Horn County | 45°13′50″N 106°59′52″W

Twenty years after the 1876 Battle of Rosebud Creek, Alvin Young and his brother Charles started ranching on the erstwhile battlefield. They joined a community of former cowhands and cattlemen who had settled in the Tongue, Powder, and Rosebud River drainages after the close of the 1876–1877 Indian Wars in southeast Montana. The Battle of Rosebud

Creek, along with the Battle of the Little Bighorn and the Battle of Wolf Mountains in January 1877, was part of a brutal campaign of displacement that isolated the Tsétsėhéstȧhese naa Suhtaio and Lakota peoples—and even the United States' stalwart allies, the Apsáalooke—on reservations much smaller than their ancestral homelands. The US government's efforts, aided by railroad companies, buffalo hunters, and homesteading legislation, paved the way for non-Indian settlement on the vast, open grasslands of southeastern Montana.

Born in Missouri, the Young brothers traveled to Montana in the 1890s by way of Nebraska, where their mother and siblings had homesteaded. Once here, they claimed 160-acre homesteads near Kirby, steadily making improvements and increasing the size of their holdings. According to Alvin's Homestead Entry case file, "I established actual residence February 1, 1896 and built my house as soon thereafter as possible. My house is a one room log house." Constructed of square-hewn logs, the sixteen-by-twenty-foot log cabin is an excellent example of a homesteader's first dwelling, and its dovetail notching reflects the work of a particularly skilled builder. Less than twenty years after its walls were stacked, Alvin moved the cabin to a new location. Faded red paint reveals that each log was numbered before the walls were dismantled and rebuilt.

In contrast to the modest log cabin, the massive stone barn reflects the influence of European builders who settled in the area. The barn is likely the work of Frederick Kollmar, Alvin's closest neighbor and an experienced German stonemason. A local supply of tertiary and red clinker sandstone and a shortage of tall timbers made stone the logical choice for the gable-roofed barn. This substantial building, constructed between 1896 and 1902, exhibits a high level of craftsmanship. So does the red clinker stone loafing shed extension, which provided shelter for stock in harsh weather.

Alvin, who remained single, knew that successful ranching meant acquiring significantly more land. When other settlers sold out or lost their property to debt, he bought their homesteads to expand his acreage. By 1916, he had increased the ranch to 520 acres, and by 1919, as drought gripped the state, he had again grown his holdings to 680 acres. When he died in 1928, Alvin owned 970 acres. His brother Albert purchased the agricultural land and ranch buildings from his mother, who had inherited the land. The remaining grazing land was put into a trust for Alvin's nieces and nephews. The Young Ranch remained in the family through the early 1980s. It serves as a fine representation of the cattle ranches that developed in southeast Montana beginning in the 1880s. *—CWB*

29. Montana State Training School Old Administration Building

Boulder | 46°14′09″N 112°07′24″W

Montana pledged its commitment to children with disabilities in 1887 when Territorial Governor Preston Leslie requested funds for what he called a Montana Deaf and Dumb Asylum. Its name, shockingly offensive by today's standards, reflected acceptable nineteenth-century terminology.

Upon statehood in 1889, Congress granted Montana fifty thousand acres of land to be sold to raise funds for the school. The 1893 legislature provided operating expenses and chose Boulder as the site. Students attended classes in a private home while the school's first campus building was under construction. State architect John C. Paulsen designed the edifice of local brick and granite, appropriately trimmed in Montana copper. Begun in 1896 and completed in 1898, it is one of the architect's few extant buildings and one of the state's best representations of Italian Renaissance Revival architecture.

Despite the connotations of its name, the school offered innovative college-preparatory instruction and training for deaf and blind youth. In 1903, the state legislature changed the name to the Montana School for the Deaf and Dumb, thereby acknowledging that it was not an asylum but rather a public school for children with special needs. By 1915, additional buildings increased the campus capacity to two hundred students, who ranged from ages five to twenty. Until the 1930s, this building served as the center of activities. It also contained dining rooms and student and staff dormitories. Blind students learned various manual industries, and deaf students learned lip-reading in addition to the usual public-school curriculum. The school also offered an extensive music program.

Around 1905, an unknown photographer snapped this image of the institution that by then was known as the Montana School for the Deaf and Dumb.
949-979, MTHS PHOTOGRAPH ARCHIVES

The population at the Boulder River School declined in the 1970s with the shift to community-based care. The south half of the Administration Building was demolished in 1976. Preservationists lobbied to save this building in the early 2000s, and it awaits a new use.

From the beginning, the institution also housed developmentally disabled youth, who were segregated south of the main campus. In 1909, the state passed legislation allowing the "feeble-minded"—a catchall term that included people with Down syndrome, cerebral palsy, and more serious disabilities, as well as a few who were accused of immorality—to remain at the school indefinitely. By the 1930s, a vast majority of residents had some form of cognitive impairment, and in 1937 deaf and blind training programs moved to Great Falls.

Those who remained at what by then was called the Boulder River School and Hospital worked as they were able. In 1904, the school purchased 194 acres, where residents worked in a dairy operation. Other residents worked in the kitchens and laundries, provided care to more severely disabled inmates, and made furniture and other goods for the school's use. In 1965, the institution was approximately 65 percent self-supporting.

Over time, the school deteriorated, and what began as part of a positive national experiment "quickly morphed into dark, dilapidated dungeons of shame," according to historian Linda Sargent Wood. "By the late 1940s . . . the Training School, largely neglected during the hard years of the Depression and World War II, suffered from inadequate funding and space, untrained staff, abuse, insufficient supplies, and little public concern." Forced sterilization was commonplace.

By the 1970s, the disability rights movement had successfully lobbied for a shift toward community-based care, and most residents returned to their home communities. In 1985, the Boulder River School and Hospital was renamed the Montana Developmental Center. The legislature voted to close the facility in 2015. Many buildings remain awaiting a new use. *—MK*

30. Montana State Prison

Deer Lodge | 46°22′58″N 112°48′04″W

Congress provided funds for a penitentiary in Montana Territory in 1870, thereby establishing a federal law enforcement presence. The prison accepted its first inmates in 1871 and its first female prisoner in 1879. Upon statehood in 1889, the federal facility passed to the new State of Montana. Architectural highlights include the 1893 perimeter wall, 1912 cell block, and 1920 theater.

The state lacked funds, so private contractors took over prison management. Warden Frank Conley's first task was to secure the facility by building a wall around it. James McCalman served as architect and builder, using prisoners' labor to construct the facility. Under McCalman's tutelage, inmates cut the quarried stone and built the forbidding, Romanesque-style fortification. Many considered the final product a monumental achievement. The massive wall, twenty feet high, features round corner towers and two square, crenelated towers. Applying the dictum "form ever follows function," its brooding presence still dominates the Deer Lodge streetscape.

McCalman and his prison laborers built a cell block in 1896 that was soon grossly overcrowded. In 1908, a small, spartan cottage, built within the walls but with its own enclosure, removed female prisoners from quarters adjacent to the men. In 1912, Helena architect C. S. Haire designed a second cell block. McCalman served as construction superintendent, teaching the inmates how to cut granite and lay the bricks manufactured at the prison's brickyard. While the primitive two-bucket system—one for human waste and one for water—was still in use in the older cell block, the new, Romanesque-style facility included two hundred double occupancy cells equipped with indoor plumbing. The crenellation on the two corner towers, which housed the guards' quarters, echoed the design of the prison wall. This cell block remained in use until the prison closed.

Warden Conley cultivated a relationship with wealthy mining magnate and politician William A. Clark and his son William A. Clark Jr. In exchange for prison labor, the Clarks endowed the prison library and band and gave $10,000 to build the W. A. Clark Theater in 1919. The first theater in the United States constructed inside prison walls, it served both inmates and the community. Traveling troupes offered matinees for inmates and evening performances for the public.

James McCalman, who drew no plans but instead created his projects entirely in his head, designed the theater and directed construction crews composed of prisoners. The elegant, classical, state-of-the-art theater was an anomaly in the dreary prison yard. Its stark white façade of brick and simulated stone—cast from white marble dust mixed with Portland cement—included three bays. Classical columns formed a portico supporting a roof that functioned as a stage for the prison band. The theater symbolizes the apex of Warden Conley's controversial regime.

Governor Joseph Dixon removed Conley in 1921 under suspicion of profiting personally from prison management. Throughout the ensuing decades, the prison decayed. In 1959, earthquakes destroyed the antiquated 1896 cell block and women prisoners were relocated off campus. In 1975, an inmate burned the theater's interior leaving only the outer shell. The prison closed in 1979 when a new facility was constructed outside of town. Today, the former penitentiary anchors a complex of five museums, including the Old Montana Prison Museum, which interprets the architectural and institutional history of Montana's penal system. *—EB*

This L. H. Jorud photograph shows the interior of the Montana State Penitentiary Theater as it appeared in 1928.
037 GOV B14 MSP, MTHS PHOTOGRAPH ARCHIVES LOT

31. University (Main) Hall

Missoula | 46°51′36″N 113°59′07″W

Since 1898, University Hall has stood at the heart—physically and symbolically—of the University of Montana (UM). More commonly known as Main Hall, its stately presence lends a sense of stability and tradition to Montana's flagship university.

Montana was only four years old when the legislature tackled the important question of where the state's institutions of higher learning would be located. With Helena and Anaconda in a heated race for state capital—and knowing that such institutions brought long-term economic benefit—other communities vied for their piece of the governmental pie. Missoula emerged victorious in its quest to become home to the "state college," while the legislature assigned the agricultural college to Bozeman, the school of mines to Butte, a normal school (teacher's college) to Dillon, a reform school to Miles City, and the school for the deaf and blind to Boulder. Accordingly, the University of Montana, as it is now named, was established in 1893. Two years later, classes began off campus with an enrollment of fifty. In February 1899, UM welcomed students to its new campus on the south bank of the Clark Fork River. From the beginning, founders perceived UM as a co-ed institution at a time when education for women was far from universal.

At the request of President Oscar J. Craig, engineering professor Frederick Scheuch drew up a campus master plan that called for a center oval onto which all university buildings were to face. Although the oval became an integral feature of the campus,

Photographer Rollin H. McKay captured this view of Main Hall after a snowfall sometime in the late 1910s or early 1920s.
PAC 2014.18.73, MTHS PHOTOGRAPH ARCHIVES

only the first two buildings constructed—Science Hall and Main Hall—followed Scheuch's plan. Science Hall was razed in 1983, leaving Main Hall singularly positioned on the oval, with Mount Sentinel rising as a dramatic backdrop.

Prominent Missoula architect A. J. Gibson designed the first five buildings constructed at UM, including Main Hall. A self-taught architect, Gibson came to Montana from his native Ohio, working in Butte as a carpenter before relocating to Missoula in 1888. In the Garden City, he initially worked as a contractor-builder, but he redefined himself as an architect by the early 1890s. Although his career spanned only two decades—he retired from architecture in 1909—Gibson built or designed nearly 150 structures in western Montana and northern Idaho. In addition to his work on the UM campus, noteworthy accomplishments include the Missoula and Ravalli County courthouses and the palatial Daly Mansion near Hamilton.

Main Hall is Richardsonian Romanesque in design. As dictated by the tenets of the style, it features round stone arches, a projecting square bell tower, symmetrically ordered windows, and an overall massive quality. While the building's foundation, columns, capitals, and entrance arch are made from Montana granite, the use of brick in place of stone as the primary building material is atypical of the style. As one of only two buildings on campus in 1898, Main Hall initially housed the president's office, biology lab, gym, library, assembly hall, literary hall, classrooms, history department, Latin and modern languages department, and rooms for a museum.

Although UM now includes more than sixty buildings, Main Hall retains pride of place in the hearts of its alumni. No campus building is more representative of the university nor a better embodiment of the ideals of public education put forth by the founders of our state. *—KL*

Plagued by extreme temperatures, poor ventilation, and the ever-present threat of cave-ins and explosions, Butte's underground miners—like the ones photographed here around 1910—formed unions in their efforts to secure better pay and improved working conditions.
LOT 8 B1.9/12, MTHS PHOTOGRAPH ARCHIVES

formally or informally in ethnically affiliated churches, fraternal lodges, and saloons, and reading foreign-language newspapers printed in the Treasure State.

Because of its economic significance, copper—and the corporations that controlled Butte's mines—had an inordinate impact across the state. The smelter towns of Black Eagle, near Great Falls, and Anaconda, twenty-six miles from Butte, processed the ore hauled out of the Butte mines. In western Montana, copper companies and their subsidiaries also built timber camps and founded towns like Bonner and Hamilton, where sawmills cut hundreds of millions of feet of logs that laborers used to shore up miles of mining tunnels threading beneath Butte. The mines' voracious demand for timber led to the sometimes-illegal clear-cutting of western Montana's forests.

Concerns about exploitative logging, not just in Montana but across the United States, led the federal government to create "forest reserves" in 1891. Millions of acres had been set aside by 1897, including the Flathead and the Bitterroot reserves in Montana. Despite corporate opposition, the US

immigrants across the state found value in joining together with others who shared the same language, customs, and beliefs. According to photographer Edgar Syverud, this "Kempa" gravestone, erected in the Danish community of Dagmar in Sheridan County, represented "the very old stone relics that are preserved in Denmark."

EDGAR SYVERUD PHOTOGRAPH, 1939. LOT 045 V1P61.09, MTHS PHOTOGRAPH ARCHIVES

Congress created the National Forest Service in 1905 and hired rangers to patrol these vast public lands.

Copper's long reach extended beyond Montana's mines, forests, and smelters. Marcus Daly, William Clark, and Augustus Heinze—collectively known as Montana's infamous copper kings—all invested in newspapers to champion their political, personal, and economic interests. Bribery, sweetheart business deals, and other forms of political corruption sullied Montana. Clark bought himself a US Senate seat, and Heinze made sure judges friendly to him were elected in Butte. Before he died in 1900, Daly sold his mining empire to the owners of Standard Oil, which ultimately consolidated the copper industry under the name of the Anaconda Copper Mining Company (ACM) and regularly strong-armed the state into passing legislation that favored its interests.

Even as Butte remained the center of wealth and influence, the rest of Montana continued to grow. About every hundred miles, transcontinental railways platted towns that

William Hall photographed these workers and their mules as they hauled away timber harvested near Marysville for use in the mines sometime around the turn of the twentieth century. Indiscriminate clear-cutting to meet underground mining's insatiable demand for lumber contributed to the need for forestry regulation and the creation of the US Forest Service in 1905.
957-924, MTHS PHOTOGRAPH ARCHIVES

served as crew change points and housed repair shops. Smaller communities also grew along the tracks, serving a growing number of farmers who had been lured west by the promise of free or inexpensive land. These towns organized schools and incorporated local governments. Women's organizations were central to community-building; creating hospitals, parks, and libraries; and advocating for "good government" and women's right to vote.

Brick buildings began to line new Main Streets, and grain elevators towered above the plains. In western Montana, the

Generally the tallest structures in rural landscapes, grain elevators not only served the important function of storing grain but also became important symbols of agricultural lifeways on the Great Plains. An unidentified photographer caught this image of the elevators in the southeastern Montana community of Mildred in 1930.
PAC 95-74.3, MTHS PHOTOGRAPH ARCHIVES

earliest homesteaders claimed land under the 1862 Homestead Act, which offered 160 acres to citizens who "proved up" by building a residence, planting crops, and staying on the land for five years. Initially, however, most homesteaders preferred the less arid and more fertile lands of the Midwest. More would-be farmers arrived in Montana after Congress passed the 1902 Reclamation Act, which funded irrigation projects, and the 1906 Forest Homestead Act. However, everything changed after passage of the 1909 Enlarged Homestead Act, which increased the size of a homestead to 320 acres and attracted a tsunami of settlers. Montana would never be the same. *—MK*

32. Chief Plenty Coups (Alek-chea-ahoosh) Home

Pryor | 45°25′40″N 108°32′53″W

Revered by his own people and highly respected by non-Indians, Plenty Coups (1848–1932) was the last principal chief (Ashakeé) of the three political divisions of historic Apsáalooke: the Mountain Crow, River Crow, and Kicked in the Bellies. As a young man, Plenty Coups went to the Crazy (Awaxaawippíia) Mountains on a vision quest. He saw that cows had replaced buffalo and a storm had destroyed a forest, leaving only one tree, "the lodge of the chickadee . . . least in strength but strongest of mind." Plenty Coups understood from the vision that to avoid destruction from the onslaught of white settlement, the Apsáalooke needed to rely on ingenuity rather than warfare. As the authors of the book *Tipis and Square Houses* explain, he encouraged Apsáalooke youth to learn and adopt American customs while preserving their unique culture.

Leading by example, the chief selected 320 acres for his homestead along Arrow Creek near a sacred spring. It was far from the government agency, so he could more easily maintain his autonomy. At the time, the homestead was at the center of the reservation; today, because of additional land cessions, it is at the western edge. The Indian agent provided materials and hired carpenters to build a Euro-American-style cabin. However, the cabin, completed in 1885, was "something of a tipi disguised as . . . a log house." Like a traditional Apsáalooke tipi, the original cabin's entrance faced east and there were no windows; the stovepipe ran through the center roof, mimicking the placement of a tipi fire pit.

In the 1890s, Plenty Coups remodeled his house, adding a small, second-story room and two windows, and in 1900, he added a one-story addition. In 1909, he added a large, two-story addition with classical-style dormers cut into the roof. While the public face of the house asserted Plenty Coups's status to white visitors, a room on the second story of the original cabin served as his ceremonial room and was arranged "tipi style." Floral and striped wallpaper echo the liners that decorated the interiors of Apsáalooke tipis. On the northwest wall, Plenty Coups kept his medicine bundles, photos, weapons, and other important items.

The house that Chief Plenty Coups—seen here on one of his trips to Washington DC—occupied near Pryor allowed him to negotiate with federal officials and meet separately with members of the Apsáalooke.
LOT 035 B12F02, MTHS PHOTOGRAPH ARCHIVES

Serving as the Apsáalooke's de facto political capital, Plenty Coups's homestead was a symbol of adaptation, what historians Peter Nabokov and Robert Easton call the "blending of European and Indian elements as the foundation of a new 'traditional' identity." In addition to the house, the homestead contained an orchard, a farm, and a small store as well as a tipi encampment and a sweat lodge built next to the sacred spring. It was a place to negotiate with government officials as well as gather with Apsáalooke friends and followers and to maintain centuries-old cultural and religious practices.

On one of his many negotiating trips to Washington DC, Plenty Coups visited George Washington's home at Mount Vernon. Understanding his home to be of similar historical significance, Plenty Coups and his wife, Strikes the Iron, deeded the house, along with 190 acres, to Big Horn County on their deaths, "as a park for my people . . . just as white men own and keep the home of their great Chief, George Washington." In 1961, the county transferred the house to the state. Now a National Historic Landmark, it remains a state park for public enjoyment, just as Chief Plenty Coups had wished. *—MK*

METALS BANK & TRVST CO.
SPORTS BAR & GRILL
ONLY
PARK ST
METALS
SPORTS BAR & GRILL
LAW OFFICES

33. Metals Bank Building

Butte | 45°54′08″N 112°39′24″W

This steel, brick, and stone high-rise building, completed in 1906, stands as a testament to the power of financial interests in turn-of-the-century Butte. F. Augustus Heinze provided most of the $325,000 that funded the construction of what is now known as the Metals Bank Building. At the time, it was among only a few steel-frame, multi-story buildings in Montana.

The bank's history intertwines with that of Montana's copper kings: Marcus Daly, William A. Clark, and F. Augustus Heinze. Marcus Daly's State Savings Bank had been located at this site in the late nineteenth century, and it was here in 1898 that Thomas Riley fatally shot wealthy bank president Patrick Largey. Riley had lost a leg copper king—owned one of the destroyed buildings, Riley falsely held him responsible.

After Marcus Daly died in 1900, his widow Margaret made a deal with Heinze, who agreed to finance a new building to house the Daly Bank and Trust Company. It was the last deal he made in Butte before he took his fortune to New York, where he proceeded to lose it after taking part in a series of fraudulent schemes. The old State Savings Bank was razed in 1906. Nationally renowned architect Cass Gilbert drew the blueprints; his associate, Gunvald Aus, supplied the engineering specifications; and Montana architects J. G. Link and C. S. Haire supervised the local work. Gilbert also designed Helena's six-story Montana Club in 1905. His early efforts in pioneering Montana's first skyscrapers led to his best-known commission: the sixty-story Woolworth Building in New York City. When the Woolworth Building was completed in 1913, it was the tallest building in the world.

In erecting the bank, Heinze and Margaret Daly spared no expense in creating an imposing house of finance. The copper-trimmed entry, ornate wrought-iron balconies, and copper-trimmed windows framed with African mahogany reflect Butte's wealth. A polished steel vault, still fully intact, recalls the building's initial use as a bank. Its installation in 1907 was no small accomplishment: A team of twenty-six horses hauled the thirty-two-ton vault door on a makeshift platform along unpaved Front Street from the Northern Pacific depot. The marble-clad elevator lobby and open wrought-iron staircase reinforced the building's association with wealth and high stature.

As Butte's economy ebbed and flowed after 1918, the bank reorganized as the Metals Bank 1920 and soon entered a new chapter involving another copper king. By 1928, the bank had acquired the assets of William A. Clark, making it the richest financial institution between Minneapolis and Seattle.

Aside from its function as a shelter for copper magnate wealth, the upper-floor offices also housed a "maternity hospital" and the medical offices of the notorious Dr. Gertrude Pitkanen and her physician husband Gust. During the 1920s and 1930s the pair performed illegal abortions and reportedly sold babies into adoption. Their longtime presence lends a darker shade to the building's history. The Metals Bank, which was fully restored in 2006, now houses a restaurant, shops, offices, and condominiums. *—EB/CWB*

The copper used to trim the building's main entry paid homage to the primary source of wealth of those who funded the construction of the bank, not to mention most of Butte's powerful and prominent citizens of the era.

34. Kero Farmstead

Carbon County | 45°17′32″N 109°13′05″W

The Kero farmstead, located eight miles north of Red Lodge, represents one of the state's finest examples of an early twentieth-century Finnish farmstead. Three generations of the Kero family farmed here while maintaining the property's distinctive Finnish character.

Difficult social and economic conditions in Finland (and much of Europe) in the 1890s and early 1900s brought many immigrants to the United States. Finnish men first arrived in Michigan and Minnesota to work in iron mines. As mining jobs opened in the West, Finns migrated westward. Coal mining in Carbon County began in 1887, not long after an 1882 agreement with the Apsáalooke tribe opened reservation lands along the Clarks Fork of the Yellowstone River to Euro-American settlement. Red Lodge developed rapidly with the arrival of railroad service in 1889, and after 1892, when another agreement with the Apsáalooke set aside additional lands for settlers, Finns and other newcomers, many of whom came first as miners, developed farms and ranches on the fertile benchlands around Red Lodge. By 1910, Finns comprised 28 percent of the foreign-born population of Carbon County.

Jacob Kero emigrated to Michigan around 1890, leaving his wife Margaret and children in Finland. He first worked in iron mines but left for Red Lodge in 1891 to mine coal. In 1899, he brought the family to Red Lodge and in 1904, he and Margaret established a 320-acre farm on the West Bench above Rock Creek. The area had many advantages, including its irrigation potential and its proximity to the railroad and Finnish cultural and religious institutions in Red Lodge.

Jacob followed traditional Finnish building methods, including arranging the buildings around a central farmyard and employing centuries-old log construction techniques. Although now mostly covered by wood siding, the house and sauna are prime examples of Finnish hand-hewn square log construction. Some exposed logs reveal that Kero used a scribe or "vara" to trace the natural curve of the upper side of each log to the underside of the log above it to ensure a tight fit. Though not unique to Finnish culture, the impressive rough-cut local sandstone barn and the substantial cobblestone root cellar exhibit traditional European-style building methods.

The sauna is a distinctive hallmark of Finnish culture. Originally built as bathhouses, saunas remain a Finnish tradition today. The Kero savusauna, or smoke sauna (pictured here), is a rare example in Montana. Instead of exhausting wood

smoke through a chimney, smoke filled the sauna room before exiting slowly through a vent in the roof. Over time, fragrant black soot stained the walls. The fire, lit early in the day, burned for hours before anyone entered the sauna. When it reached over one hundred degrees and the smoke cleared, the Keros poured cold water on the hot sauna stones and enjoyed a long and cleansing steam bath.

The second and third generations of Keros added a new house and outbuildings to the farmstead after World War II but maintained the original buildings and the courtyard plan. Their efforts to modernize and keep pace with changes in equipment and efficiency kept the farm in the family until 2007. Although many of the original Finnish homesteaders are gone, their legacy is still well represented in a few distinctive log and stone buildings in and around Red Lodge. *—CWB*

35. Carpenters' Union Hall

Butte | 45°54′08″N 112°39′24″W

Miners organized Butte's first union in 1878, when they struck for a wage of $3.50 a day and won. Other trades soon followed, including carpenters, who established the United Brotherhood of Carpenters and Joiners Union Local No. 112 in 1890. By the turn of the century, thirty-four unions representing eighteen thousand members made up the Silver Bow County Trades and Labor Assembly, and Butte had become known as "the Gibraltar of Unionism" for its strength as a union town.

In 1906, amid a citywide building boom, the Brotherhood of Carpenters, whose membership had grown to over seven hundred, decided to replace their one-story, wood-frame headquarters with a building that remains as a testament to Butte's labor history. N. T. Nelson designed the elegant and imposing hall. Located just across from the courthouse—a prominent position that spoke to unions' centrality and power—it was labor's answer to the Hennessy Building, the sixth floor of which housed the Anaconda Copper Mining Company's offices.

Sandstone from Columbus, less than two hundred miles east of Butte, trims the Renaissance Revival–style building's arched entryways and windows on the first floor, while the union's emblem, which incorporates tools of the trade and the motto *Labor omnia vincit* (Labor Conquers All), appears over the main door. The interior boasted modern plumbing, hot and cold water, and steam heat; a finished basement; and three stories of meeting halls, offices, reception rooms, and a banquet hall.

Unions representing several other trades operated from the building, including ironworkers, stationary engineers, clerks, streetcar men, machinists, boilermakers, and typographers. After disenchanted members of the Butte Miners Union dynamited and destroyed their own union hall in 1914, the group temporarily relocated here. The building was also home to the Women's Protective Union, which represented Butte's female wageworkers, from the bucket girls who packed lunches for the thousands of miners who worked underground, to hotel and hospital maids, dishwashers, waitresses, carhops, laundresses, and salesclerks.

Carpenters' Union Hall, often touted as the oldest union hall still in use in the United States, was more than a site for union offices and a symbolic expression of union power. It was also where members gathered—for weekly union meetings, of course, but also for lectures, memorials, ceremonies, fundraisers, and socializing. Between these various events, the hall was in use nearly every day. Anarchist Emma Goldman spoke at the hall in 1910. Zita Dillon's Orchestra played for the Harmony Dancing Club every Friday night in 1916. In 1918, the Labor Day parade began at the hall. Men paid fifty cents and women a quarter to attend a dance sponsored by the Anaconda Clerks Union in 1929, and the Engineer's Union social club hosted a "New Year's Eve Frolic" in 1935. Many fraternal organizations also met at the hall, from the Woodmen of the World to the Brotherhood of American Yeomen. In other words, the building was central to Butte life—just as the unions themselves were central to the daily lives of Butte workers. *—MK*

The keystone over the building's main entrance is emblazoned with the United Brotherhood of Carpenters and Joiners' emblem which features a rule, compass, and jack plane as well as the Latin motto *Labor omni vincit* (Labor Conquers All).

1906
CARPENTERS UNION № 112.
KBMF
102.5 FM

Right: This 1918 photograph shows Charles M. Russell at work in his studio on the painting *Lewis and Clark Reach Shoshone Camp Led by Sacajawea the "Bird Woman."*
944-706, MTHS PHOTOGRAPH ARCHIVES

Bottom right: Through her acumen as a business manager, Nancy Russell, seated here at her desk in the couple's home around 1907, played a critical role in her husband's success.
PAC 2000-40.23, MTHS PHOTOGRAPH ARCHIVES

Opposite page: Today—filled with the artist's collection of cowboy gear and Indian artifacts—Russell's studio looks much as it did when he painted there.

36. Charles M. Russell Home and Studio

Great Falls | 47°29′30″N 111°17′21″W

As a youngster growing up as a member of a prominent St. Louis family, Montana's celebrated "Cowboy Artist" Charles M. Russell succumbed to the romance of the West. From the earliest age, he was always drawing western scenes—on any paper at hand, including his schoolbooks—or modeling horses and wild animals from clay and wax. In 1880, when he was just shy of his sixteenth birthday, Russell's parents relented to his persistent pleading and let him venture west. They hoped that the reality of an oftentimes harsh life on the frontier would persuade him to return to St. Louis and the family business. It did not.

For a time after arriving in Montana Territory, Charlie, as he was widely known, supported himself by working as a cowboy. Although he was not generally regarded as the best hand, his company was treasured for his expertise in spinning yarns to entertain his companions. Adding to his appeal was his ability to convincingly capture cowboy life in his artwork. In 1894, Russell quit cowboying to pursue art full time. Two years later he married Nancy Cooper, gaining not only a wife, but an expert business manager who would play a crucial role in transforming the self-taught artist into a national celebrity.

In 1897, Charlie and Nancy moved from Cascade, where they had met and married, to Great Falls. There, in 1900, on the corner of Fourth Avenue North and Thirteenth Street North, they built a modest frame house. Three years later, they constructed "a log studio . . . just a cabin like I [Charlie] used to live in"—only this time it was built of telephone poles. Thereafter, as Nancy noted, "to the end of his life he loved that . . . building more than any other place on earth and never finished a painting anywhere else." In 1912, Russell had to raise the studio's roof to accommodate his masterpiece, *Lewis and Clark Meeting Indians at Ross' Hole*, which measures twelve feet high by twenty-five feet wide and hangs in the Montana State Capitol.

Russell had arrived on the frontier just in time to witness its closing. Despite his late entrance, he spent his career chronicling—through art and story—what he termed "The West That Has Passed," a rugged, but beloved, landscape inhabited only by cowboys, Indians, horses, cattle, and wildlife. In doing so, he depicted a mythic past, equal parts reality and romance, that still resonates with citizens of the Treasure State. As noted by Montana Historical Society director K. Ross Toole in 1952, "Montana is terribly proud of her adopted son, 'Charlie' Russell. No one has ever painted her portrait so vigorously or so well. No one—in word, picture or by any other device—has yet captured the pioneer flavor of her formative years more vividly." Today, no place provides a more direct link to Montana's favorite son than his cherished log-cabin studio and the unassuming home that he shared with his beloved wife. *—KL*

37. Wah Chong Tai and Mai Wah Buildings

Butte | 46°0′40.2″N 112°32′9.8″W

Overpopulation, famine, and the Taiping Rebellion (1850–1864) prompted thousands of men from southern China's Guangdong Province to leave their families and join America's western gold rushes. Most never intended to stay, hoping instead to return home with newfound wealth. "Overseas Chinese" were among the first arrivals at Montana's booming gold camps. By 1870, these sojourners made up 10 percent of the territorial population. As placer mining waned, just before the 1882 federal Chinese Exclusion Act prohibited Chinese laborers' entry into the United States, a second wave of Chinese workers joined crews building the Northern Pacific Railroad.

"Chinatowns" sprang up in most of Montana's urban areas to support this large, temporary population. Butte's Chinese community settled along West Mercury Street. By 1885, Chinese physicians, druggists, tailors, laundries, stores, and restaurants crowded the block. While many Chinese people returned to China, others could not afford to do so. In larger communities like Butte, a few generational Chinese families continued to provide goods and services.

The Wah Chong Tai was Butte's premier Chinese mercantile, stocking a general line of goods including groceries, porcelain, teas, herbal remedies, and silk. The company, established by Chin Hin Doon around 1893, built this brick commercial building in 1899. In 1909, Butte architect George De Snell designed the adjacent Mai Wah Noodle Parlor. These two businesses, operated by the prominent Albert Chinn family until the 1940s, were at the heart of Butte's Chinatown.

The Wah Chong Tai housed the mercantile on the first floor. The second floor contained living quarters for Albert Chinn, his wife Lou, and their eleven children. In the Mai Wah building next door, a series of small stores divided the first floor into retail spaces. Between the Mai Wah's first and second stories, a "cheater story" offered small lodging rooms where, in 1920, Dr. Sang Kong and his two grown sons boarded. On the second story, the Mai Wah Noodle Parlor offered a mixed menu of Mandarin and American fare as well as hot tamales and chili. The original dining room, kitchen, and food storage area of the Mai Wah, which means "beautiful, luxurious," remain intact.

The Chinn family left Butte in the 1940s. Montana legislator Charles Bovey, who advanced the state's tourism industry by preserving the mining camp of Virginia City, purchased the Wah Chong Tai inventory to display in his re-created Chinatown in Nevada City, where he had moved a variety of historic buildings. The State of Montana purchased the Bovey properties in 1997 and returned the Chinese collection to the Wah Chong Tai in 2011.

The Wah Chong Tai and Mai Wah Noodle Parlor now house the Mai Wah Museum. The museum's temporary and permanent exhibits interpret Butte's Chinese history. The Wah Chong Tai and its 2,500 artifacts, displayed as they appeared in the early twentieth century, comprise one of the nation's most complete Chinese stores and is the only establishment of its kind in Montana that survives in its original setting. *—EB*

This rare, early photograph of Butte's Chinatown was taken between 1899 and 1908. The Wah Chong Tai building (third from right) is wedged between log cabins on its left and China Alley on its right. The Mai Wah Noodle Parlor building replaced the log buildings in 1909.
TPC 001 BUTT-MS 29, MTHS PHOTOGRAPH ARCHIVES

38. Judith River Ranger Station

Judith Basin County | 46°50′51″N 110°17′25″W

Snowcapped mountain ranges and expanses of lush grass drew vast buffalo herds and Indigenous hunters to the Judith Basin area long before the US Forest Service built this remote ranger station in 1908. A well-worn trail nearby leads to a rock shelter where these early travelers stopped to paint images on the rock walls. In May 1805, Captain Meriwether Lewis gave the Judith River its present name in honor of his fiancée Julia (Judith) Hancock. In the early 1880s, sixteen-year-old tenderfoot Charles M. Russell spent time not far from the ranger station under the tutelage of trapper Jake Hoover. The area is where the beloved Montana artist found his artistic soul. Gold and sapphire mining and cattle and sheep ranching are also part of the rich and varied tapestry of the Judith Basin.

Thomas Guy Myers arrived at this remote mountain meadow in 1906. Armed with a pocket-sized "use book" of forest regulations, Myers's task as a ranger at the newly created Jefferson National Forest was to interpret and administer policies regarding public use of "federal" timber, range, water, and mineral resources in the Judith District. An abandoned sawmill and 1876 miner's cabin offered lonely reminders of long-gone occupants and their reliance on natural resources. Taking up residence in the primitive cabin, Ranger Myers set to work building a field office and permanent lodging. Completed in 1908, his handiwork embodies the ideal image of the early Forest Service, as the building represents conservation in both feature and function.

Starting with a basic mail-order house kit, Myers also used materials at hand, including native logs and chinking of hand-split wood billets supplemented by willow saplings as mortar stops. Myers scrounged barbed wire, scattered through the timber by the sawmill outfit that had operated in the area, to reinforce the lime-mortar daubing. Crude corners and a simple square shape with a hip roof further demonstrate the conservation ethic. The corrals and tall log barn (1909) illustrate the ranger's need for self-sufficiency, while the garage (1925) demonstrates modernization.

Myers married second-grade teacher Emily McLaury in 1910, and together they made their remote quarters warm and inviting. Emily put her own touches on the interior. Beadboard walls and elegant wallpaper added an urban flair to the simple rustic style. The Myerses' son Robert, born in 1914, grew up at the station, where the family lived year-round until 1935. Rangers then occupied the site seasonally until 1981.

When Forest Service preservationists began extensive restoration, carpenters discovered remnants of the Myers family everywhere. The house kit's shipping crate, stamped with Myers's address, framed the living and dining room doorway. Wallpaper samples and opened mail filled in gaps around the windows and doors. A teaching tool in young Robert's upstairs bedroom, forgotten beneath a layer of sheetrock, depicted a timeline of Stone Age and ancient Mediterranean history.

The Forest Service has fully restored the station to its early 1900s appearance and has made this historic site available for public rental. *—EB*

39. Power Mercantile Building

Lewistown | 47°02′53″N 109°28′58″W

Lewistown owes its moniker "the City of Stone" to the Croatian master craftsmen who made it their home. Born and trained in the Dinaric Alps, Peter Tuss, Peter Drazich, and John Plovfanic arrived in Great Falls in 1897, quickly moving to the growing community of Lewistown, where stone was prevalent and timber scarce. The "men from Bribir" soon recruited other countrymen; by 1910, of Lewistown's twenty-two stonemasons, sixteen were from Croatia. Women and children followed, creating a vibrant Croatian community.

For every building project, these skilled immigrants began by quarrying sandstone from nearby Upper Springs Creek, which they transported to the construction site on "stone boats," or small-wheeled, flatbed wagons. They also mixed their own mortar from locally produced lime, sand, and water. Peter Tuss employed three shifts of men who worked around the clock to stoke the wood fires at his lime kilns, since high-quality lime required extremely hot, even temperatures. At the construction site, craftsmen precisely chiseled rough stones into identical blocks using specialized tools they had brought with them from Croatia. Stacking the stone to create perfectly straight walls was its own art form.

Although the Power Mercantile lacks the elaborate embellishment evident on some of Lewistown's other stone buildings (for example, the Carnegie Library, Masonic Temple, and St. Joseph's Hospital), the massive, well-appointed business block is the community's most visible example of Lewistown's stone architecture. The mercantile was an offshoot of the Fort Benton wholesaling firm T. C. Power and Brothers—headed by powerful Montana businessman Thomas C. Power—which, in 1883, took over the business of Lewistown founder and merchant Francis Janeaux, who was deeply in debt to the firm. As Lewistown grew, the mercantile expanded. In 1901, masons constructed this two-story, dressed stone building at the corner of Third and Main Streets. A block carved with "PMCo-1901" marks that original section of the building, which boasted running water, elevators, and electric lights. In 1908, the firm, which sold everything from clothing and shoes to fresh fruits and furniture, added a stone warehouse on Third Avenue, facing Broadway.

As homesteaders flocked to central Montana to take up land under the 1909 Enlarged Homestead Act, Fergus County grew from almost seven thousand people in 1900 to over twenty-eight thousand people in 1920. In 1913, at the height of the boom, Power Mercantile hired noted architectural firm Link and Haire (which designed the wings of Montana's capitol building) to triple the size of its building. Built at an estimated cost of $70,000, the two-story addition connected the store on Main Street with the firm's warehouse on Broadway. The foundation was engineered to support a full four stories if Lewistown continued to grow as anticipated and the business warranted another expansion.

Drought and plummeting commodity prices devastated central Montana's economy after World War I, spelling the end to this grand vision. However, the Power Mercantile continued to serve Lewistown and surrounding communities until 1957. *—MK*

Delivery trucks line up at Lewistown's Power Mercantile in this mid-1920s photograph.
PHOTO 01105, LEWISTOWN PUBLIC LIBRARY

40. Farmers and Merchants State Bank

Eureka | 48°52′36″N 115°02′44″W

Before 1934, banking was risky business. Underdeveloped infrastructure and minimal regulation meant that, in the days before federal deposit insurance, customers could lose their life savings to fire, burglary, or bank failure. To reassure potential patrons, banks made every effort to promote an image of security and permanence. They advertised their fireproof vaults, the capital they had on hand, and the well-respected community members who served as the bank's directors. They also consciously chose architectural styles that expressed safety and stability.

Typically, banks were among the most imposing buildings in their town, and the Farmers and Merchants State Bank was no exception. Incorporated in 1907 with $25,000 of capital ($5,000 more than required by state banking regulations), the bank hired Blake and Son of Kalispell to construct a business block using bricks from local clay deposits. The second masonry building to be constructed in Eureka, the new bank featured elegant brickwork, including a distinctive central arch with a multi-paned cut-glass transom. The *Tobacco Plains Journal* pronounced it "without doubt the handsomest brick structure" in the western part of the county, and the *Kalispell Journal* declared the town quite fortunate since "the most important factor in the development of a new country is a solid banking institution."

The $12,000 bank building featured a modern, secure safe and interior furnishings from Chicago. The Townsite Company shared the bank's ground floor while the town rented the upstairs for the police court and council chambers. The bank's investors had promised a "good, wide awake man at the helm" and named one of their own, C. A. Hamann of Kalispell, bank president. Deposits of more than $7,000 on opening day were a grand prelude to the bank's early success.

Established to serve area farmers and merchants, as its name implied, the bank's prosperity was linked to that of the community. Eureka was only four years old when the bank opened, but it already had a lumber mill, and community boosters envisioned the town as the center of a booming agricultural district.

As long as Eureka prospered, the bank prospered, but like many Montana communities, Eureka struggled in the 1920s. Between 1921 and 1925, over half of Montana's banks failed as exuberant dreams and overly generous lending policies collided with the bitter realities of economic downturn. In much of the state, banks closed after drought and low commodity prices caused farmers to default on their loans. For its part, the Farmers and Merchants State Bank closed in 1925, doomed by heavy investments in a failed irrigation scheme and the closure of Eureka's lumber mill in 1923.

Even as Eureka's population fell from two thousand to nine hundred residents, the Farmers and Merchants State Bank building remained a community showpiece. Dentists, a dance studio, and New Deal rural electrification and soil conservation projects operated from its offices. Through it all, the former bank building remained remarkably unchanged, fulfilling the implicit promise of its architecture: permanence. *—MK*

19
BANK
07
MONTANA
FARMACY
FOOD TRUCK
HERBS
SPICES
OPEN

41. Daly Mansion (Riverside)

Ravalli County | 46°14′54″N 114°09′40″W

The spectacular Daly Mansion, also known as Riverside, was the summer residence of Margaret Evans Daly, widow of copper magnate Marcus Daly. Completed in 1910, the sprawling home is a unique Montana example of early twentieth-century revival styles that affluent capitalists used to display their wealth. Since the Panic of 1893 destroyed many mining-based fortunes, such grand homes were mostly a thing of Montana's past by 1909, when Daly hired Missoula architect A. J. Gibson to remodel her sprawling 1897 Queen Anne–style mansion.

Gibson's Georgian Revival–style design is relatively restrained compared to mansions of this period on the East and West Coasts. Its outstanding features include a monumental, classical portico; symmetrical façade; hipped roof; and balustraded roof deck. The home's twenty-four thousand square feet included twenty-four bedrooms, fifteen bathrooms, three dining rooms, imported Italian marble adorning seven fireplaces, call bells to summon thirteen servants, and bathtubs edged in gold.

Margaret Evans Daly was born in Ohio and moved with her parents to Nevada. At seventeen, she visited the Walker Brothers' Ophir Mine with her miner father, who was inspecting the operation. When she lost her balance and tumbled into the arms of the foreman, Marcus Daly, the pair began a lifelong romance. The couple married in 1872; Margaret was eighteen and Daly was thirty.

Daly rose from a penniless fifteen-year-old Irish immigrant to a massively wealthy man. He had an uncanny ability to locate copper, and, just as importantly, he realized it would become an essential resource in a world reliant on electrical and telephone wires. Daly's intuition won him investors; with their backing, he purchased Butte silver mines that he soon developed into copper mines. He then built the largest smelter in the world and founded the town of Anaconda to serve it.

The rich timberland of the Bitterroot Valley shored up Daly's mines and fueled his smelter. He built a sawmill and platted the town of Hamilton in 1890. He brought in professionals to run his business concerns and erect fine homes and business blocks for his employees. But it was Daly's love of horses that kept him close to the Bitterroot Valley.

Believing horses developed better stamina at higher altitudes, Daly began buying Bitterroot Valley land in 1887, eventually combining five ranches totaling twenty-two thousand acres. He built an indoor racetrack, hired the best veterinarians, and imported young African American jockeys. Daly's Bitter Root Stock Farm produced national champions.

Unlike Montana's other copper kings, who took their wealth elsewhere, the Dalys remained tied to Montana and the Bitterroot Valley. After Marcus died in 1900, Margaret Daly managed the family syndicate that oversaw Daly interests, and Riverside remained her beloved summer home and social hub. Until her death in 1941, Mrs. Daly was a cherished benefactor and gracious hostess to local guests regardless of social status. The house sat empty for more than forty years after her death, but a local group formed the Daly Mansion Preservation Trust in 1986 and restored the home for use as a museum and event space. *—EB*

Left: This 1897 Queen Anne–style home preceded A. J. Gibson's Georgian Revival mansion as the Daly's summer residence at Riverside.

87.0035, ARCHIVES AND SPECIAL COLLECTIONS, MANSFIELD LIBRARY, UNIVERSITY OF MONTANA

Opposite page: This photograph shows the front of Marcus Daly's home near Hamilton as it appeared in 1925.

87.0038, ARCHIVES AND SPECIAL COLLECTIONS, MANSFIELD LIBRARY, UNIVERSITY OF MONTANA

42. Montana State Capitol

Helena | 46°35′47″N 112°01′35″W

Perhaps fitting for a building devoted to politics, much of the early history of the capitol building is a story of conflict. From the time that Montana became a state in 1889 until the wings of the statehouse were completed in 1912, Montanans argued about nearly every aspect of the building. They quarreled about which town deserved the honor of becoming capital; about the location of the building within Helena; and about the hiring of "recognized" architects and artists from the East versus resident artisans with less experience. They even fought about the selection of the stone to face the wings, a dispute that ultimately required a special legislative session to resolve.

However acrimonious, those early battles resulted in a grand edifice that has greatly benefited succeeding generations. Charles E. Bell and John H. Kent designed the capitol after relocating to Helena from Iowa to meet the requirement that the architects be residents of the state. The original building—with its Butte-copper-topped dome and Columbus sandstone—owed its exterior aesthetics to the American Renaissance, a Neoclassical revival movement that reinterpreted the architecture of ancient Greece and Rome as a testament to the ideals of American democracy. In contrast, the capitol's opulent interior, masterminded by the Cincinnati, Ohio, firm of F. Pedretti and Sons adhered to the Gilded Age dictates of the French Renaissance. Dedicated with great fanfare on July 4, 1902, the new building was hailed as a "Triumph of Architect and Decorator" by the *Montana Daily Record*, which praised the combination of the exterior's "severe dignity" and its "highly ornate, rich interior."

Within a decade, demands for more space led to the construction of wings on the east and west ends of the original building. The symmetrical additions were designed by New York architect Frank M. Andrews in conjunction with the Butte architectural firm of Link and Haire. The demand to incorporate Montana materials, even though they were more expensive than out-of-state options, forced Governor Edwin Norris to convene a special session of the legislature, which ultimately allocated additional funds for Montana granite, a harder and more durable choice than the building's original

The rotunda includes depictions of (clockwise from the top right) prospector Henry Finnis Edgar, Chief Charlo, an archetypal cowboy, and fur trapper Jim Bridger, all painted by the Cincinnati-based firm F. Petretti and Sons.

sandstone. The question of how to select the artists who would paint murals to adorn the interior spaces likewise sparked a Montana versus out-of-state battle. Fortunately, the pro-Montana faction prevailed and Charles M. Russell, Edgar Paxson, and R. E. DeCamp created, according to the 1913 legislature, "enduring monuments to themselves, and a lasting source of pride for the people of this commonwealth."

Since 1912, the capitol has retained its overall exterior character. Restoration work in 1999–2000 returned the grandest interior spaces, which had been altered by renovations in the 1930s and 1960s, to their original appearance. Over the decades, the state has added art to reflect themes of evolving importance including select statesmen, the Lewis and Clark bicentennial, and women's history. In 2020, a tribal flag plaza was constructed in front of the building to recognize the contributions of Native nations to Montana's history and culture. *—KL*

43. Railroad Depots

Railroads transformed Montana, making it possible to haul in heavy mining equipment and everyday consumer goods and to ship out ore, coal, timber, cattle, and crops. Most Montana towns owe their creation to the railroad and, according to railroad historian Dale Martin, trains made up 98 percent of intercity travel around World War I. Railroads connected Montanans to the rest of the nation and to each other.

In 1905, the legislature passed a law requiring railways to build and maintain facilities both for passengers and freight at every town along a rail line populated by at least one hundred people. Rural depots, which occupied pride of place on every railroad town plat, were community hubs and social centers. In larger cities and tourism centers, architecturally striking depots housed restaurants and barbershops as well as waiting rooms and railroad offices. These urban depots symbolized the railroads' power and influence while providing necessary amenities for travelers.

Men posed next to Northern Pacific engine no. 418 and train near the depot at Cinnabar, Montana, 1895. Construction of a branch line from Livingston in 1883 made Cinnabar a hub for passengers and freight until workers completed the last three miles to Yellowstone National Park's north entrance twenty years later. F. JAY HAYNES PHOTOGRAPH, 1895. H-03303, MTHS PHOTOGRAPH ARCHIVES

Livingston Depot

Livingston | 45°39′41″N 110°33′45″W

As the transcontinental railroads laid tracks across the Northern Plains, they stopped every hundred miles or so to plat a town, which served as crew change points and housed repair shops and railroad offices. Livingston was one such town, founded by the Northern Pacific Railroad in 1882. Its first depot was a utilitarian wood-frame building, replaced by a brick building in 1888.

Located halfway between Minneapolis and Seattle, Livingston was a logical place for the Northern Pacific's Central Division headquarters. It was also the gateway to Yellowstone National Park, a destination the railroad promoted heavily to wealthy tourists who expected luxury. The Northern Pacific contracted the St. Paul architectural firm Reed and Stem—which specialized in depots—to design a suitable station in 1901. The central, three-story, Renaissance Revival–style building, decorated with terra-cotta ornamentation, housed passenger waiting rooms on the first floor and division offices on the upper stories. A curved colonnade connects the exuberant blond and red brick depot (now a museum) to what was originally the baggage room on one side and a café on the other.

Missoula Milwaukee Road Depot

Missoula | 46°52′03″N 113°59′53″W

This splendid brick passenger depot was built in 1910, marking the completion of Montana's third and final transcontinental railroad and solidifying Missoula's role as a major urban trading center. Designed by J. A. Lindstrand, an architect in the Chicago, Milwaukee, St. Paul and Pacific Railway Bridge and Building Department, the depot is notable for its castle-like appearance and Mission Revival–style detailing. Its grand interior still boasts fifteen-foot coffered ceilings with milled wood beams, relief-paneled wainscoting, and elegant molded wood trim.

Kevin Depot

Kevin | 48°44′44″N 111°58′5″W

The Kevin Depot, built in 1903, typifies the small-town station. As in other "whistle-stop towns," community life centered around the depot, which housed the post office and telegraph office as well as a ticket office, waiting room, and freight room. The utilitarian, wood-frame depot was quickly assembled according to a standard plan. A projecting windowed bay housed the ticket office, which adjoined the passenger waiting room. Large sliding doors provided access to the freight room. In 1925, the Great Northern added living quarters for the station agent.

In 1979, the Kevin Economic Development Corporation moved the building from the railroad right-of-way and converted it into a senior center. Although now divorced from its original location, the depot remains instantly recognizable as a railroad property due to its long, narrow form, which once paralleled the tracks.

Above: This bracket is all that remains of a signal that stationmasters at the Kevin Depot used to let conductors know whether they needed to stop at the station to pick up new orders.

Oregon Short Line Depot

Dillon | 45°13′32″N 112°37′38″W

The Union Pacific Railroad was the first railroad to enter Montana Territory, completing a branch line connecting the Utah main line to Butte in 1881. Although it was one of the main stops on the line, the original Dillon depot, dismantled from another location and moved to Dillon in sections in 1880, was inconveniently located and, according to one contemporary assessment, "dingy, dirty and absolutely unfit." Local businessmen lobbied the Union Pacific for a depot more suited for the town's size and significance.

In 1908, the railroad funded this Arts and Crafts–style brick depot, which features cast concrete corner quoins and string courses, multi-paned windows, and wide eaves supported by wooden brackets. Railroad depots are one of the few types of buildings for which the back (facing the town) is as important as the front (facing the tracks). The stylish façades on both front and back of this depot—now housing the county history museum and a theater—reflect its railroading history. *—MK*

Cut into the steep hillside below the family's mausoleum, these "fairy steps" provided Alicia Conrad private access from a carriage path to her husband's gravesite.

44. Charles E. Conrad Memorial Cemetery

Kalispell | 48°12′12″N 114°17′20″W

On a fine fall day in 1902, Kalispell founder Charles E. Conrad and his wife Alicia took their last horseback ride together. When Charles, diabetic and ill, became tired, the couple rested on a narrow overlook where the valley spread below. Charles told his wife there could be no lovelier place for his final rest. Before his death several weeks later, Charles sketched the mausoleum he wanted Alicia to build on the promontory.

Alicia Conrad worked tirelessly to establish a community cemetery serving all people and all faiths as a memorial to her husband. She traveled extensively to find the right design. At her invitation, A. W. Hobert, superintendent of the famed Lakewood Cemetery in Minneapolis, Minnesota, visited the site and agreed there was none more beautiful. He designed the cemetery in 1903 as a classic Rural Garden Landscape. This concept in urban cemetery planning, first employed at Père Lachaise Cemetery (1804) in Paris, France, and later in the United States at Mount Auburn (1831) in Cambridge, Massachusetts, offered a park-like setting for the enjoyment of nature as well as the burial of loved ones.

Hobert's careful, artistic planning is based on the rural garden concept, but the design goes further, incorporating lawn, or memorial park, elements. The classic features include a focus on nature enhanced by carefully planned landscaping; open grassy spaces with flat, embedded markers; and artistically pleasing spatial arrangements of upright tombstones and monuments.

Alicia Conrad laid the foundation for thoughtful stewardship, initiating a legislative bill, passed in 1905, that established cemetery management and perpetual care, meaning the creation of a fund that would ensure the long-term upkeep of the public grounds. The Conrad Cemetery became the prototype for perpetual care cemeteries in Montana. Today, 104 acres of winding driveways and sweeping lawns include more than eighteen thousand burials. The Fairy Steps are a unique feature, cut into the steep hillside below the Conrad mausoleum. The steps afforded Alicia private access from a carriage path to her husband's gravesite and have since delighted generations of Kalispell children.

The Conrad family played a key role in the settlement of northwestern Montana and the founding of the town of Kalispell. Charles Conrad's far-reaching business endeavors spanned the 1860s to the time of his death, from freighting buffalo robes to banking, real estate, and civic improvements. Alicia Conrad likewise was beloved by people regardless of social status and always ready to help those in need. From her contributions to the Red Cross to hosting disadvantaged children, her concern and graciousness left an indelible impression wherever her travels took her.

The Conrad legacy coalesced in the founding of the Conrad Cemetery. Because of Alicia Conrad's planning and management, the cemetery remains open to all. Advertised as "Your Last Best Place," it is a living landscape and a well-deserved tribute to Kalispell's founding family. *—EB*

TESLOW
INC.
GRAIN
HAY
BNSF
BNSF
489525

45. Billy Miles & Bros. Grain Elevator (Teslow Elevator)

Livingston | 45°39′42″N 110°34′49″W

During the early decades of the twentieth century, as homesteaders attempted to transform the high plains from "the great American desert" to a cultivated heartland, grain elevators rose as icons of the prairie. Their recognizable silhouettes—visible for miles—came to symbolize the small towns that served as farming hubs and the agricultural enterprises that brought these communities into being.

Livingston was incorporated on December 21, 1882, by the Northern Pacific Railroad near an earlier settlement first known as Benson's Landing and later as Clark City. Named after a Northern Pacific executive, it became both an important railroad division point and a gateway for Yellowstone-bound tourists. Especially after the turn of the twentieth century, Livingston also became increasingly important as a shipping hub for local farmers and ranchers.

Grain elevators were essential components in transporting Montana wheat and barley to outside markets. Once harvested, farmers hauled their crops—initially by wagon, later by truck—to trackside elevators where the grain was dumped into a basement-level "pit." From there, it was conveyed by a "leg"—a continuously looping belt to which cups or buckets were attached—to the "headhouse," or top of the elevator. There, it was fed via a "gerber," or distribution spout, into one of several "bins" segregated by grain type and grade (large elevators could hold as many as twenty bins). Once in the proper bin, the grain was stored until the farmer was ready to sell it. Prior to sale, the grain was released into a "hopper," from which it was loaded into railcars for shipment to national and international buyers.

The homesteading boom dramatically increased the number of farmers looking to ship grain. Seeing an opportunity, in 1906 Billy Miles & Bros. built what is now known as the Teslow Elevator in the heart of Livingston's railroad district.

A former Texas cowboy, Billy Miles arrived in Clark City in 1881 and opened a livery and sale stable in Livingston the following year. His brothers Tom and Boyd joined him, and, among other ventures, the three brothers provided feed for the Northern Pacific's Livingston stockyards and bought and sold horses; customers included the British Army. The Miles brothers would also eventually become Park County's largest grain dealer.

Construction of the Billy Miles & Bros. elevator held enough significance to the community to merit newspaper coverage. When completed, it stood seventy-five feet in height and held seventy-five thousand bushels of grain. Except for a concrete foundation, it was constructed entirely of wood, then clad with galvanized sheet metal panels. The Miles brothers sold their elevator to the Gary Hay and Grain Company in 1918, which, in turn, sold it to the Teslow family in 1952. The Teslows sold the elevator to the Minnesota-based Peavey Elevator Company in 1971 before it ultimately ceased operation altogether.

While at one time fixtures of most rural communities, by the twenty-first century many wood-frame elevators faced demolition as changing technology made the historic structures obsolete. When high winds damaged the Teslow in 2016 a similar fate seemed to be inevitable. However, recognizing the importance of the elevator to Livingston's past, citizens rallied and raised enough money to purchase the grand old "prairie skyscraper." Today, the Teslow stands as a prime example of a remarkable preservation victory as well as a beacon of Livingston's agricultural history. *—KL*

46. Deer Lodge American Woman's League Chapter House

Deer Lodge | 46°23′54″N 112°44′00″W

In 1890, twelve Deer Lodge women gathered to create a literary club—the Deer Lodge Woman's Club—for "mental stimulus and uplifting influence." At a time when few women attended college, club members took their studies seriously, even hiring a history teacher. As they studied, they learned new skills—such as how to run meetings and speak in public—and gained self-confidence.

While it was the first women's club in the Treasure State, the Deer Lodge group was part of a much larger national movement. Both in Montana and across the country, participants in women's organizations soon began looking beyond their own personal development toward ways to improve their communities. Adapting the language of "social housekeeping," they asserted that their womanly duties toward their homes and children required them to become involved in community affairs and politics. Many became active in the fight for women's suffrage, helping to win the vote for Montana women (excluding American Indians) in 1914.

The American Woman's League (AWL) was among those clubs devoted to promoting women's suffrage. Alma Higgins, a member of the original Deer Lodge Woman's Club, organized the AWL's Deer Lodge chapter in 1909. Unlike other women's clubs, the AWL was founded by a man—Edward Lewis—who owned a St. Louis–based publishing company. White women could gain membership in the segregated AWL by selling, or pledging to sell, $52 worth of magazine subscriptions. Half the subscription price belonged to the publisher; the other half, Lewis promised, would fund league activities. These included study courses; a mail-order lending library; an exchange through which members could sell handicrafts; a retreat for widows, orphans, and the elderly; and a loan and relief fund. In addition, Lewis promised to build a chapter house for any town with enough AWL members, providing the community donated the lot.

Unfortunately, the scheme failed. Beset by accusations of fraud, Lewis declared bankruptcy, but not before work had begun on the Deer Lodge Woman's League Chapter House, one of only thirty-nine (of the seven hundred promised) chapter houses ever built. Designed by the St. Louis–based Helfensteller, Hirsh and Watson, the homey clubhouse follows the firm's Class III plan, except for the addition of a central chimney and partial basement. The original plan did not include a furnace. Its wide-bracketed eaves, heavy piers, and low side planters emphasize the horizontal orientation typical of the Prairie style, while inside, exposed beams, dark moldings, and original stenciling reflect the Craftsman style.

Lewis's bankruptcy declaration occurred before the Deer Lodge workmen were paid. Alma Higgins approached her father, pioneering stockman Nicholas Bielenberg, for help. He paid for the project and donated the building to the women of Deer Lodge in memory of daughter Augusta Kohrs Bielenberg, who had died in 1901.

Ever since, the building has hosted women's civic and cultural activities: art, music, literary events, city beautification projects, well-baby clinics, and flower shows. The Deer Lodge Woman's Club also raised money for a variety of causes, from tuberculosis research and domestic violence prevention to animal welfare. Club work continues to this day, making this one of the oldest continually active women's clubs—and one of the few women's club buildings—in Montana. *—MK*

WOMAN'S
CLUB

47. Grandey School

Terry | 46°47′32″N 105°18′45″W

Terry's beloved Grandey School recalls the influence of its namesake, Charles W. Grandey. "Pop" or "Prof" Grandey was a local teacher, school principal, superintendent, community activist, farmer, and state legislator who shaped the future of education not just in Terry but across Montana. The building, little changed in over one hundred years, symbolizes Grandey's lasting impact on local and state education, athletics, and community development.

Grandey, suffering from a lung ailment, headed west from Illinois in 1907 on doctor's orders to find a drier climate. He accepted a job in Terry, teaching in a two-room schoolhouse. The budding community quickly embraced Grandey's energy and enthusiasm, and in January 1908, the school board offered to build a new grade school if Grandey would stay on. He agreed, and voters unanimously passed a $15,000 bond issue. The board hired respected Montana architects John G. Link and Charles S. Haire to design the building.

Completed in 1908, the school's buff brick walls, red brick trim, and stately central bell tower offered an imposing yet welcoming prairie edifice. Inside, pine wainscotting, a central staircase with oak railings, and maple floors presented a home-like atmosphere. Contractors and architects alike noted that the new building endowed Terry with "better school facilities than any other town of the same population . . . in any of the northwestern states."

The school's opening marked the beginning of Grandey's long career improving education and community life in Montana. Under his direction, the Terry grade school gained a strong academic and athletic reputation, which brought more families to the area. In 1910, Grandey organized a horse-drawn school bus for rural students—the second district in the state to offer the service. He also petitioned the county to build a new bridge over the Yellowstone River, allowing students north of the river access to the school. In 1916, Grandey oversaw construction of a large addition that doubled the school's size. As county superintendent and basketball coach, in 1929 he directed construction of Terry High School nearby, which included a regulation-size basketball court.

In addition, Grandey spearheaded most of the town's community organizations, including the Commercial Club, Rotary Club, telephone co-op, Masonic Lodge, and Terry Community Church. He was also a wheat farmer, Sunday school teacher, occasional newspaper editor, and town council clerk.

Statewide, Grandey helped revise Montana school law in 1912, taught teachers at various normal schools, helped rewrite Montana's high school English curriculum, and stopped proposed cuts to humanities instruction during World War II. Grandey was a founding member and president of both the Montana Education Association (now the Montana Federation of Public Employees) and the Montana High Schools Association. After he ostensibly retired in 1947, he worked as a sales representative for textbook company MacMillan Publishing and, from 1952 to 1960, as a state senator who advocated to improve education policy and funding.

A newspaper reporter wrote of Grandey's accomplishments in 1947, "To be sure there was a Terry before Grandey came west. There would have been a Terry if he had never migrated, but it would have been a different Terry." And without Grandey, it would have been a different Montana. *—CWB*

Several children stand outside of the Grandey School in this photograph from around 1915. While its surroundings have changed in the past 108 years, the school building itself has barely been altered.

LOT 048 TERR, MTHS PHOTOGRAPH ARCHIVES

CHAPTER FIVE

PLOWING TOWARD PROGRESS 1911–1918

"Montana has long been famous for its copper and its cattle. . . . Within the next few years, Montana will be as well known for enormous crops of wheat and oats." So promised the Great Northern Railway in one of its many promotional pamphlets, this one advertising farmland in the Judith Basin, which it dubbed "one of the most fertile sections in the entire northwest."

Having built transcontinental lines across Montana to connect the coasts, railroads foresaw profit in filling what they perceived as vast, empty tracts. Prosperous farmers would need railroads to ship their grain to market, and almost everything purchased in their local market towns—from agricultural implements and furniture to buttons and Bibles—would have to be brought in by train. To the railroad companies, the equation was simple: more people equaled more traffic and, correspondingly, more profits.

In addition to promoting homesteading on government-owned lands, the railroads joined area businessmen to push the US government to open Indian reservations to homesteaders. The first step was allotment, the policy of surveying and parceling out (or allotting) reservation land to individual tribal members, typically 160 acres to the head of household and 80 acres to unmarried men and women. After all tribal members were assigned their allotments, the Department of the Interior sold the remaining land, which it deemed "surplus," at below market value. Another tool of forced assimilation, the ostensible goal of allotment was to transform Indians into successful farmers. In reality, it resulted in increased poverty for Native families, and by 1918, non-Indians owned the best agricultural sections on many Montana reservations.

Lured by the vision of free or inexpensive land, newcomers arrived in Montana in droves. While some had farming experience, others had no background in agriculture. "Between 1909 and 1923, settlers filed 114,620 homestead claims on almost twenty-five million acres of land," note historians Michael P. Malone, Richard B. Roeder, and William L. Lang in *Montana: A History of Two Centuries*. About 18 percent of these would-be farmers were single women. Railroad promoters traveled across Europe and the United States lecturing on "dry farming," which they claimed would turn the semiarid West into the "last and best grain gardendry [*sic*] of the world." Brochures published in multiple languages explained how to claim 320 acres and how—after only three years of living on a homestead part time—the land would be yours to keep. Cheap fares across the Atlantic by boat and then to Montana by train sealed the deal.

It was a time of optimism and expansion among Montana's non-Indian population. Across the Hi-Line and throughout eastern and central Montana, towns invested in infrastructure, schools, libraries, and community halls.

Above: The federal government's allotment policy benefited non-Indian homesteaders, who—like this crowd of recently arrived homesteaders photographed by Herman Schnitzmeyer in 1914—flooded onto the Flathead Reservation. Allotment, which broke up reservation lands across the state and nation, devastated Indigenous nations by reducing their resource base and eroding traditional lifeways.
950-561, MTHS PHOTOGRAPH ARCHIVES

Right: Promotional postcards like this one, published in the early twentieth century, aimed to entice farmers to move to the Treasure State. Railroads often produced these cards, as they had a vested interest in increasing the amount of people moving into and products moving out of the state.
LOT 032 B4F07.08, MTHS PHOTOGRAPH ARCHIVES

Congregations constructed churches, and fraternal organizations erected lodges, sometimes large enough to house additional businesses. Billings—called the Magic City because of its rapid growth—became the "heart of the Midland Empire," a wholesale center that served much of eastern Montana and northern Wyoming. Entrepreneurs constructed hotels and business blocks, and almost every Main Street boasted a brick or stone Neoclassical bank, the

To encourage Americans to "See America First" (and, not incidentally, increase railroad profits), the Great Northern Railway promoted Glacier National Park as "America's Alps," complete with its very own Matterhorn, seen behind these hikers. Dubbed the Little Matterhorn, this peak looks out over Avalanche Lake on the park's west side.
N. A. FORSYTH PHOTOGRAPH, 1906. ST 001.270, MTHS PHOTOGRAPH ARCHIVES

very appearance of which promised to keep depositors' money safe for the ages.

The homesteading boom came at the height of the Progressive Era, a time of intense ideological disagreement about the appropriate role of government in the economy and the way immigration was shaping American culture. For a time, progressive ideals seemed to be in ascendance. Montana women (excluding most American Indians) won the right to vote in 1914, six years before passage of the national suffrage amendment. Women put their votes to work in 1916, electing Jeannette Rankin to Congress and passing statewide Prohibition. Believing that government was most responsive if it was closer to the electorate, Montanans also repeatedly voted to form new, smaller counties. Big Horn, Blaine, Carter, Fallon, Hill, Mineral, Musselshell, Phillips, Prairie, Richland, Sheridan, Stillwater, Toole, Wheatland, and Wibaux Counties all formed between 1911 and 1918. In heady expressions of local pride, residents generously funded tax levies to construct courthouses in the towns newly designated as county seats.

White Montanans' optimistic views toward the role of government in improving people's lives echoed national efforts to use state power to protect the environment and regulate big business. The federal government founded Glacier National Park in 1910, a victory for conservationists and the Great Northern Railway, which stood to profit from increased tourism, but a blow to members of the Piikuni (Blackfeet) Nation, who lost hunting rights and access to important sacred sites. At the same time, the US Forest Service continued to expand its conservation mission, especially after the "Big Burn," a wildfire that raged across three million acres in northern Idaho and western Montana in August 1910.

Demand for grain increased markedly in 1914 with the onset of World War I, as European wheat production fell by over 50 percent. Prices for copper—an essential component in every weapon, ship, and tank—also soared, even as wages stagnated and pressure to "get the rock in the box" made mining more dangerous. Radical union organizers decried the conflict as a "rich man's war but a poor man's fight," joining immigrants from Ireland, Germany, Austria, and Finland in opposing US entry into the war on the side of England and Russia. After the United States declared war against the Central Powers in April 1917, tension between war opponents and supporters—and between labor and capital—grew, sometimes erupting into violence. Complicating matters, drought hit scattered counties in northern Montana in 1917. The next year, hot, dry weather held all of central and eastern Montana in its grip, a preview of even harder times to come. *—MK*

With America's entry into World War I, patriotic fervor swept over many Montanans, including these Red Cross nurses who paraded down the streets of Miles City. They were among the roughly twenty thousand women nationwide to volunteer for service.
DOUBLEDAY-FOSTER PHOTO CO., 1918. LOT 048 MICI, MTHS PHOTOGRAPH ARCHIVES

48. Miles City Water Works

Custer County | 46°24′22″N 105°52′5″W

Tucked away in a park along the Yellowstone River, the Miles City Water Works building symbolizes the town's forward-thinking approach to growth and development. The plant sits near the site of Colonel Nelson A. Miles's original 1876 Tongue River cantonment, which became Fort Keogh after being moved farther west in 1877.

With the arrival of the Northern Pacific Railroad in 1881, Miles City grew rapidly, but city services such as streetlights, water, sanitation, and fire safety developed in fits and starts. Various wells supplied drinking and washing water to businesses and houses but provided little protection against a wind-blown fire. While the Miles City Water and Light Co. was organized in 1886 and a combined light and water plant near Eighth and Pacific Streets was operational by 1888, the town still lacked water lines and hydrants. Sanborn Fire Insurance Company maps for Miles City prominently posted on the title page that the town's water facilities were "Not Good."

In 1890, the city began pumping water from the Tongue River and authorized construction of two reservoirs, a deep well, storage tank, pumps, water lines, and thirteen fire hydrants. By 1894, the downtown and residential areas had a constant water supply, and the system proved successful in extinguishing more than one large building fire. Nevertheless, calls for better supply were perennial, and by 1904, the city had added a large cistern and an auxiliary pumping plant.

The water supply problem worsened in 1906, when land on the Crow Reservation opened to homesteading and the Chicago, Milwaukee, St. Paul and Pacific Railroad announced plans to build a depot and shops in Miles City. The ensuing population boom stressed the town's already ailing system. After many complaints about polluted well water and typhoid fever, voters approved a 1910 bond issue to build a new waterworks plant on the Yellowstone River.

City architect and engineer Grover C. Pruett designed the waterworks in the French Eclectic style, a revival style recalling rural architecture from the French Renaissance. The style fit well into the natural landscape along the Yellowstone River. Significant stylistic hallmarks include the building's expansive hipped roof, overhanging bracketed eaves, and decorative concrete keystones and corner moldings above each window. Pruett also likely drew architectural inspiration from the City Beautiful movement, a Progressive Era effort that sought to improve social and economic conditions through architecture and urban planning. The movement favored the French Beaux-Arts style, which incorporated European Renaissance design motifs.

The Miles City Water Works was as functional as it was beautiful. Technologically state-of-the-art for the time, the system served Miles City from December 1911 until 1974 when the Custer County Art and Heritage Center remodeled the facilities into an art gallery and studio space, now called the WaterWorks Art Museum. It became a model for other communities as one of Montana's first historic industrial adaptive reuse projects. —***CWB***

49. Daniels County Courthouse

Scobey | 48°47′27″N 105°25′12″W

Mansfield Daniels and his brother-in-law Jake Timmons founded a cattle ranch along the Poplar River flats in 1900. The ranch was situated along the Wood Mountain Trail, which generations of Native people had used to travel between the United States and Canada, hunting buffalo and later trading furs. Daniels and Timmons were the first white settlers in the area. Major C. R. A. Scobey, the Indian agent at the nearby Fort Peck Reservation, assisted in establishing a post office there. Daniels named the settlement in Scobey's honor in 1901. The newly christened community first served travelers and then hundreds of homesteaders who arrived after the Enlarged Homestead Act of 1909.

When the Great Northern Railway planned its Hi-Line route across northern Montana, it bypassed the original Scobey settlement in favor of a route on the east side of the river, a mile and a half away. As the tracks approached in the summer of 1913, the town relocated. Residents moved existing buildings and constructed new ones, including the Commercial Hotel. When the first train arrived in Scobey on Thanksgiving Day, the two-story, Western False Front–style hotel—today the south half of the courthouse—was the new townsite's largest building.

The Commercial Hotel accommodated passengers and visitors as Scobey became a key grain shipping point. Minnie "One-Eyed Molly" Wakefield—so named for the glass eye she wore—arrived at the booming metropolis from Kansas City in 1915. Anticipating a rare business opportunity, she purchased the hotel from the Northern Town and Land Company.

Wakefield immediately expanded her business to include gambling and live entertainment. She and her sons kept pit bulls for fighting staked between her hotel and the Tallman Hotel next door. In addition to drinking, gambling, and dog fighting, women were a main attraction at the Commercial. Wakefield used the hotel's first floor for prostitution, while a large sleeping room upstairs accommodated legitimate overnight guests.

Federal closure of red-light establishments and the threat of Prohibition put a damper on Wakefield's business. She sold the hotel in 1917. In 1920, voters chose Scobey 964 to 358 over Madoc as the seat of the newly designated Daniels County, named for rancher Mansfield Daniels. County officials purchased the hotel for use as a courthouse and remodeled the interior.

In 1927, a frame addition on the north doubled the building's size, preserving and extending the original false front and ground floor porch. New clapboard siding and a second-story porch spanning the front unified both halves of the building. The upper porch functioned as a speaking platform for governors, senators, and other visiting dignitaries. The first floor housed offices, and the second story held the judge's chambers, courtroom, and offices. Original interior finishes include paneled doors with transoms. One first-floor office retains its corner sink, a telltale souvenir of its bawdy past.

The Western False Front architectural style, once common across Montana, gave young communities like Scobey the look of instant prosperity. The building is Montana's last functioning false-front frame courthouse and perhaps the West's only bordello converted to government use. *—EB*

50. Anna Scherlie Homestead Shack

Blaine County | 48°51′01″N 108°23′26″W

The Missouri River on the south and Canada on the north form the boundaries of Blaine County where a vast 132,000 acres is so level one can see for miles. The Enlarged Homestead Act of 1909 drew homesteaders to this area, appropriately dubbed "the Big Flat." Watered by the Milk River from east to west, it proved a good place to grow grain.

Neil J. Scherlie, the son of Norwegian immigrants, was among the first to file a homestead claim on the Big Flat. Over the next four years, his brothers Viggo and Bernard and sisters Martha, Nora, and Anna also filed claims on nearby homesteads, a common practice among families coming to Montana to farm.

Thirty-two-year-old Anna, a single woman who had previously served as a nurse to railroad magnate James J. Hill's newborn grandson, arrived from Minnesota in 1913. She and her sisters were part of a long tradition of women homesteaders in Montana. In fact, in the four surrounding townships, women made up about one-fourth of the total homestead applicants.

Two days after Anna filed her claim, she took up residence on her homestead. Within a month she had built a shack, the term used to describe dwellings hastily built to fulfill immediate occupancy requirements. The tiny, wood-frame building—probably built with her brothers' help—measures only fourteen-and-a-half feet on the long side.

Anna put twenty acres under cultivation in 1913. By 1916, when she proved up and earned her land title, Anna had forty acres planted in wheat, oats, and flax. It was a lonely existence. Isolation on the Big Flat and lack of income led many settlers to winter elsewhere. Anna followed suit, spending winters in St. Paul, Minnesota, where she worked as a nurse.

Over the decades, Anna made few changes to her small shack, adding only a vestibule for use as a summer kitchen, storage shed, and laundry. The house rests on a dry-laid "foundation" of stones filling the space between the shack's floor and the ground. Clapboard siding with corner boards covers the outer walls while imitation brick siding of asphalt in the gable ends adds a bit of ornamentation. A metal roof has replaced the original wood shingles. Inside, tongue-and-groove boards form the walls and ceiling of the single room; linoleum covers the floor.

During the hardest times, when one out of every two Montana farmers lost their land, Anna persevered. Long after her neighbors had built modern homes, Anna stayed in her shack, insisting that she was "too old for modern conveniences." Leon and Nellie Cederberg purchased the homestead when its seasoned resident retired and moved to Havre in 1968. Anna died in 1973, leaving an estate of more than $100,000 to be divided among eighteen nieces and nephews. Friends scattered her ashes beneath a lilac bush on the property. Rather than return the site to crop land, the Cederbergs maintained the homestead exactly as Anna left it, and so it survives today. *—EB*

51. Milwaukee Road Substation #10 (Primrose Station)

Missoula County | 46°54′45″N 114°09′03″W

The Primrose Substation was one of thirteen electrical substations built in Montana between 1915 and 1916 to convert and transfer power to locomotives on the Chicago, Milwaukee, St. Paul and Pacific Railroad's electric line between Harlowton and Avery, Idaho. The entire line, nicknamed the Milwaukee Road, was constructed mainly by Japanese contract laborers between 1906 and 1909. Even before the line was complete, railroad officials were planning to convert it to run on electricity. Operating steam locomotives along steep grades, often in frigid temperatures, was slow and expensive. With abundant hydropower in Montana and a ready source of copper in Butte, electrifying the line through the rugged mountain West would decrease fuel costs and speed travel times.

In 1912–1913, the railroad contracted with the Great Falls and Thompson Falls power companies to supply power to a series of substations positioned every 37 miles along the 440-mile route. Power line construction began in 1914 with the installation of one-hundred-thousand-volt lines along the tracks. Twenty-two substations built in the next two years converted three-phase alternating current to a three-thousand-volt direct current. A pantograph mounted on the roof of the locomotive ran along the wires, collecting the power needed to propel the train. A regenerative braking system (similar to the technology used in electric automobiles today) recovered about 60 percent of the energy required to travel up steep grades.

Once completed in 1916, the line's Rocky Mountain Division was the longest electrified railroad in the United States and a technological and economic triumph. Company historian August Derleth later reported that compared to steam locomotives "the tonnage per train was virtually doubled, and the operating maintenance expense, owing to the regenerative braking process, was significantly reduced. Overall efficiency was increased to such an extent that, in the initial eight years of operation, the road estimated a savings of $12,400,000 had been affected by electrification."

The Primrose Substation—named for a wildflower proliferating in the area—reflects the Milwaukee Road's standard substation design. The two-story front section housed two or three motor-generator sets, low-tension switching equipment, and a combination switchboard, ticketing office, and waiting room since most substations also served as railroad stations. The rear two-and-one-half-story section housed high-tension transformers and switching equipment.

Lightning arresters and horn gaps on the roof of the rear section dissipated occasional lightning strikes. Though mostly devoid of ornament, patterned brickwork above the foundation and windows and decorative tiles along the cornice add interest to the building's industrial character. The Primrose complex also included a water tank, pump house, shed, outhouse, tower, coal and oil house, stone house, icehouse, garage, two residences, and a two-story section house. Three men, each working eight-hour shifts, operated the substation continuously.

In 1950, the Primrose station began to operate via remote control from a substation in Tarkio. Despite initial cost efficiencies, over time the power lines and substation complexes became expensive to maintain. The substation closed in 1974 when the Milwaukee Road converted to diesel-fuel locomotives. Though the tracks were abandoned in 1980, this substation and three others remain, recalling the Milwaukee Road's innovative approach to rail transport in the early 1900s. —*CWB*

52. Carnegie Public Library

Big Timber | 45°49′57″N 109°57′7″W

In 1914, Big Timber Library Association president J. A. Lowry wrote to Andrew Carnegie's personal secretary James Bertram about the importance of its new library to the community: "Big Timber is . . . the center of a large ranching, stockgrowing, and farming district. They come to Big Timber from 25 to 30 miles from all directions . . . and we are quite anxious to do our part to take care and interest these people." He continued: "There is not a place in Big Timber for them to spend the evening unless it is hanging around the hotel or, what is the same thing here, a saloon, or pool hall, so we thot [*sic*] that by opening the Library building each evening . . . we would not only be educating them in the right way, but keeping them from falling by the wayside, as so many do in these western towns."

As Lowry's letter suggests, for the young town of Big Timber, the new library was more than just a book repository. It was a symbol of moral uplift and refinement, "visual proof" according to library historian Theodore Jones, of a "commitment to education, and to the community's history and future."

Big Timber's first library, a branch of the Parmly Billings Library, was a shelf of books in a local store in 1901. However, according to Montana historian Kate Hampton, the community was determined "to keep pace with other progressive cities in the state." In 1905, its citizens founded the Big Timber Library Association, which joined forces with the Big Timber Woman's Club to raise money for the library's permanent home. The involvement of the woman's club was typical; historians estimate that women's clubs founded approximately 75 percent of libraries across the United States.

By 1911, the library, then housed in the town hall, had grown to 1,300 volumes, and the community asked industrialist and library patron Andrew Carnegie to fund a new building. By this time, Carnegie was well known for funding libraries; ultimately, he paid for the construction of over sixteen hundred libraries, including seventeen in Montana. Carnegie provided $7,500 to Big Timber, stipulating, as he did with all his library grants, that the community provide a building site and commit tax funds to support free library services.

Designed by the Montana architectural firm of Link and Haire, this "temple of learning" embraces Classical Revival elements that became popular for civic buildings following the 1893 Columbian Exposition in Chicago. The library follows the "Plan A" design for small libraries provided in the *Notes on the Erection of Library Bildings* [*sic*] published by the Carnegie Corporation in 1911. It features large windows to bring in natural light, a main floor with a circulation desk flanked by two reading rooms, and a daylight basement with a meeting room for lectures. Embellished with Tuscan columns and a pedimented entry, the symmetrical building is a fine example of "Carnegie Classic" design, personalized by a façade of river rock at the basement level. *—MK*

CARNEGIE LIBRARY
Celebrating
1914-2014
"Sharing the Story"
by Dave Hodges

53. Lincoln Community Hall

Lincoln | 46°57′20″N 112°40′22″W

Since 1918, this distinctive octagonal structure has served as the heart of the Lincoln community. Here, generations of Upper Blackfoot Valley residents have come together for dances, talent shows, Christmas pageants, plays, reunions, weddings, and funerals. At one point, the building was even equipped for roller skating and used as a gymnasium.

Lincoln owes its beginnings to the discovery of gold in August 1865. Prospectors named the site of their strike Lincoln Gulch to honor America's recently slain president. As more miners, workers, and businessmen moved in, the small community of Lincoln developed along the Blackfoot River approximately four miles east of the eponymous gulch. By the 1880s, timber and agriculture had replaced mining as the region's primary economic drivers, while the unincorporated hamlet of Lincoln—which, in 1920, had a population of 119—continued to serve as its commercial and social hub.

Given the preeminence of the timber industry, it was natural that, when efforts began to construct a new community center in 1916, citizens chose logs as a building material. As longtime Lincoln resident and musician Carter Rubottom recalled in a 1962 *Great Falls Tribune* article, "An association was formed and plans began to take shape. We agreed to build it of logs, but the size and shape required a lot of discussion." Ultimately, Rubottom continued:

> Final plans [for an octagonal structure] were drawn up. . . . We cut logs and decked them in the woods on Stonewall Creek, about five miles from the site of the hall. The cement foundations were poured before freezing weather. Ira Tuck and I offered to haul down the logs and by the time we started the snow was more than three feet deep in the hills . . . We hauled down 120 logs and then started the building. We dug a trench in the deep snow, exposing the foundation, then set up trestles and peeled the logs. We mortised the ends to make the joints. This was some job, as the logs were 27 feet long and at least 10 inches in diameter at the small end.

Leonard Lambkin, a prominent businessman and Lincoln booster, donated most of the land—conspicuously situated on Highway 200—upon which the Community Hall sits. Volunteers, supervised by local carpenter Tom Hensler, provided most of the labor for the project. Others donated their services to raise needed funds; women raffled needlework and held "basket socials," while Rubottom and his band organized dances. As Rubottom reminisced, "People came from miles away and we had a fine time [dancing]. . . . We often had large crowds from Helena and Great Falls. . . . At the close of the war, everyone was crazy to dance."

By 1920, the dances had raised enough money to construct a log addition on the rear of the building to house a dining room/kitchen. Over time, shed additions on the east and west sides of the rear wing increased the building's functionality, and the original hipped-roof porch was replaced in 1956 when Highway 200 was widened. Even with these relatively minor physical alterations, the spirit of the building has never changed. During the building's centenary celebration in summer 2019, locals and visitors alike came together to dance, watch performances, worship, eat, and enjoy each other's company, just as they had been doing since the lodge's construction. —***KL***

Around 1925, Edward M. Reinig took this photograph of the Lincoln Community Hall, then well known for the popular dances it hosted to raise money for the construction and expansion of the building.
LOT 048 LINC, MTHS PHOTOGRAPH ARCHIVES

54. Churches

Churches are more than houses of worship. They are also places of community that demonstrate settlers' dreams for the future. Constructing a dedicated church building, with a full-time minister or priest, was an expression of a community's coming of age and the result of much hard work and fundraising. It asserted that settlers were here to stay—and expressed the value they placed on the cultural and religious traditions they brought with them.

St. Wenceslaus Catholic Church in Danvers

Cathedral of St. Helena

Helena | 46°35′24.53″N 112°1′57.15″W

By 1905, Helena had fully matured from a mining camp into Montana's financial and political center. With a congregation numbering 2,500, Bishop John Carroll purchased a lot near downtown Helena to build a grand, new cathedral to replace the modest, brick building constructed in 1876. Wealthy and influential men, including three US senators, two bank presidents, and other prominent businessmen and attorneys, made up the building committee. Mining magnate Thomas Cruse, an Irish immigrant who discovered and developed the Drumlummon lode and founded the town of Marysville, was its president. Cruse donated over $200,000 to the costly $550,000 project.

Architect A. O. Von Herbulis modeled the Gothic-style church after the Votivkirche in Vienna. Dedicated in 1914 and completed in 1924, its spires rise 230 feet in the air, symbolically reaching for the heavens. Inside, over eleven thousand square feet of art glass, purchased from the world-renowned artisan F. X. Zettler of Munich, Germany, make up the fifty-six stained glass panels, retelling scenes from the Old and New Testaments and church history—reviving the Medieval tradition of using stained glass to create a "Bible for the Poor." —***MK***

St. Wenceslaus Catholic Church

Danvers | 47°13′42″N 109°42′47″W

Grand edifices like the Cathedral of St. Helena were out of reach for most congregations. However, the Gothic style was so strongly associated with church architecture that almost no church design was complete without pointed-arch windows, bell towers, vestibules, and steep gable roofs. St. Wenceslaus Catholic Church in Danvers, twenty-three miles northwest of Lewistown, exemplifies the rural, community-constructed churches commonly built by all denominations during the homesteading boom. It also reflects how important these churches were to immigrant communities.

In 1910, slightly more than half of Montanans were either immigrants or had at least one immigrant parent. Lured by the 1909 Enlarged Homestead Act's promise of free farms, extended families and friends often settled near one another, creating ethnic and religious enclaves. Such was the case in Danvers, which boasted twenty-two Czech families by 1920.

Danvers Catholics initially held services in the schoolhouse, private homes, and even the railroad depot. In 1915, they raised $2,650 to build a church. Carpenter Frank Snider oversaw construction, and the congregation pitched in to excavate the basement and complete the interior. Named for the patron saint of Czechoslovakia, Saint Wenceslaus features distinctively Czech decorations, including a replica statue of the Infant of Prague, which adorns the ornately constructed wooden reredos (the screen behind the altar). *—MK*

Above left: Union Bethel African Methodist Episcopal Church; Above right: Melville Lutheran Church

Union Bethel African Methodist Episcopal Church

Great Falls | 47°29′30″N 111°17′21″W

Ethnic communities in larger cities also worshiped in their own churches; as with St. Wenceslaus, urban churches served both as religious homes and community centers. A pillar of the African American community in Great Falls for more than a century, the Union Bethel African Methodist Episcopal Church began holding regular services in the Electric City's first fire station in 1890. The following year, African American residents gathered with white supporters to lay the cornerstone of their new building. Built on swampy ground on donated land, the building was hard to maintain, and by 1915 the wooden church had fallen into disrepair.

As in many church congregations, women took the lead in raising funds to construct this brick church. Completed in 1917, the new Gothic-style edifice incorporated the cornerstone of the original structure. In addition to providing a home for worship, Union Bethel also provided meeting space for Black secular organizations like the Dunbar Art and Study Club and offered institutional support for members who took leading roles in the fight against segregation in Great Falls. *—MK*

Melville Lutheran Church

Melville | 46°6′11″N 109°57′14″W

Norwegian immigrants from Minnesota established Montana's first Norwegian colony north of Big Timber in 1881. Originally dubbed "The Settlement," residents later renamed it Melville after Arctic explorer George Wallace Melville. In 1885, locals gathered to create a Lutheran congregation. They worshiped in homes and in a one-room schoolhouse until 1914, when sheep ranching was at its peak. Parishioners raised $2,600 to construct this classic vernacular Gothic church and donated much of the labor to build it. Unlike many small rural churches that lost membership following World War II, Melville Lutheran retained its congregation through the late twentieth century. It still opens its doors for Sunday and holiday services as of 2024. *—CWB*

55. Masonic Temple

Havre | 48°32′34″N 109°40′49″W

Several hundred Masons from across the state helped dedicate the Havre Masonic Temple, which the newspaper grandly called "the finest of its kind to be found in the entire northwest." Dedicated in 1916 at the height of the homestead boom, the imposing, five-story, Revival-style building expressed confidence in Havre's future by providing needed space for large Masonic gatherings as well as modern store and office space. As Havre's tallest building at the time of its construction, its stout massing followed a longstanding Masonic tradition of erecting lodges whose size symbolized the permanency and solidity of masonry itself.

Fraternal organizations were an important facet of life in territorial Montana towns, helping to establish social and civic stability. The Ancient Free and Accepted Masons established its first lodge in Virginia City in 1866, offering its members support, connections, and a close-knit community. Frontiersmen and women, accustomed to transience, valued these bonds. Fraternal societies flourished in Montana and throughout the United States in the nineteenth and early twentieth centuries. By 1897, approximately six million Americans were members of a fraternal group and over two hundred

This photograph of the Havre Masonic Temple dates to around 1916, shortly after it was constructed.

AL-916-491-1002, AL LUCKE COLLECTION, VANDE BOGART LIBRARY, MONTANA STATE UNIVERSITY-NORTHERN

The frieze above the building's main entrance features a winged sun flanked by two cobras—one of many ancient motifs found in Egyptian Revival architecture—in the center of which is the Mason's Square and Compass symbol.

thousand new members joined every year. Whether new lodges rented rooms or erected their own temples, their presence was integral in the development and longevity of numerous Montana towns.

Members of Havre Lodge #55, first organized in 1901, contributed to their community's development by building a multi-use facility that would provide space for businesses as well as for ceremonial and social functions. Havre architect Frank Bossuot, who also planned the nearby Hill County Courthouse, carefully designed the building to fulfill its multiple functions.

Various merchants, including an undertaker, grocer, and dry goods salesman, occupied the first-floor storefronts. Behind the plain façade and double-hung windows of the second and third floors, many Havre lawyers, doctors, and businessmen had their offices. The top two stories—reserved exclusively for Masonic use—included a grand lodge room, a large kitchen and dining area overlooking the lodge room, and a chapel.

Bossuot and the organization's building committee chose a mix of styles that freely melded a blend of ancient architectural design elements, creating a distinctive appearance. The diamond-patterned brick, blue tile, and bracketed cornice at the temple's roofline illustrate Italian and Mediterranean influences, evoking the Masons' philosophical ties to ancient Greece and Rome. More subdued, but equally important, the entrance's tapered sandstone pilasters and winged frieze employ Egyptian iconography. More Egyptian motifs decorate the fourth-floor lodge room. In the early 1900s, renewed attention to Napoleon's 1798–1799 Egypt campaign sparked European and American interest in Egyptian history, culture, and decoration. The Havre Masonic Temple's Egyptian aesthetic is one of only a handful of examples of that craze ever realized in Montana. —***CWB***

56. The Atlas Block

Columbus | 45°38′05″N 109°14′45″W

For many, saloons were—and are—an integral part of life in the West. The Atlas Bar in Columbus is among Montana's most historic and colorful establishments. When the state legislature created Stillwater County in 1913, voters chose Columbus as the new county seat. Already a well-established trade center and Northern Pacific shipping point, the small community was favorably positioned to assume its role in government. Correspondingly, between 1907 and 1920 sandstone and brick buildings largely replaced the wood-frame buildings that had characterized its commercial district. Significant among these new stone edifices was the two-story Atlas Block, constructed in 1915–1916 by quarry operator Michael Jacobs and saloon keeper Thomas Mulvihill.

Jacobs had learned masonry in his native Italy. After immigrating to Chicago in 1877, he added studies in architecture to his considerable skill as a stonecutter. He moved to Columbus in 1900 to assume management of the quarry northeast of town when the Montana Building Company secured the contract to provide sandstone for the state capitol building, then under construction in Helena. Under his supervision, quarry operations expanded and contractors used Columbus sandstone for numerous notable buildings not only in Stillwater County but across the state.

Jacobs and Mulvihill hired German-born Billings architect Curtis C. Oehme to design their new building. While Oehme's career in Montana was cut short by anti-German hysteria during World War I, his design, according to historians Jon Axline and Joan L. Brownell, resulted in an "excellent example of Western Commercial Architecture," which was prevalent in the late nineteenth and early twentieth centuries. The street level housed commercial enterprises, while the upper levels provided office space, meeting halls, and rented rooms. Additionally, Oehme's design incorporated rusticated pilasters projecting above the roofline and a checkerboard-patterned frieze enlivening the cornice, features that that the skilled masons working on the project crafted using local sandstone.

Of the original occupants of the Atlas Block—which included Annin and Banks Dry Goods in the east side—the Atlas Bar, housed in the west side, would prove to be the most enduring. Jacobs and Mullvihill arranged their establishment into five "departments." A smoking room and cigar stand offering "the best Smoke in Town" greeted customers as they entered the building's main floor. In a narrow barroom running down the saloon's east side, men were encouraged to order a drink but not linger. Instead, they were expected to take their libations to a billiard parlor, in the rear of the building, which a local newspaper declared "the most beautiful and attractive in the whole state" due in large part to the "wonderful array of heads and other taxidermy specimens" that adorned the walls. Women were accommodated in a "ladies sitting room" accessed through a separate "ladies entrance." The basement housed a lunchroom and a three-lane "duckpin" bowling alley where smaller balls and pins were used on lanes of standard dimensions.

During Prohibition, owners sold soft drinks, ice cream, cigars, and sporting goods. Following the repeal of the Eighteenth Amendment in 1933, alterations to the saloon's interior left intact most of its historical character, including an ornate Brunswick-Balke-Collender mahogany front and back bar, pressed metal ceilings, and the storied taxidermy mounts. Members of the Mulvihill family continued to operate the Atlas until 1997, preserving a Stillwater County institution and its traditional hospitality. —*KL*

Above left: In the saloon's original configuration, seen in this ca. 1920 photograph, men were encouraged to order a drink from but not linger in the narrow barroom.

946-558, MTHS PHOTOGRAPH ARCHIVES

The Atlas Block (left) and adjoining Columbus Mercantile Co. are among the business blocks built of locally quarried sandstone lining the north side of Columbus's main street.

57. First National Bank of Glasgow

Glasgow | 48°11′57″N 106°37′55″W

Merchant brothers John and Robert Lewis faced little competition when they opened a bank in a corner of their general store in Glasgow in 1891. Their new bank was the only one within a two-hundred-mile radius. Despite an initial lack of experience, the brothers successfully steered the enterprise through economic shoals that doomed many other Montana banks: the panics of 1893 and 1907. During Glasgow's early years, the bank thrived, moving to a brick building in 1900 and obtaining its national charter in 1905.

The Lewises sensed even greater opportunity when the US government opened the Fort Peck Indian Reservation for settlement in 1913. Thousands of non-Indian, would-be farmers purchased the former reservation lands left over after the government had surveyed the reservation and assigned each tribal member between 320 and 380 acres of land, a policy known as allotment. Believing that Glasgow would prosper with this influx of dryland farmers, the Lewises purchased five lots on the corner of Fifth Street South and First Avenue South, a few blocks north of the county courthouse and across the street from the railroad depot. The choice to build on the primary thoroughfare was strategic not only for customer convenience but also for security; like other bankers, the Lewises hoped the busy location would deter bank robbers.

Technically, national banks were not allowed to speculate in real estate, for fear that their directors would overestimate their town's prospects and fall prey to the boosterism that defined young communities. To get around this prohibition, bank boards often authorized construction of large buildings with surplus office space. The First National Bank of Glasgow was no exception. Designed in 1914 by prominent St. Paul architects Charles Buechner and Henry Orth, the building housed retail stores and the bank itself on the first floor and business offices and an apartment for Robert Lewis on the second floor. The classic Beaux Arts–style building features a symmetrical façade, entry porches with roofs supported by graceful Corinthian columns, second-floor balconies, and exuberant decorative terra-cotta detailing.

The First National Bank building helped mark Glasgow's coming of age. The stability reflected in its style symbolized safety and permanence both for the bank and for the community itself. In fact, both the bank and the community survived the agricultural depression of the 1920s and the ravages of the Great Depression, when over half of Montana's banks closed. And unlike many Montana communities, Glasgow boomed in the 1930s, with the construction of Fort Peck Dam, and again in the 1950s when establishment of the Glasgow Air Force Base bolstered the local economy. The bank's directors responded by renovating the building's interior: expanding the lobby, covering the original mosaic tile floors with linoleum, and installing acoustic tiles on the ceiling to create a "sleek, modern design." In 1971, the First National Bank moved into a new, larger building one block west. *—MK*

Disregarding the inconvenience to others from blocking the street, contractors Leigland, Kleppe & Co. erected these two makeshift structures to store their tools, take a break from the weather, and complete paperwork in the same way that construction companies use trailers today.

UNKNOWN PHOTOGRAPHER, CA. 1914. MONTANA STATE HISTORIC PRESERVATION OFFICE FILES

58. Rosebud County Courthouse

Forsyth | 46°16′01″N 106°40′30″W

Although scandal ultimately surrounded the construction of Rosebud County Courthouse, the building's origins were uncontroversial. Recognizing the need for a new courthouse ten years after Rosebud County was carved from Custer County, voters passed a $125,000 bond issue to fund construction in 1911. The *Forsyth Times-Journal* praised the outcome as a sign "that the taxpayers of Rosebud County stand for progress."

To design a suitable replacement for the original courthouse—a wood-frame former schoolhouse—county commissioners hired Butte architects John G. Link and Charles S. Haire, who designed courthouses for eighteen of Montana's fifty-six counties. Featuring a colossal portico and an octagonal tower topped by a copper dome, Link and Haire's design was well received, and Gray's Construction Company of South Dakota began excavation in 1912.

Trouble commenced when it became clear that the project was more than $40,000 over budget. In September 1913, the editor of the *Forsyth Times-Journal* lambasted the commissioners for the cost overrun and sued to restrain them from further expenditure. Such overspending often plagued courthouse and capitol construction projects, sometimes because of graft or, as in Forsyth's case, the impulse to spend lavishly on temples of democracy. The requested changes that led Gray's Construction to exceed its original estimate included siding the courthouse's exterior with Columbus, Montana, sandstone and specifying a marble stairway and marble wainscotting in the restroom and ground floor. The cost of artwork, furniture, and landscaping also added to the expense.

In September 1913, District Judge Charles L. Crum responded to the newspaper's accusation that the county had illegally exceeded its spending authority by issuing a temporary injunction, preventing the commissioners from acting on courthouse matters. He then called a grand jury to hear the case and ordered the sheriff to take possession of the new courthouse. Apparently worried that his company would not be paid in full, Gray's foreman refused to turn over the keys to the completed building, despite the court order. The clash had moments of high drama: At one point, the foreman locked himself inside the building and hid between the ceiling and the roof.

The undersheriff retrieved the keys so that Judge Crum and the county commissioners could move into their new quarters. Soon, however, Judge Crum found himself under attack for his opposition to World War I. Although Crum, who had German ancestors, insisted he was a loyal American merely exercising his First Amendment rights, the Montana State Senate impeached him in 1918. He was posthumously exonerated by a unanimous vote of the Montana Senate in 1991.

The *Forsyth Times-Journal*'s case against the commissioners ended less rancorously, with the grand jury ultimately dismissing all charges against the county. In fact, the grand jury ruled that the building's design was "imposing and attractive" and its interior "very harmoniously and artistically decorated." It also declared that the county received "full value for the money expended." That verdict still stands. The elegant Neoclassical building remains one of Rosebud County's architectural jewels. *—MK*

Unidentified citizens float past the *Times-Journal* office and the Rosebud County Courthouse as waters from the Yellowstone River flood the streets of Forsyth on June 16, 1918.

WALTER DEAN JR. PHOTOGRAPH. ROSEBUD COUNTY LIBRARY

This uncredited 1911 photograph shows the nearly completed Red Lodge Brewery building. A three-story wood-frame addition (opposite page) was constructed in 1927 to house needed canning equipment.
MONTANA STATE HISTORIC PRESERVATION OFFICE FILES

59. Red Lodge Brewery/Cannery

Red Lodge | 45°11′36″N 109°14′55″W

Because beer was heavy to transport and easy to manufacture, many communities had their own breweries before Prohibition halted the sale of alcohol. According to Montana beer historian Steve Lozar, prospectors brewed beer in German Gulch in 1861, and Henry Gilbert opened Montana's first brewery in Virginia City in 1863. There were over twenty breweries in the state in 1910, when Bozeman beer baron and German immigrant Julius Lehrkind incorporated the Red Lodge Brewing Company with his nephews Fred and Paul. The Lehrkinds hired the prominent architectural firm of Link and Haire to design the monumental brick brewery as well as the bottling plant next door. Red Lodge contractor Anton Roat constructed both buildings in 1911.

The brewery's design—modified from plans John Link created for the Washoe Brewery in Anaconda—reflected the owners' prosperity, pride in their product, and European heritage. It also reflected the building's function. Engineered to support heavy equipment, breweries also required easily cleanable surfaces, fresh air, and light. The four-story tower was ornamental but also an integral part of a gravity flow system that moved huge quantities of liquid through the brewing process without the use of pumps.

Pure Rock Creek water and a ready market of thirsty coal miners proved a recipe for success, and the Lehrkinds' widely advertised decision to use union labor tied the brewery to the Red Lodge patrons it hoped to serve. The large plant, which had a capacity of thirty-five thousand barrels annually, distributed its product throughout Carbon County and into Wyoming.

With the advent of Prohibition, the brewery initially limped along selling "near beer" and soft drinks before closing permanently in 1921. However, the building's sturdy construction, proximity to an established railroad spur, connection to city water, and room for expansion made the property the perfect site for a factory, and in 1925, Billings investor Guy Myers purchased the complex. He hired experienced cannery operator M. H. Mann to oversee the brewery's conversion into a pea cannery, including the hasty construction of a three-story wood-frame addition in 1927 to house needed canning equipment.

According to Blain Myers, who took over management from his father, the cannery worked with regional farmers to stagger production. Up to three hundred people—mostly older women, teachers on summer break, and college students looking to pay their way through school—worked furiously to preserve the highly perishable product within three days of harvest. A machine cleaned the peas in the shed addition before an external freight elevator carried them to the third floor. There, sieves separated them by size. Then, on large picking tables, workers removed Canadian thistle and other debris before passing them to the second floor for blanching. The cooked peas then traveled through an opening to the first floor where they were combined with water, placed in cans, sealed, and pressure cooked.

In 1926, there were about sixty other canneries in the Northern Rockies, but this was one of the largest, packing 55,144 cases of peas per year. That number grew to 80,000 cases in 1947 and 263,000 cases in 1963, which was enough peas to serve all of Montana, Idaho, Wyoming, and most of North and South Dakota. It was the last cannery in the region when it closed in 1975. *—MK*

SALEM
EXIT

60. Jersey Lilly Bar & Cafe

Ingomar | 46°34′36″N 107°22′20″W

Completion of the Chicago, Milwaukee, St. Paul & Pacific (Milwaukee Road) across Montana brought hundreds of hopeful homesteaders to eastern Montana during the 1910s. In Rosebud County and elsewhere, the Milwaukee Road platted towns along its line and enticed new homesteaders with advertising campaigns.

Ingomar was one such town, platted in 1912, and already the site of a small community. By 1914, it boasted several wood-frame homes and a small commercial district. On July 2, 1914, the *Ingomar Index* announced that a bank would soon open, marking an important milestone in the community's development. Miles City and Melstone bank cashiers H. B. Wiley and C. W. Greening, along with Miles City lumberman E. B. Clark, incorporated the bank and hired bookkeeper W. T. Craig to manage it. All, declared the *Index*, were businessmen of "sterling reputations."

Completed that October and clad in multi-hued brick manufactured in Hebron, North Dakota, the distinctive new bank was Ingomar's first masonry building. Instead of the usual columned Classical-style bank found in urban centers, the partners specified a more restrained façade for the rural location, embellished by contrasting light and dark brick courses. Its dignified outward appearance reflects an era when Ingomar shipped out hundreds of thousands of pounds of wool annually.

Upon its opening, the bank prospered. Total deposits reached an impressive $185,548.47 by 1916. The partners reorganized in 1917 as the Ingomar State Bank and again in 1921, under federal charter, becoming the First National Bank of Ingomar.

After 1918, however, long periods of drought forced many homesteaders to leave. Then, in July 1921, a devastating fire destroyed every wood-frame building in Ingomar, sparing the masonry bank. Nearby sheep ranching and oil drilling offered some promise for the town's future, but it was not enough to sustain the local economy. Despite efforts to stay open, the bank closed suddenly in July 1922 and never reopened.

For more than a decade, the building stood empty, a painful reminder of delinquent loans and failed homesteads. In 1933, the Oasis Bar opened in the former bank, and an ornate back bar imported from a saloon in Forsyth replaced the teller cages. Texas native Bob Seward purchased the bar in 1948, renaming it the Jersey Lilly Bar and Café, after a notorious Langtry, Texas, courthouse and saloon named for British actress Lilly Langtry.

Under Seward's ownership, the former bank became a Montana institution with a devoted local clientele. Subsequent owners made minimal changes and, although Ingomar nearly became a ghost town after the railroad pulled out in 1980, the Jersey Lilly's time-capsule Western character remained a draw for tourists. As of 2021, visitors from around the globe stopped in to soak up the vintage atmosphere and fill up on Texas chili and the unusual, but delicious, sheepherder's hors d'oeuvres: saltine crackers topped with a slice of orange, cheddar cheese, and white onion. —***CWB***

61. Armour Cold Storage Building

Billings | 45°46′50″N 108°30′12″W

For the past century and a half, the romantic image of rugged cowboys astride their trusty steeds trailing cattle from Texas to Montana has captured the imagination of young and old alike. A far less glamorous, but more crucial, part of the story involved getting those beeves—once fattened on Montana's rich rangelands—to slaughterhouses in the Midwest and, from there, delivering the processed meat to customers all over the country, including back in Montana. Railroads dominated this shipping process, and the built environment of commercial hubs like Billings reflected that supremacy.

By 1916, the convergence of three major rail lines in Billings positioned the Magic City to become a regional distribution center. Workers offloaded trainloads of incoming freight into the warehouses that lined the tracks along Minnesota Avenue. There, goods of every kind were stored until they could be redistributed to merchants across eastern Montana and northern Wyoming. In addition to the warehouses, facilities for processing agricultural products and other industrial buildings developed south of the tracks while civic structures, churches, and "cleaner" businesses populated the commercial district north of the tracks.

Because its products were perishable, Chicago-based meatpacker Armour and Company required specially designed warehouses that ensured cool storage temperatures. Beginning in 1883, following the lead of rival meatpackers George Hammond and Gustav Swift, Armour mastered the use of refrigerated train cars to get its meats to market. Being able to ship greater distances without fear of spoilage allowed the company to centralize its operations in places like Chicago and East St. Louis, Illinois, increasing efficiency and, correspondingly, profits at the expense of its workers, who labored in often gruesome conditions for little pay. By century's end, Armour operated twelve thousand units of rolling stock, making it the largest private refrigerator car fleet in the nation. Not incidentally, Armour was also one of the country's largest employers.

This cold storage facility, built by Armour in 1918 to house its Billings operations, serves as a classic example of a Western Commercial–style warehouse. Constructed of red brick with a raised concrete foundation, its two façades—one facing South Broadway and one facing Minnesota Avenue—feature simple brick corbelling at the cornice, regularly spaced double-hung windows, and cast stone windowsills. The building's recessed entrance, on Broadway, is also framed by cast stone, while the loading dock that originally provided access from Minnesota Avenue has been replaced by an aluminum-and-glass-grid storefront window. Inside, the building is structured around a concrete refrigeration shaft with cold rooms on each level.

The Armour Company used the building into the 1930s. Subsequently, the former cold storage warehouse accommodated other businesses including hardware and furniture stores. In 2001, the owners converted it into lofts and office space. The success of the renovation—which focused on maintaining the building's historical integrity while ensuring that it met twenty-first-century needs—spurred the development of other historic properties along Minnesota Avenue. *–KL*

R R

62. Savenac Nursery Historic District

Mineral County | 47°23′7″N 115°23′47″W

The creation of the US Forest Service in 1905 brought Elers Koch, one of the nation's first professional foresters, to Montana to inspect and evaluate its forest reserves. Appointed forest supervisor of the Bitterroot and Lolo National Forests in 1907, Koch happened upon the abandoned homestead of a German settler named Savennach. Surrounded by timber-covered hills and with ample water from Savenac Creek, Big Creek, and the St. Regis River, Koch thought it was a perfect spot to establish a tree nursery.

Work began in 1908. Just as the first pine seedlings were ready for transplanting in 1910, wildfires swept through the region, scorching three million acres of timberland and destroying the nursery. The disaster, later dubbed the Big Burn, influenced how the Forest Service, which had adopted conservation as its primary mission, approached fire prevention. The agency's emphasis on reforesting burned and logged areas guided its decision to promptly rebuild the nursery.

Savenac Nursery was ideally situated along two railroad routes, and the historic Mullan Road ran right through the property. Around 1912, national road improvements incorporated the new Yellowstone Trail into this segment of the Mullan Road. The location along the popular trail and the nursery's unique work brought tourists, but the nursery was a serious endeavor. By 1916, Savenac shipped several million western white pine, ponderosa pine, and eastern white pine seedlings to the Forest Service's vast Northern Region.

The facility began to modernize. After World War I, it hired its first women workers and, in 1922, the staff bought a Ford truck, sending Mike and Dick, its team of workhorses, elsewhere. Horses, however, proved more efficient, and they were returned in exchange for the truck.

Between 1932 and 1941, the Civilian Conservation Corps rebuilt and further modernized the facility. Ultimately, the nursery complex included visitor/administrative and service areas connected by a symmetrical network of roads and sidewalks, outlying seed beds, an irrigation system, an arboretum, and exotic ornamental trees planted throughout. At its peak, Savenac was one of the largest tree nurseries in the United States, producing up to twelve million seedlings annually.

National forests in different geographical regions required specific species of trees. Each forest that requested seedlings provided its own cones. Nursery workers at Savenac extracted the seeds and planted them in seed beds, where they usually spent about two years before being transplanted. The seedlings then were lifted, separated, and replanted in transplant beds for another two years. Burlap proved most effective in shipping quantities of young trees. Fifty trees were bundled together in burlap, packed in wet sawdust, and shipped to national forests across the country for planting.

The nursery operated until regional reorganization brought about its closure in 1969. As a site where scientists pioneered much of the theory and practice of silviculture, Savenac Nursery reflected the conservation ethic of the Forest Service. Although no longer functioning as a nursery, its grounds and facilities remain intact and host various groups and camps seeking to learn about reforestation and the large-scale cultivation it requires. *—EB*

This 1916 photograph shows a Savenac Nursery wagon reportedly loaded with one hundred thousand western white pine saplings.

950-826, MTHS PHOTOGRAPH ARCHIVES

A nurses' dormitory added in 1916 and demolished in 1964 is visible behind the main hospital building in this ca. 1920 black-and-white postcard.
PAC 96-83.33, MTHS PHOTOGRAPH ARCHIVES

63. Holy Rosary Hospital

Miles City | 47°23′7″N 115°23′47″W

In 1907—a year before the Chicago, Milwaukee, St. Paul and Pacific Railroad extended its line to Miles City—a converted two-story house still served as Custer County's hospital. That facility proved inadequate once the railroad established large repair shops in Miles City; the town's population boomed as railroad workers and their families joined the thousands of homesteaders settling Custer County.

With encouragement from the railroad, which needed a place to treat injured workers, the county decided to build a larger facility. The architectural firm of Link and Haire designed this thirty-five-bed hospital circa 1910. The building's trussed porticos reflect the era's popular Craftsman style, and its hipped roof and distinctive curvilinear parapet evoke the Mission style. Inspired by Spanish missions—an important source of medical care in the early Southwest—the style was a popular choice for hospitals. Other Mission-style hospital buildings in Montana include ones built in Helena and Missoula during the same era.

The county soon realized it did not have the expertise to manage a hospital, so it invited the Presentation Sisters of Aberdeen, South Dakota, to administer the facility. Originally a teaching order, the Presentation Sisters entered nursing after a 1900 diphtheria epidemic, establishing hospitals in Aberdeen, Mitchell, and Sioux Falls, South Dakota, as well as in Miles City.

The Presentation Sisters were relative latecomers to Montana and to hospital work, but they followed in a long and significant tradition of religious women serving the sick. Mobilized by their faith, "they went," according to medical historian Todd Savitt, "where others might not—cities threatened by epidemics, rough mining and lumber camps, unruly towns in the newly settled west." The first to arrive in Montana were the Sisters of Charity of Leavenworth (Kansas), who established a hospital in Helena in 1869, just five years after the discovery of gold. The sisters soon opened hospitals in Deer Lodge (1873), Virginia City (1875), Butte (1881), Anaconda (1889), and Billings (1898). Not to be outdone by the Catholics, the Methodists embraced the idea of women's religious service through the Deaconesses Movement; after the turn of the twentieth century, trained deaconesses established hospitals and nursing schools in Great Falls, Butte, Sidney, Havre, Billings, Glasgow, Bozeman, and Forsyth.

In Miles City, the Presentation Sisters quickly established a nursing certificate program, and in 1916, the city passed a $36,000 bond to build a nurses' dormitory for both active and student nurses. The dormitory, which connected to the hospital by a narrow corridor, was demolished in 1964.

The 1918 influenza epidemic increased support for the hospital, allowing the sisters, who had purchased the building from the county in 1919, to expand their operation. Link and Haire designed a compatible, flat-roofed annex. Built in 1922, it boasted modern medical and surgical units and increased the number of available beds to eighty-five. The Presentation Sisters managed the hospital through drought, depression, and war before constructing a new facility in 1948. A herculean rehabilitation project completed in 2007 converted the building to low-income housing while maintaining its architectural integrity. *—MK*

This contemporary photograph shows the hospital with its flat-roofed annex, constructed in 1922.

64. Slayton Mercantile

Lavina | 46°17′42″N 108°56′20″W

Every budding Montana town in the late 1800s and early 1900s had a general store, but few remain as well preserved or symbolic of area history as Lavina's Slayton Mercantile. As railroad lines began to spread across Montana in the early 1880s, merchant prince Thomas C. Power hired agents to establish stage stations at crossroads between railroad depots. In 1882, Power's agent Walter Burke built the Lavina stage station, a combination log dwelling, hotel, store, and post office on the Musselshell River between Billings and Great Falls. Burke shamelessly named the station after a former girlfriend rather than his wife.

Lavina remained a small but important stop north of Billings, serving travelers, freighters, and sheep ranchers on the arduous trip to Great Falls. When the Milwaukee Road built a train depot east of Lavina in 1907, its businesses relocated near the new depot. After Power closed the stage station, prominent sheep rancher Daniel W. Slayton, in partnership with George "Herb" Belcher, built the Slayton Mercantile Co. in 1908. Their two-story, wood-frame store joined the handsome Adams Hotel nearby. In 1909, Slayton built the First Bank of Lavina, a sheep shearing plant, and a wool warehouse.

Disaster struck on June 9, 1910, when the Slayton Mercantile burned. Undeterred, Slayton and Belcher rebuilt immediately—this time in fireproof brick—and reopened the store in early August. Its grand Western Commercial style gave the town a heightened feeling of permanence. The *Roundup Record* reported, "Since the magnificent new building of the Slayton Mercantile Co. has been completed, Lavina seems to have taken a new lease on life."

Many of the store's then-modern design features remain intact, including its tall glass display windows, pressed tin ceiling, rolling oak ladders, hardwood floors, an elevator, and a money trolley to convey cash from the register to the rear,

second-floor office. In addition to groceries, meat, clothing, household goods, and hardware, Slayton Mercantile offered furniture storage, mail-order service, grain processing and shipping, and a harness shop. In 1916, it also began selling Ford cars and, in 1917, Titan Tractors and other farm implements.

With the store under Belcher's able care, Slayton focused on community building. Always active in town and county business, social, and political life, Slayton used his connections not only to boost Lavina's businesses but also to win a seat in the Montana legislature in 1910. As state senator, Slayton was instrumental in the formation of Musselshell County in 1911 and was reelected twice to represent it in the legislature.

Just as a long period of drought and depression began in Montana in 1917, Belcher sold his interest to Slayton. During these difficult years, Slayton sold his sheep herd but kept the store running, despite heavy debts, until his death in 1927. The building, shuttered for more than thirty years, reopened as a grocery store in 1960. Subsequent owners continued to operate the small community store with minimal changes to its original features until 2003. —*CWB*

The lodge's Swiss chalet–style exterior belies the Western-themed décor inside the building.

65. Lake McDonald Lodge

Glacier National Park | 48°37′2″N 113°52′44″W

Since its completion in 1914, Lake McDonald Lodge has served as a prime attraction for tourists visiting the west side of Glacier National Park. Nestled on the scenic shores of glacier-carved, crystal-clear Lake McDonald, the hotel combines Swiss chalet–style architecture with rustic detailing to provide guests with a unique, Western park experience.

After the Great Northern Railway reached the area in 1891, homesteader George Snyder realized the value that his property held as a destination for overnight visitors. In 1895, he constructed a simple, two-story frame hotel near the head of the ten-mile-long lake. Eleven years later, Columbia Falls businessman John E. Lewis and his wife Olive acquired Snyder's holdings and added cabins to their operations. When Congress made Glacier a national park in 1910, the Lewises—anticipating ever-growing numbers of tourists—decided to replace Snyder's original hotel with a much grander structure.

The Lewises hired Spokane, Washington, architects Kirtland Cutter and Karl G. Malmgram to design the three-and-one-half-story Swiss-style lodge. Their design complemented other park buildings then being constructed by the Great

Northern in what it hailed as "America's Switzerland." When completed, the exterior of the new Lewis Glacier Hotel featured clipped-gabled roofs, jig-sawn detailing, stone walls (now stuccoed) on the ground floor, upper floors of painted clapboard siding, and a ground-floor veranda and upper-story balconies overlooking the lake.

Inside, a three-story lobby showcased a trio of massive, unpeeled cedar log columns in each corner; a stone inglenook-style fireplace; upper-floor balconies; taxidermy mounts; large-scale landscape paintings; and Indian-themed light fixtures and other décor.

At the time the hotel was built there was no road into the park's west side. Consequently, construction materials not gathered locally had to be hauled from the Belton (now West Glacier) depot to Apgar by wagon, then skidded over the frozen lake in winter or carried by boat other times of the year. Likewise, once the hotel opened, guests arrived by boat. Accordingly, the architects designed the side of the building that faced the lake as its front, and most striking, façade.

By the early 1920s, tourists were increasingly traveling to the park by automobile. To accommodate motorists, the Park Service constructed the Going-to-the-Sun Road, which reached as far as the Lewises' hotel in 1921 and delivered guests to what had been designed as the back of the building. To remedy this unimposing welcome, beginning in the 1930s, balconies were added to the rear façade, horse corrals and other support structures were moved, and a new approach—featuring a two-lane boulevard that culminated in a circular drive—was designed to create a "front-door impression" for those arriving by automobile.

The Lewises sold their hotel complex to the Great Northern in 1930, and two years later the National Park Service acquired the property from the railroad. After name changes to Lake McDonald Hotel in 1930 and Lake McDonald Lodge in 1958, it was designated a National Historic Landmark in 1987. *—KL*

Since Lake McDonald Lodge was built at a time when patrons arrived by boat, its original "front," or most impressive façade, faces the lake, as depicted in this postcard printed around 1915.

PC 001 GLNP, MTHS PHOTOGRAPH ARCHIVES

CHAPTER SIX

DIMINISHING RETURNS
1919–1932

After a 1923 Fourth of July celebration, William Alexander of Culbertson wrote in his diary: "In 1913 people had just come to Montana. They were well dressed; had plenty of money; they were hopeful, spirited, and energetic. In 1923 every face looked careworn." Alexander's neighbors had lost loved ones in the Great War and had survived the 1918 flu epidemic. They were also coping with a devastating combination of high debt, low commodity prices, and drought.

The debt was a legacy of World War I. After the United States entered the war, the federal government pushed farmers to increase food production, declaring that "Food Will Win the War." Insisting that increasing crop production was "a patriotic obligation," the Montana Council of Defense offered farmers help getting seed and equipment. Where farmers were short of funds, county Councils of Defense urged local banks to loan the money, even if the applicant "might not ordinarily be entitled to credit."

Patriotic farmers mortgaged land to purchase tractors so they could cultivate more acreage. Then the war ended, and commodity prices fell. Wheat sold at $3.30 a bushel in the early 1920s but dropped to $1.46 by the end of the decade as European agricultural production increased. Beef prices also declined. Equally damaging, Montana farmers discovered that the 1910s had been exceptionally wet years. Farmers had been able to harvest about twenty-five bushels of grain per acre, but drought dramatically reduced yields. In 1919, Montana farms averaged only 2.4 bushels per acre.

The occasional wet year raised hopes, only for them to be dashed by the next drought. Over the course of the 1920s, tens of thousands of desperate Montana farmers abandoned their homesteads. Counties took possession of farms for back taxes, and banks seized livestock, land, and equipment in lieu of loan repayment. The assets were not worth much. Having liberally loaned money during the war years, banks found themselves in a tenuous position. Nearly half of Montana's banks closed between 1921 and 1925, a staggering blow to Montana's economy.

Farmers with the means to weather hard times took advantage of low prices to increase their holdings, buying land and livestock, sometimes for back taxes. Choteau homesteader J. C. Cronk, for example, purchased his neighbors' places as they went broke. By 1921, he had three thousand acres, which he mostly used to run cattle. "The fellow that has no stock can't do anything but sit around and look at his wheat wilt," he explained. "It's stock . . . that will make this country." Such consolidation of agricultural land happened across Montana.

Montana's sluggish economy and agricultural depression made it the only state in the nation to lose population

Across Montana, abandoned homesteads such as this windblown shack still stand as silent reminders of the often-insurmountable hardships faced by earlier generations of Montana farmers.

during the 1920s. The result can be seen on Montana streetscapes by the scarcity of 1920s-era buildings. Craftsman and Colonial Revival–style houses, which were stylish in the 1910s, are still found in abundance in Montana's cities and towns. Much harder to find are Tudor and French Eclectic buildings, styles fashionable in the 1920s.

Since other parts of the country were "roaring," tourism became a lifeline for some Montana families. Dude ranches capitalized on easterners' fascination with the Old West, and both Yellowstone and Glacier continued to attract tourists from across the nation, with railroads building ornate stations in both West Yellowstone and Whitefish.

While some tourists continued to arrive by train, increasing numbers came by car. Henry Ford introduced the Model T in 1908, and by 1915, there were over twenty thousand cars, trucks, and motorcycles registered in the Treas-

Tudor Revival architecture reached its zenith in the 1920s, by which time competition from automobiles was beginning to impact railroad ridership. Consequently, Whitefish's 1928 Great Northern depot—seen in this photomechanical postcard from roughly 1932—is one of the few such stations designed in the Tudor style.
PC001 WHFI, MTHS PHOTOGRAPH ARCHIVES

During the 1920s, tourist camps like this one in Deer Lodge sprang up across Montana to accommodate the ever-growing numbers of enthusiastic automobile drivers.
PAC 76-105.27, MTHS PHOTOGRAPH ARCHIVES

ure State. Combustion engines increased demand for oil and gas, providing a bright spot in Montana's struggling economy. In 1923, Great Falls saw the construction of the Sunburst Oil Refinery to process crude from the Kevin-Sunburst field, north of Shelby, and a strike at Cat Creek near Winnett led to the creation of Petroleum County in 1925.

In addition to fuel, motorists required infrastructure: roads, bridges, gas stations, and repair shops. Initially, individual counties were responsible for road and bridge construction, and even after the Montana legislature created the state highway commission in 1913, building and maintenance remained a piecemeal affair. Beginning in 1916, federal subsidies for highways helped, as did gas taxes, which Montana voters passed to build and repair roads and bridges: one cent per gallon in 1923, three cents in 1926, and five cents in 1929.

Despite this influx of funds, most of Montana's roads remained barely passable. "The roads of Montana are, I believe, the poorest of any state in the Union. Even the glorious scenery of the Rockies can't entirely make up for the ruts, chug-holes, mud and detours—to say nothing of broken springs or stone-bruised tires," motorist and writer Hoffman Birney proclaimed in 1930. Of Montana's 8,148 miles of primary and secondary roads in 1930, only 1,846 miles (less than one-fourth) were graveled, and fewer than 80 miles (less than 1 percent) were surfaced with asphalt or concrete. It would take massive federal investment by way of the New Deal to finally lift Montana drivers out of the mud. *—MK*

Above: Drillers struck oil at a Toole County ranch in 1922, leading to the development of the Kevin-Sunburst oil field, which, for a time, ranked first in Montana crude oil production. The Great Falls Photo View Co. caught this gusher in action in 1924.
957-556, MTHS PHOTOGRAPH ARCHIVES

Left: While Harlem Motor Company auto mechanic Harris M. Olson (right) might have been prepared to deal with mechanical breakdowns, his expertise was of no assistance when his 1925 Model T Ford became stuck in the mud in Blaine County. Also pictured are Burt Simons (left) and Walter C. Olson (center).
957-323, MTHS PHOTOGRAPH ARCHIVES

66. Sacred Heart Church

Fort Belknap Reservation | 48°31′55″N 108°47′05″W

Sacred Heart Church sits atop a small hill along Highway 2 on the Fort Belknap Reservation in the north-central part of the state. The abandoned, Mission Revival–style "Pink Church" (Owacegiya Sá'imna/ba' ééí'biibíthiiníiin'ć) maintains a silent vigil over an adjacent cemetery and the rolling hills of the Milk River valley below. For almost four decades the church served the spiritual needs of the area's predominantly American Indian Catholic community. Since its closure in 1964, it continues as a distinctive landmark on Montana's Hi-Line.

Today's Fort Belknap Reservation represents only a small portion of the once-vast homelands of the Nakoda (Assiniboine) and Aaniiihnen (White Clay People/Gros Ventre) peoples, nomadic hunters, gatherers, and traders whose lifeways centered around the buffalo. In 1885, three years before Congress established the reservation, Father Frederick Eberschweiler, S.J., built the region's first Catholic mission near present-day Harlem. In the ensuing decades, the Jesuits continued to expand their operations, including, in 1911, the construction of a log church along the Milk River southeast of Harlem.

By 1923, the priests had declared that location unsuitable due to seasonal flooding and poor accessibility and announced plans to move the mission to a higher site. To that end, according to family history, Takes Prisoner, a member of the Aaniiihnen Nation, donated a portion of her eighty-acre allotment in memory of her daughter Wa tzin'i tha (Plume Woman), who died in 1901 shortly after taking her final vows to become a nun. The cemetery was established in 1924, and construction of the church began sometime thereafter.

According to historian Joan L. Brownell, the finished building represented a "local interpretation" of Mission Revival architecture, "with curvilinear parapets, stucco cladding, and little ornamentation while incorporating lancet windows to evoke the ecclesiastical purpose of the building." As elsewhere in the West, Mission Revival–style architecture—inspired by early Spanish missions in southern California—was popular in Montana during the first decades of the twentieth century. Other examples range from the Fergus County Courthouse (1907) to Boulder Hot Springs (1910–1913) and Butte's Columbia Gardens Pavilion (1908). The style is also evident in two additional Hi-Line churches, St. Jude Thaddeus in Havre (1924) and Thomas the Apostle in Harlem (1932).

Local father-and-son contractors Emil and Elmer Nelson led construction efforts while "labor was all done with horses digging the basement and much donated help." Harlem resident Thomas O'Hanlon built the free-standing bell tower (now missing its bell) and, although the interior was still unfinished, great ceremony attended the dedication of Sacred Heart on September 23, 1928.

For the next thirty-six years the church played a central role in the life of the reservation's Catholic families, both Indian and non-Indian. Today, the cemetery continues to hold special meaning to those who have family members buried there. Near its center, a large, mortared stone monument bears a brass plaque dedicating the cemetery "to All Members of this Parish and to the Veterans of WWI, WWII, Korea, Vietnam, and Persian Gulf Wars." Those buried are memorialized by a variety of markers—including wooden crosses; marble, granite, and slate headstones; military markers; and rocks and logs laid on the ground to outline graves—as well as offerings of colorful artificial flowers and items significant to the deceased. *—KL*

67. Howard Lepper Memorial Hall/Flatwillow Hall

Petroleum County | 46°49′59″N 108°24′01″W

Since 1921, the Howard Lepper Memorial Hall has served as the social center of the rural Flatwillow community. During the 1870s, mining opportunities and the search for livestock range attracted Euro-American settlers to Indian lands in the Musselshell River valley. Efforts by the federal government and railroad companies to remove Indigenous nations to reservations succeeded, and by 1883, stockmen and woolgrowers fully occupied the "Flat Willow Range" east of the Little Snowy Mountains in what was then part of Fergus County. Freight haulers and stage lines heading west crossed at Flat Willow Creek. That site, initially known as Flat Willow Crossing, later would be just called Flatwillow.

An influx of new homesteaders arrived in the area after 1910. The newcomers fenced the open range and forced many ranchers to reduce their herd sizes or go out of business altogether. Longtime Flatwillow wool grower Benjamin F. Lepper was one who sold out in 1912. With his nephew Howard Lepper and business partner George Davis, he purchased the Flatwillow store and later, in 1917, established the First State Bank in Winnett.

Both Howard and Benjamin were benevolent bankers who loaned money to help homesteaders stay on their land. Sadly, Howard died suddenly at age thirty-four in 1918—a victim of the influenza pandemic. In 1920, as plans for a dedicated community hall solidified, Benjamin donated $1,000 toward construction of a community hall to be named in Howard's honor. Flatwillow resident Jim Wilson donated land for the hall, and community members gave modest contributions to purchase materials.

More than three hundred Flatwillow community members attended the grand opening dance at the partially completed hall on June 28, 1921. A few days later, a July 4 celebration brought residents from all over the county. A reporter from the *Winnett Times* described the community as "one large family" and declared their new gathering place a fitting tribute to its namesake.

Lepper Hall board members threw another party to celebrate the completion of the building in November 1925, then it mysteriously burned down on May 3, 1926. Luckily, no one was hurt, but an investigation suggested arson. Community members speculated that at least one resident who was unhappy that Saturday dances ended in the early hours of Sunday morning—the "Lord's Day"—may have set the fire; however, officials never indicted anyone for the suspected crime.

Undeterred, Flatwillow residents moved rapidly to rebuild "bigger and better," holding the first dance on the subfloor less than three months later. Carpenter Ted Svinland recentered the stage on the wide side of the building, creating a much larger dance floor. When fully finished in 1929, the Craftsman-style hall featured exterior stucco walls and an interior tin ceiling aimed at improving fire safety. Since then—with only a brief closure during World War II—this historic hall has continued to serve the community as a welcoming place for celebrations and public events. —***CWB***

68. Bones Brothers Ranch

Rosebud County | 45°17′16″N 106°29′16″W

Welcoming "dudes," or tourists from the East, to work on cattle ranches saved many Montana ranches from bankruptcy during the depressed 1920s and 1930s. One of Montana's most popular dude ranches, the Bones Brothers Ranch near Birney, offered patrons the Western experience they desired, fulfilling their romantic visions of "cowboys and Indians," magnificent scenery, and adventure. From 1924 to 1964, the ranch offered eastern families a working vacation complete with horseback riding, roping, branding, rodeos with the Tsétsėhesėstȧhase naa Suhtaio (Northern Cheyenne), dancing, baseball, and fishing.

The ZC Bones TH brand is clearly visible on the roof of the barn, a reminder of the late 1880s when Zachary Cox purchased and claimed government land along Hanging Woman Creek, a tributary of the Tongue River. Zachary and his wife Peachy ran cattle; by 1928, they had amassed more than four thousand acres. In addition to rearing their own four sons, they also fostered three nephews after Peachy's sister died in 1907: Floyd "Bones," Allen "Big Bones," and Irving "Little Bones" Alderson. Their nicknames—acquired when they were teenage cattle wranglers—matched their statures.

Following a particularly frigid winter roundup in 1919, Big Bones and Little Bones headed south in search of more hospitable ranch work. At the Eaton Ranch in Wyoming, one of the original and most successful dude ranches in the West, they found they loved working with people as much as with cattle and horses. After three winters, the brothers combined their Wyoming experience with their "winning personalities," handsome looks, and gracious manners to start their own dude ranch at the Cox place.

Promotional brochures described the Bones Brothers Ranch as "just a typical western outfit, comfortable and hospitable, without the slightest pretense." The Rustic-style sandstone barn and corrals and several log guest cabins, built to launch the operation, fit perfectly with tourists' expectations for comfort. Most often, dudes started and ended their day at the impressive stone barn. Its sandstone walls served as a diary of sorts for riders who scratched their names into the soft stone, leaving their mark while waiting for their horses. After long days on horseback, guests relaxed in cabins with log walls and exposed rafters, stone fireplaces, and shady front porches.

A ranch vacation included room and board, a horse and a saddle, and corral service. In 1928, weekly rates began at $50 for July and August, $40 for June and September, and $30 for the rest of the year. Spring roundup and branding and fall roundup to winter pastures became a main attraction, while trail rides occupied many dudes' days. The brothers added an "Amusement Hall" in 1927 to host dances and group activities. Eventually, the ranch was so successful they allowed veteran families to build private cabins and only let returning clients make reservations. Though the ranch closed to guests in 1964, the barn remains in use, part of a Wagyu cattle operation carried on by descendants of Allen and Irving Alderson. *—CWB*

BONES

69. Billings Communal Mausoleum

Yellowstone County | 45°46′04″N 108°33′40″W

Perched high atop a hill at the western edge of Mountview Cemetery, the Billings Communal Mausoleum endures as an impressive reminder of the community mausoleum movement. Rooted in early twentieth-century Progressive Era ideals of social and civic improvement, the mausoleum concept sought—ultimately unsuccessfully—to shift American funerary practices from traditional earthen burials to aboveground crypts held within the walls of monumental Classical Revival–style buildings. The movement satisfied Victorian-era desires for more dignified gravesites and supported emerging efforts to improve sanitary conditions. Importantly, the cost was comparable to in-ground burial, making it affordable for the masses.

After the country's first community mausoleum opened in 1907 in Ganges, Ohio, interest quickly spread throughout the United States. By 1915, with more than two hundred mausoleums built nationwide, these buildings became markers of civic pride in communities large and small. The movement reached Montana in early 1919 when Arthur L. Rankin, president of the Montana Mausoleum Company, began promoting mausoleums in eastern Montana as "the Better Way" to honor loved ones.

“If a Mansion in Heaven for the Soul, Why Not a Palace on Earth for the Body” read one advertisement for the Billings Communal Mausoleum. The idea especially appealed to Billings residents who for years complained to city officials that the privately owned Billings Cemetery was deteriorating “into a wilderness of weeds and unsightly mounds.” Intrigued by the “opportunity . . . to sleep through eternity . . . secure against the ravages of time,” more than two hundred people reserved crypts before construction began. Prices ranged from $270 to $400, which included the promise of perpetual maintenance.

In July 1920, the City of Billings authorized Rankin to build a gleaming $100,000 community mausoleum in the city’s then-new Mountview Cemetery. Prominent Montana architect John Gustave Link—who was later entombed within—followed standardized mausoleum plans for a 330-crypt, Classical Revival–style, reinforced concrete building. Link’s austere design—which featured a symmetrical cruciform (cross-shaped) plan, barrel-vaulted roof, a columned portico, and marble-clad interior walls—recalled ancient Roman architecture and reflected the mausoleum’s promise of permanence.

Upon its dedication in 1924, Reverend Raymond Walker proclaimed, “When other buildings of our community, in which we take just pride, have yielded to the ravages of fire, flood and the deterioration of time . . . this quiet home of the dead will, here on the hillside, endure.” Walker painted a rosy picture that did not foretell the mausoleum’s future. Rankin’s company never raised sufficient endowment funds to cover perpetual care costs, which led to decades of legal battles with the city and the Mausoleum Cemetery Association over maintenance and land ownership.

By 1980, the mausoleum was in severe disrepair. Fortunately, Landmark, Inc., a local historic preservation group, stepped in to raise funds to restore the building, rebuild its perpetual care fund, and convey the building to the city. It remains one of three historic community mausoleums in Montana; two others, in Red Lodge and Great Falls, also still stand. *—CWB*

70. Troy Jail

Troy | 48°27′47″N 115°53′21″W

The first Troy Jail was a ten-by-ten-foot wood-frame building. Constructed before 1912, it only had enough room for a single cell, which may have been adequate to control disorder early in the community's history. In 1916, however, the population jumped from three hundred to seven hundred when the Snowstorm Mining Company started extracting lead, zinc, and silver for use in World War I. Before the mining company arrived, Troy was a "beautiful town," according to Jesse Walters, wife of Snowstorm's superintendent. After 1916, however, Troy became "a boom town with the usual drunks, prostitutes, even a murder or two."

The next year brought more strife to Troy when an Industrial Workers of the World (IWW) strike for better pay and improved living conditions shut down the entire northwest timber industry. After thousands of loggers left the now-idle camps in mid-June 1917, the IWW worked to convince sawyers, miners, and railroaders to join the strike. On July 17, Troy police detained IWW organizer Frank Thornton for "creating a disturbance." While Thornton was imprisoned, a mysterious fire broke out at the jail. Although the official story was that Thornton accidentally started the fire, many believed he was murdered for union activity.

After the fire, the City of Troy repaired its jail, which continued to serve the community—however inadequately—until 1924. That year, the city contracted with local builder D. E. Crissey to construct a new, fire-resistant, twenty-by-forty-foot jail from reinforced concrete. Barred windows and the words "Troy Jail" stamped beneath a bracketed cornice make the building's function clear, as does the almost complete absence of windows to the side and rear of the building. Three jail cells, an exposed primitive toilet, and bare hanging lightbulbs define the sparse interior.

Troy's original jail was set back from Yaak Avenue. The new jail was situated more prominently as a visual warning to the mostly single miners, sawyers, and railroad workers who populated the town. Four brothels bordered the jail, which served as a barrier between the small red-light district and the main street's more respectable blocks.

Soon after the jail was completed, Troy's promising economy collapsed. In 1926, the Great Northern Railway removed its freight division point. Then, in 1927, the mining company's concentrator burned. A year later, fire destroyed the sawmill. Today the solid, three-cell jail remains as a reminder of Troy's boom years and of town leaders' desire to assert social control over their working-class community. *—MK*

71. Anaconda Smoke Stack

Anaconda | 46°06′36.58″N 112°54′48.92″W

Preserved at the behest of a community determined to protect this symbol of their industrial past, the Anaconda smoke stack—now a state park—towers over the former smelter city. As Bob Vine explained the stack's importance to the city and its workforce: "Everybody would get up in the morning and then look and see if there was smoke coming out of that stack and if there was, God was in His heaven and all was right with the world, and we knew we were going to get a paycheck."

Copper king Marcus Daly founded the town of Anaconda, named after his mine in Butte. In 1883, he built his first smelter on the north side of Warm Springs Creek; it handled five hundred tons of ore a day. By 1887, he had opened another smelter that could handle three thousand tons a day. Smelting—which involves melting ore to 2,700 degrees Fahrenheit—produced thick poisonous clouds of arsenic oxides and sulfur dioxide as it separated copper from unwanted elements.

The Anaconda Company ultimately became the largest copper producer in the world. In 1902, "the Company," as it was known, built the Washoe smelter, closing the "Old Works." The new smelter initially treated 8,000 tons of copper ore a day, eventually raising that total to 12,500. However, its location at the south end of the Deer Lodge Valley meant that prevailing winds carried billions of cubic feet of smoke each day over the valley, poisoning farmers' livestock and killing their crops.

In response to farmers' complaints, the company replaced the Washoe's four smaller stacks in 1903 with a gigantic flue and stack system. They promised that as the smoke slowly traveled through the horizontal flues, it would drop condensed particles of arsenic and that the remaining smoke, streaming from the three-hundred-foot-tall stack, would be diluted to harmless levels in the atmosphere. According to historian Timothy LeCain, it worked, but not well enough.

N. A. Forsyth took this photograph of the blast furnace department at the Washoe Smelter ca. 1910. It shows the tapping either of molten copper matte to be carried to the converter department to further remove impurities from the copper, or of molten slag to be granulated and carried by a launder with flowing water to the slag dump.
ST 001.006, MTHS PHOTOGRAPH ARCHIVES

Farmers filed an unsuccessful lawsuit. Then in 1910, the federal government filed its own suit, charging that the operation had damaged national forest lands. As part of an agreement to suspend litigation, the company built this 585-foot-tall stack, among the tallest free-standing masonry structures in the world. Seventy-five feet wide at its base, the stack tapers to sixty feet wide at the top; six-foot-thick walls support its crushing weight. At its base were "precipitators," which held 111 miles of electrified chains that hung between a series of hanging sheets of corrugated iron. They were designed to capture particulates from the smoke, including valuable metals—gold, silver, and copper—as well as the less valuable arsenic.

"When I worked up in the stack . . . they used to furnish us three pairs of leather gloves, and fifty yards of gauze every week, and one pair of wool coveralls every month, and all the arsenic you could eat," Thom Dickson remembered. Lung cancer and heavy metal poisoning killed many smelter workers, even as the high-paying and, after 1934, union jobs helped them provide for their families. The stack is all that remains of the massive smelter complex, which helped electrify America and employed thousands of men before it closed in 1980. *—MK*

72. Bridges

Montana's first timber bridges provided critical access to mining areas and agricultural markets. According to Montana transportation historian Jon Axline, "A good bridge could mean the difference between prosperity and oblivion" for a new community. As railroads crisscrossed Montana beginning in the 1880s and the state's population expanded, county officials hired bridge companies to build hundreds of reinforced concrete, steel truss, and steel stringer bridges through the 1910s.

Bridge building after 1913 changed considerably with the creation of the State Highway Commission in 1913, the arrival of federal highway funds in 1916, and the creation of the Montana Highway Department in 1919. With the highway department overseeing both bridge design and contracting, bridge construction across the state became standardized. Though Montana's economy suffered after 1918 and bridge construction slowed, several spectacular bridges built before 1932 reflect the Montana Highway Department's formative era.

A crowd gathers around the Forsyth Bridge in this 1905 L. A. Huffman photograph. American flags fly from surrounding wagons, horses, and the bridge itself, and a sign advertises a riding contest.
981-339, MTHS PHOTOGRAPH ARCHIVES

Bell Street Bridge

Glendive | 47°6′20″N 104°43′9″W

Glendive, established by the Northern Pacific Railroad in 1882, was an ideal supply and distribution point along the Yellowstone River. Located where the railroad first met the river, the town looked to ranchers and farmers on the river's opposite side for economic support. The county erected the town's first bridge in the mid-1890s, but in 1899, an ice jam and flood destroyed it. A second bridge replaced it and sufficed until better technology rendered the structure obsolete. The third bridge, constructed between 1924 and 1926, consists of six riveted Warren through trusses. Characterized by the "W" configuration of its diagonal members and its above-roadway trusswork, the 1,352-foot bridge is one of the longest of its kind in Montana. In 1992, the Montana Department of Transportation built a new bridge three hundred feet to the north and preserved the 1926 bridge for pedestrian use.

Wolf Point/Lewis and Clark Bridge

McCone and Roosevelt Counties | 48°4′2″N 105°32′6″W

Straddling the McCone and Roosevelt County line, this was for many years the only bridge over the Missouri River between Fort Benton and Williston, North Dakota—a distance of 350 miles. The Wolf Point Bridge connected residents to distant markets and Canadian neighbors. The site was long considered a strategic point. Lewis and Clark camped here in 1805, and an army engineer noted in 1860 that it was a logical place to build a bridge. But even after 1887, when the Great Northern Railway arrived, and 1913, when homesteaders poured onto the Fort Peck Reservation, the only river crossing was by ferry or over the ice in winter. In February 1926, when two teenagers crossing the ice drowned, county officials finally convinced the legislature to build a bridge.

Christening ceremonies for the massive, three-span Pennsylvania through truss bridge in 1930 drew approximately fifteen thousand people. Renamed the Lewis and Clark Bridge in 1945, it carried traffic until a nearby bridge replaced it in 1998. Its symbolic importance, however, prompted its preservation, and that same year the Montana Historical Society accepted ownership of the historic structure.

This uncredited photograph of the Wolf Point/Lewis and Clark Bridge shows two unidentified men standing atop the span as it appeared around the time of its 1930 completion. LOT 028 B08F11.1, MTHS PHOTOGRAPH ARCHIVES

Tenth Street Bridge

Great Falls | 47°31′14″N 111°17′25″W

When this critical connection between Great Falls and Black Eagle opened in December 1920, the *Great Falls Tribune* described it as "a carved monument above the water." The Montana Highway Commission proclaimed that the Tenth Street Bridge represented "the most advanced ideas of modern bridge building." By this time, the Montana Highway Department had standardized plans and procedures for building one- and two-span bridges, but for longer spans such as this one over the Missouri River, the commission hired Spokane structural engineer Ralph Adams and prominent Great Falls architect George Shanley. Their aesthetically pleasing design provided the model for other bridges in scenic locations such as the St. Mary's River Bridge near Babb and the Carter Bridge in Park County. Though the bridge was technologically advanced in 1920, the highway department flagged it for replacement in the 1990s. After an adjacent traffic bridge replaced it in 1996, heroic local preservation efforts in the early 2000s restored the Tenth Street Bridge for pedestrian use in time for its hundredth birthday. —***CWB***

Evaro School House
and
Community Center

73. Evaro School

Missoula County | 47°04′16″N 114°00′12″W

Montanans have always valued education, whether it took the form of the holistic education the tribes offered their children before Euro-American settlement or formal, Western schooling. After statehood in 1889, four residents of any community could petition the state government for financial assistance to pay a teacher's salary and room and board. Settlers in Evaro, at the southern tip of the Flathead Reservation, established their school in 1902. For the first eighteen years, the school held classes in area homes and barns. In 1920, however, the district purchased this site and constructed a one-story frame building from lumber donated by a local sawmill. The first class in the new building included twenty-seven first through eighth graders, but turnover was high and only thirteen students attended the entire school year.

The design of this one-room building was based on plans developed in 1919 by W. R. Plew for the State Department of Health and Public Instruction. As per Plew's recommendation, the design avoided "cross-lighting," considered harmful for pupils' eyes, by placing windows on only one wall. Since all students were required to write with their right hands, situating the windows to the students' left meant sunlight could illuminate their papers without casting shadows. After 1926, the district added two shed additions: living quarters for the teacher (called a teacherage) and a storage room. The school also boasts a belfry. Common to nineteenth-century schools, bell towers—normally associated with church architecture—had moral overtones, and many twentieth-century school administrators considered them to be outdated relics. The Evaro school board disagreed.

Initially, many students came from families associated with the local sawmill. Then, in 1910, over the expressed objections of the Confederated Salish and Kootenai Tribes, the US Department of the Interior opened the Flathead Reservation to non-Indian farmers. These new farm families also contributed students. In addition, a number of tribal members attended Evaro School. In 1891, Chief Charlo's band of Bitterroot Séliš (Salish) had settled at the southern end of the Flathead Reservation after being forced from the Bitterroot Valley. Some of them enrolled their children in the Evaro School, which for the course of its existence catered to both Indian and non-Indian students. In fact, Evaro's school's most famous graduate was Chief Charlo's grandson Louis. Private Louis Charlo was one of the Marines providing cover for those who raised the American flag at Iwo Jima during World War II. He died in fighting a week later.

Good roads, cars, and buses and the desire to offer students a wider curriculum than a single teacher could provide led to school consolidation across Montana. An early victim of this trend, Evaro School closed in 1944. However, the building continued to serve as a community center and polling place. Longtime residents also fondly remember dances at which they spread cornmeal on the wood floor to make it more slippery and danced in stocking feet. In 1987, a nonprofit group assumed ownership of the building, which fosters the Evaro community by remaining a place where residents gather. *—MK*

74. Romney Hall

Bozeman | 45°40′06″N 111°03′00″W

Built in 1922 to serve as the gymnasium at the college now known as Montana State University (MSU), Romney Hall, as it was renamed in 1973, is one of seven Renaissance Revival–style brick buildings built between 1920 and 1925 during a post–World War I campus building boom. While agriculture, engineering, and domestic sciences were the impetus for creating what was originally named the Agricultural College of the State of Montana in 1893, the gymnasium endures as a reflection of the school's progressive growth from its founding to the present.

The campus's earliest brick buildings, including Montana Hall, arose from a field of grass on a hill south of Bozeman in 1896. The first gymnasium was a one-story, wood-frame "Drill Hall" completed in 1898 west of the first chemistry building. For more than twenty years, the simple drill hall served both men and women's athletic activities and hosted large gatherings, including graduation ceremonies.

In 1917, the Montana State Board of Education hired renowned New York architect Cass Gilbert to create a master plan for MSU. Gilbert's plan expanded the campus to the south, aligning Montana Hall on the north with a new gymnasium to the south across an expansive lawn. Agricultural and scientific buildings were planned to fill in the east and west lawns. Though World War I curtailed any new building plans and the influenza epidemic of 1918–1919 practically closed all Montana campuses, enrollment at MSU reached 607 students by the fall of 1920, just over a 100 percent increase from 1915.

Fortunately, voters in 1920 approved a property tax increase and a $5 million bond issue to fund state college expansion. MSU administrators hired George Carsley to design the new chemistry building (Traphagen Hall); respected local architect Fred Willson to design the engineering building (Roberts Hall), the domestic science building (Herrick Hall), the heating plant, and engineering shops; and the Great Falls firm of Shanley & Baker to design the biology building (Lewis Hall) and the new gymnasium.

The buildings all shared clay tile roofs, intricate brick and tile work, and graceful arched entrances and windows, which recalled monumental buildings constructed during sixteenth-century Italy's artistic and intellectual rebirth. As a group, the seven new buildings gave the campus an air of stability and refinement, addressed increasing enrollment, and carried out Gilbert's Classical master plan.

From the start, the three-story gym played an outsized role in campus life. Its imposing barrel-arched roof and prominent position across the green from Montana Hall boosted its physical significance. Adding in the energetic leadership of Coach George O. Romney and the building's function as an uplifting gathering place for athletic activities, it quickly became a beloved MSU icon. In 1923, Coach Romney sang its praises in the college's student newspaper, promoting it as a "laboratory for the development of manhood and womanhood" and a place where athletics encouraged "the centralizing, spirit-firing, unifying, loyalty-inspiring agent in the student body."

The gymnasium functioned in that spirit—providing a home away from home for athletes—into the late twentieth century. It steadily fell into disuse after the new 1958 fieldhouse and 1973 fitness center opened and was largely unoccupied by 2010. Intent upon revitalizing the historic building, a complete renovation in 2020–2021 transformed the former gym into seventeen classrooms, a writing center, and a veterans' services center. Though it no longer caters to athletes, the building's new use, along with its innovative geothermal heat and solar energy systems, perpetuates the school's commitment to advances in engineering and technology. *—CWB*

The concrete frame and imposing barrel-arched roof of the future Romney Hall take shape in this construction photograph taken on October 3, 1922. PARC-000261, MONTANA STATE UNIVERSITY LIBRARY

75. Shelby Town Hall

Shelby | 48°30′26″N 111°51′37″W

May 1923 saw some five hundred buildings under construction in Shelby. "Main Street resembles a freight yard, [with] lumber and material being strewn about," the *Great Falls Tribune* reported. The cause of the boom? The upcoming 1923 World Heavyweight Championship Fight between titleholder Jack Dempsey and challenger Tom Gibbons.

Shelby's mayor—a real estate developer, rancher, and oilman named Jim Johnson—secured the fight by contributing $100,000 of his own money and raising $200,000 more, paid as an advance to Dempsey's manager. Johnson also convinced the city council, the Great Northern Railway, and local businesses to build the necessary infrastructure, including a forty-thousand-seat stadium (demolished within the year), miles of sidetrack for special trains to deliver anticipated fight fans, a number of "temporary hotels," and a town hall.

The city council hired Havre architect Frank Bossuot to design an Art Deco–style hall in April 1923. Bossuot's design included sleek stucco walls and distinctive domed pilasters decorated with relief triangles. The building was completed in just two months, in time to serve as press headquarters for the July 4 fight. The actual event, however, was a financial disaster. Only 7,966 people bought tickets at full price; an additional 17,000 bought heavily discounted tickets, and thousands more simply crashed the gate. The fight left the promoters heavily in debt, and some asserted that four local banks folded under the weight. Nevertheless, the fifteen-round match went down in sports history.

Shelby never became the "Tulsa of the West," as enthusiastic boosters anticipated, but the Kevin-Sunburst oil field and the community's role as a regional distribution center helped Shelby survive not only the fight but the agricultural depression of the 1920s. The "town fathers" quietly paid off their debts and the community embraced its modern town hall, which provided space for city offices, public meetings, and even a jail.

Backers of the 1923 Jack Dempsey-Tom Gibbons fight erected an octagonal forty-thousand-seat arena in Shelby to accommodate the throngs of paying spectators who unfortunately failed to buy tickets. Today, the site, known as Champions Park, offers visitors an opportunity to learn more about the historic event. 76.102, ARCHIVES AND SPECIAL COLLECTIONS, MANSFIELD LIBRARY, UNIVERSITY OF MONTANA

In 1938, Shelby used money made available from the Works Progress Administration—a New Deal program designed to provide employment—to enclose the original entrance. The building gained its place in Cold War history when residents constructed an observation tower on the building's roof in 1956. For the next two years, members of the Shelby Ground Observer Corps used the tower to scan the skies for enemy aircraft as part of the US Air Force's Operation Skywatch. Organized by the Shelby Business and Professional Women's Club, volunteers—who were mostly women—regularly staffed the post in two-hour shifts, looking for low-flying Soviet planes sneaking below US radar. Although they had trouble meeting the goal of 24/7 coverage, observers tracked aircrafts most days and evenings. This was one of 340 such posts in Montana and one of 16,000 nationwide. *—MK*

76. Union Pacific Dining Lodge

West Yellowstone | 44°39′44″N 111°06′25″W

Although most of Yellowstone National Park falls within the borders of Wyoming, Montana is home to three of the park's five entrances. Consequently, the histories of these gateway communities are inexorably linked not only to the history of "Wonderland" itself but also to the histories of the transportation routes that delivered the tourists upon whom the towns relied. For Cooke City, it was the Beartooth Highway; for Gardiner, the Northern Pacific Railway; and for West Yellowstone, the Union Pacific Railroad (sometimes working through its subsidiary, the Oregon Short Line) that dictated in large part the early stories of these hamlets.

Seeking to cash in on the tourist traffic generated by America's first national park, in 1905 the Union Pacific (UP) began constructing a branch line from Ashton, Idaho, to the then-wilderness on the west side of the park. Two years later, as the tracks approached their terminus, the Forest Service surveyed and platted a six-block townsite that would, in time, become West Yellowstone. The first train arrived in 1908, and the following year the UP opened its new depot, which it heralded as being "built of stone, very substantial, spacious, and artistic."

In the 1910s and 1920s, the UP sought to improve its operations and increase its share of the tourist monies being spent in West Yellowstone by expanding the services it offered. As it planned for additional facilities, ranging from a baggage

The Union Pacific's dining hall mixed upscale amenities, like tablecloths and china, with a rustic Western atmosphere created by the architect's use of rhyolite and peeled and unpeeled logs. LOT 048 WEYE, MTHS PHOTOGRAPH ARCHIVES

building to employee dormitories, the UP called upon Gilbert Stanley Underwood to design its buildings. Underwood was a Yale and Harvard-educated architect who—in creating lodges for Cedar Breaks, Bryce Canyon, Zion, Yellowstone, Yosemite, and the North Rim of the Grand Canyon—helped define the naturalist Rustic style that has now become synonymous with national park architecture.

Most notable among Underwood's new buildings in West Yellowstone was the UP Dining Lodge, which he designed at the same time he was working on Yosemite's Ahwahnee Hotel. Constructed in 1925, the dining lodge replaced an earlier "beanery" restaurant that was both too small to accommodate the growing number of diners and architecturally unimpressive. In contrast, Underwood's new structure—which could seat 350 people in its cavernous main hall—was intended to serve as a fitting complement to the park experience. It featured rhyolite gathered from the railroad's right of way for the foundation, piers, walls, chimneys, and massive fireplaces, while peeled and unpeeled logs were used for posts, beams, trusses, ridgepoles, and brackets. Additionally, the dining lodge incorporated a former "rest pavilion" (where diners waited to be seated) enclosing it, rotating it ninety degrees, and attaching it to the east side of the lodge to serve as a lounge.

The UP ended rail service to West Yellowstone in 1960, but its architectural legacy continues. Today, the depot is home to the Museum of the Yellowstone, the men's dormitory houses the community medical clinic, and the dining lodge continues its tradition of hospitality by providing a truly distinctive setting for special gatherings and events. *—KL*

77. Dave's Texaco

Chinook | 48°35′24″N 109°13′55″W

Although expensive "horseless carriages" had been around since the 1880s, at the beginning of 1908, fewer than two hundred thousand Americans drove automobiles. Between 1908 and 1927, however, Henry Ford's mass-produced Model T roadster brought fifteen million affordable cars to middle-class owners and to US roads. This revolution in personal transportation led to the demand for new and improved roads and safe, clean places to refuel and service automobiles.

In 1914, Montana had just twenty-six miles of paved road, which ran between Butte and Anaconda. Summer travel on oiled dirt roads was bumpy and dusty, and winter travel could be nearly impossible. Efforts to improve transportation started in earnest in 1910 with Good Roads Congresses, which eventually led legislators to create the State Highway Commission in 1913 and finally the State Highway Department in 1918. By 1920, several of the state's paved and "improved" dirt roads had become part of a growing network of interstate "trails." The longest US highway at the time was the Theodore Roosevelt International Highway—part of the northernmost intercontinental road across America and parts of Canada—linking New England with the West Coast. Federal legislation in 1926 created the US Numbered Highway System, and in 1927 the Roosevelt Highway became US Highway 2 (known in Montana as the Hi-Line).

While Montana slowly worked to develop reliable paved roads, oil companies began building gas stations at road junctions. Basic curbside pumps appeared first but proved to be safety hazards. During the mid-1910s, lone pumps gave way to drive-in fuel stations. By the 1920s, the City Beautiful movement influenced oil companies to design gas stations that projected a clean and efficient appearance. Shell Oil first introduced standardized station designs in the mid-1910s, and other companies soon embraced the effort. Pure Oil's Carl A. Petersen designed the first "cottage style" station in 1925, and by the late 1920s, these picturesque drive-in stations became ubiquitous in towns across America.

Perhaps anticipating increased traffic and tourism on the newly christened US Highway 2, oil dealer Al Rasmussen built this well-preserved cottage-style Texaco station in Chinook in 1927. The original station, which was positioned diagonally to the corner, consisted of a small gable-roof cottage with a long, perpendicular, gabled canopy covering the office and extending over the driveway to the pump island. The building's proportions, clean white stucco walls, green and red trim, and red gas pumps caught motorists' eyes and harmonized with Chinook's downtown buildings.

Rasmussen sold the station to Curly Graham in 1935, and in 1938, young service station attendant David Sprinkle became the station's third and eventually its longest-tenured owner. From 1938 until 1978, Sprinkle sold Texaco gas and oil products and serviced cars traveling along the Hi-Line. He then sold Exxon products for another twenty years before retiring. Sprinkle added an enclosed service bay to the southwest side in the late 1940s and recent owners added a metal roof, but little else has changed since 1927. Even after Highway 2 was rerouted two blocks north, and Sprinkle saw two generations of modern gas station designs emerge, he maintained the original design of his Texaco gas station. Though cars no longer stop for gas or repairs, the building is still clearly recognizable as one of Montana's early gas stations. —***CWB***

Eponymous gas station owner Dave Sprinkle, seen here in July 1993, supplied Hi-Line drivers with gas and oil products for sixty years.
JOSEPH M. ASHLEY PHOTOGRAPH. MONTANA STATE HISTORIC PRESERVATION OFFICE FILES

the better banking
altana
fcu
alternative

1931
YUCCA THEATRE
SUNDAY MOVIES
SEPT. 23
OUT OF AFRICA

78. Yucca Theatre

Hysham | 46°17′26″N 107°13′48″W

An optimistic, cheerful nature and keen sense of humor helped make legislator, contractor, inventor, and engineer Dave Manning instrumental in getting Montana "out of the mud." The Democratic champion of the Treasure State's rural communities initiated significant improvements across Montana's sparsely populated areas: electricity, paved roads, dams, and irrigation systems. Nicknamed "The Fox" for his clever solutions to difficult problems, Manning was a fair and patient leader who often crossed political party lines when others would not. He served in the Montana house and senate from 1932 to 1985—longer than any other legislator in the nation at the time of his retirement.

Just before embarking upon his long political career, Manning and his brother Jim designed and built this Hysham landmark. The brothers owned a silent picture theater called the Idle Hour as one of their many businesses. (They also ran a construction company and invented a machine to load sugar beets onto railcars.) By 1931, however, "talkies" had replaced silent films, and the brothers decided that Hysham needed a state-of-the-art theater, with an "arctic Nu-Air ventilator," "acoustical plaster," and "Masterphone sound equipment."

Hysham had been hit hard after World War I. Grain prices plummeted as Europe started to grow its own food again and drought wiped out crops across the northern plains. Many homesteaders left the area, but for those who remained, the Yucca's construction in 1931 was a welcome show of faith in the town's future. The week the theater opened, the *Hysham Echo* newspaper published congratulatory messages from other local businesses who not only wished the Mannings luck but thanked them for the "tangible expression of their confidence in the future of southeastern Montana."

The Yucca Theater expresses the flamboyance typical of 1920s and 1930s theater design. Its exotic façade features a balcony flanked by two battered (tapered) towers crowned by gently peaked polygonal domes. Its ornamental vigas (protruding wooden beams), stucco siding, and a curvilinear parapet are all common Mission-style details.

No one knows exactly why the Mannings chose the Spanish Mission style, which they called the "Sante Fe style," for their theater. Dave undoubtedly encountered it while working construction in the Southwest in the early 1920s. The style was a relatively common choice for theater design because of its association with romance and leisure. Certainly, movies offered an escape from the cares of daily life, and the Yucca's architecture promised to transport all who entered its doors into a different world, at least temporarily.

The building originally had a stage that allowed it to double as a venue for live acts, but in 1936, Manning removed the stage when he built his family home at the back of the theater. After Dave's death in 1990, the Manning heirs donated both the theater and residence to the Treasure County '89ers, a local history group. Now a museum, the Yucca continues to commemorate Hysham's early development and the productive career of a widely acclaimed Montanan. *—MK*

79. Going-to-the-Sun Road

Glacier National Park | 46°17′26″N 107°13′48″W

Montana is replete with scenic drives. But for drama and splendor, Glacier National Park's Going-to-the-Sun Road, a fifty-mile route that provides a breathtaking experience for those who traverse it, remains unsurpassed. One of the first national park roads created specifically for automobile travel, its construction greatly influenced subsequent road design throughout the park system.

When Glacier National Park was established in 1910, most visitors traveled by train to the small communities of Midvale and Belton—now East and West Glacier, respectively. From there, travel inside the park was limited to exploration on foot or horseback, or by tour boat on the park's larger lakes. From the beginning, however, Glacier officials envisioned a road across the park's interior that would link the east and west sides. When automobiles began to rival trains as a means of reaching Glacier, interest in such a road increased, leading Congress to appropriate the first funds to build a "Transmountain Highway" in 1921. That year, work began on both the east and west ends of the road, which were comparatively flat.

Construction across the "Backbone of the World," as the Piikuni (Blackfeet) called the Continental Divide, loomed as a far more daunting challenge.

Initially, the road followed a route proposed by National Park Service (NPS) engineer George Goodwin in 1918. In 1924, however, NPS landscape architect Thomas Vint raised objections to Goodwin's plan to build fifteen switchbacks on the western approach to Logan Pass. Fearing that the switchbacks would make it "look like miners had been there," Vint successfully proposed a longer, more expensive route—carved into the cliffs of the Garden Wall—with more gradual grades and only one switchback (now known as the Loop).

In accepting Vint's costlier alternative, the NPS reiterated its dedication to "harmonizing park improvements with the landscape." Additionally, in 1925 the Park Service entered into an agreement with the Bureau of Public Roads (BPR), the precursor to the Federal Highway Administration. That agreement successfully joined BPR's engineering and construction expertise with the NPS's sensitivity to topography and scenic features. This partnership—which continues today—had a lasting impact not only in Glacier but in sites nationwide through the Park Roads and Pathways program.

Constructing a road over such mountainous terrain presented a variety of unique challenges: sheer cliffs, a short construction season, sixty-foot snowdrifts, and overwhelming amounts of trees, stumps, and solid rock that had to be removed or excavated. The physical labor involved was backbreaking and treacherous. Surveyors had to climb three thousand feet to reach work sites where they perched along narrow ledges or had to be suspended over cliffs to take measurements.

Hauling in supplies and heavy equipment provided its own logistical challenge. Three workers died, and many others resigned in the face of the difficult conditions. Ultimately, however, laborers persevered, and the first automobile crossed the park's new Transmountain Highway in October 1932. The following July, several thousand people gathered on Logan Pass for the road's dedication. Officials christened it Going-to-the-Sun Road after a nearby mountain peak of the same name. Today, this remarkable achievement is recognized as both a National Civil Engineering Landmark and a National Historic Landmark. *—KL*

Thousands of people—and their automobiles—crowded Logan Pass for the official dedication of the Going-to-the-Sun Road on July 15, 1933.

GEORGE ALEXANDER GRANT, LANTERN SLIDE NO. 22. GLAC_5540, GLACIER NATIONAL PARK ARCHIVES

CHAPTER SEVEN

RISING FROM THE DUST

1933–1945

"The thirties I don't want to remember at all. That was bad all the way through," Custer County's Wallace Lockie recalled. The end of the 1920s ushered in a period of brief prosperity, with adequate rain and high copper prices. However, the October 1929 stock market crash and a series of disastrous droughts and insect infestations sent Montana's economy into a tailspin. According to historian Mary Murphy, Montana farm income dropped by 53 percent between 1930 and 1932, while copper prices plummeted from eighteen cents per pound in 1929 to five cents in 1933. The next year, a dust storm blew topsoil from Montana and Wyoming all the way to the Atlantic Coast. Throughout the 1930s, grasshoppers darkened the skies, and cars killed so many Mormon crickets on Highway 87 south of Billings that the state entomologist posted signs warning motorists of slippery conditions.

Unlike the droughts and low commodity prices that had devastated Montana's farming communities in the 1920s, the Great Depression was an international phenomenon that spurred a national response. In 1932, Americans elected Franklin Delano Roosevelt as president, attracted by his promise of a "New Deal for the American people." Roosevelt poured money into Montana—a politically important state—through his administration's "alphabet soup" agencies and programs, so called because of the acronyms commonly used in place of their unwieldy names. His administration delivered approximately $530 million in loans and grants, making Montana second only to Nevada in per capita New Deal investments. The AAA (Agricultural Adjustment Acts) authorized the government to purchase crops at inflated rates and paid farmers to reduce production, while the FCA (Farm Credit Administration) offered farmers easy lines of credit, and the REA (Rural Electrification Administration) supported nonprofit cooperatives to bring low-cost electricity to Montana's farms and ranches. The RA (Resettlement Administration), for its part, constructed entirely new communities; 129 families from Prairie, Musselshell, and Petroleum Counties traded

As part of the New Deal's Resettlement Administration, Montana families were relocated from "submarginal" dryland farms to irrigated farms complete with newly constructed (or newly renovated) houses and outbuildings, including chicken coops. In 1939, Arthur Rothstein photographed this unidentified farm wife as she fed chickens on the Fairfield bench, which benefited from the establishment of the Greenfields Irrigation District in 1926.

LC-USF34- 027289-D [P&P] LOT 500, LIBRARY OF CONGRESS

Much as gold camps had in the preceding century, boomtowns of hastily constructed shacks sprang up around Fort Peck to house dam workers and their families, as this ca. 1937 image credited to Coles Photo shows.
PAC 2008-024-A1P17B, MTHS PHOTOGRAPH ARCHIVES

their unproductive homesteads for small, irrigated farms in Teton and Chouteau Counties.

Aided by the 1934 Silver Purchase Act, which authorized the federal government to buy silver at substantially higher prices than market value, Montana's mining and smelter industries continued to offer employment, albeit for far fewer men than before the crash. Miners worked two weeks on and two weeks off to spread the jobs around; even so, over 25 percent of Butte families were receiving some kind of relief in 1935 and 1936. To aid them and others, the federal government initiated a series of programs designed to put Americans back to work. It's no overstatement to say that these jobs programs changed the face of Montana. The largest public works project was the Fort Peck Dam, which employed fifty thousand people while also subsuming 245,000 acres of farm and ranchland to create the fifth-largest man-made lake in the United States. The effects of other projects were more diffuse but no less meaningful.

The CCC (Civilian Conservation Corps) hired young men, ages seventeen to twenty-five, to work in national parks, national forests, state forests, and campgrounds. Of the twenty-five thousand men stationed in the Treasure State, 62 percent were Montanans; the rest were from elsewhere, mostly New York, New Jersey, and Kentucky, including all–African American units stationed near Libby and Troy. The men fought fires and dug firebreaks, restored parks and recreational areas, built truck trails and airport runways, strung telephone and electric wires, planted trees, surveyed for blister rust (a fungus that infects pine forests), and erected fire lookout towers. The CCC also had an Indian division, whose enrollees worked on Montana reservations building dams, fences, and community halls;

Civilian Conservation Corps (CCC) workers man a sawmill near Camp Thompson River in Sanders County during the mid-1930s.
PAC 2003-47.29, MTHS PHOTOGRAPH ARCHIVES

working as hospital orderlies; eradicating weeds and pests; tilling community gardens; fighting fires; stringing telephone and electrical lines; and constructing trails.

The Works Progress Administration (WPA) had an even larger impact on Montana's built environment than the CCC. Under its auspices, the state gained 7,300 miles of paved roads and 1,360 bridges. The 14,000-plus WPA workers employed in Montana also built outhouses, fish hatcheries, playgrounds, and community centers; installed storm sewers and airway beacons; staffed libraries; fed children; canned food; and sewed clothing for distribution to Montanans in need. According to historians Michael P. Malone, Richard B. Roeder, and William L. Lang, men employed by the WPA in Montana constructed "301 school buildings, 31 outdoor stadiums, 81 athletic fields, 30 swimming pools, 40 skating rinks, 16 golf courses, 10 ski jumps, and 10,000 rural privies." Montanans continue to benefit from this outsized federal investment.

With the onset of World War II, events far beyond Montana's borders once again shook the Treasure State to its core. Agriculture rebounded, both because of increased demand and because the war years coincided with abundant rainfall. The war machine also hungered for timber, oil, coal, and strategic metals, including Butte copper, zinc, lead, and manganese. Montana's northern latitude and high altitude offered strategic advantages as well. Military investments in Montana included an expansion of Fort Harrison, just outside of Helena, as a training ground for the Devil's Brigade;

Above left: Of the 2.3 million outhouses that the Works Progress Administration (WPA) built in locations across the country, nearly ten thousand of them were in Montana. The WPA produced this poster promoting outhouse construction in 1938.
98508956, PRINTS AND PHOTOGRAPHS DIVISION, LIBRARY OF CONGRESS

Above right: At the smelter in Anaconda, workers cast anodes by pouring molten copper from a converter into forms on a Walker casting wheel, which rotates to move the forms into position to receive the molten copper. Photographer Russell Lee captured this process in action in September 1942. LC-USW3- 008610-D, FSA/OWI COLLECTION, LIBRARY OF CONGRESS

With so many men away fighting in World War II, Malmstrom Air Force Base relied on women—like the crew here working on a P-63 in the processing hanger in June 1945—to get the job done.
341ST MISSILE WING MUSEUM, MALMSTROM AIR FORCE BASE

construction of a "War Dog Reception and Training Center" at Camp Rimini; and Great Falls Army Air Base (informally known as East Base and later changed to Malmstrom Air Force Base), which built satellite air bases in Lewistown, Cut Bank, and Glasgow. Initially established to move equipment and supplies to the Soviet Union as part of Roosevelt's "Lend-Lease" program, Malmstrom grew to become a mainstay of Great Falls' economy.

Even as jobs became plentiful and profits high, many Montanans left the state. Almost 10 percent served in the military, a higher percentage than any other state. Others headed to the West Coast, where war work was plentiful, not to mention more lucrative and less risky than underground mining. Montana's population dropped 16 percent between 1940 and 1943. Many of those who left never returned. *—MK*

80. Fort Peck Dam

Valley and McCone Counties | 48°00′10″N 106°24′58″W

At two hundred and fifty feet high and four miles long, Fort Peck is the largest hydraulically filled dam in the United States. More importantly, its construction brought much needed work to tens of thousands of unemployed Americans during the Great Depression, and it continues to provide essential flood control, improved navigation, hydroelectric power, water-quality management, and recreational resources for the Upper Missouri River region.

President Franklin D. Roosevelt signed the bill authorizing construction of the dam in October 1933 as part of his New Deal, which aimed to create jobs and stimulate America's devastated economy. Using funds made available through the National

Industrial Recovery Act and channeled through the Public Works Administration, the US Army Corps of Engineers immediately set the project in motion as desperate workers flocked to the area from all parts of the country. According to the Corps of Engineers, "The dam directly employed as many as 10,546 men at one time at the site and thousands more across the country [manufacturing the needed] fleets of earth-moving equipment, rolling stock, electrical equipment, and other machinery."

As many as fifty thousand workers found meaningful employment as a result of the project. Before work on the dam itself could begin, laborers had to build roads and lay railroad track from the Great Northern line at Wiota, construct power lines from Rainbow Dam in Great Falls, and remove four million cubic yards of overburden from the dam site. Ultimately, men working in around-the-clock shifts installed 125,628,000 cubic yards of fill to form the dam; built and operated pump boats and dredges; laid five miles of pipe to carry slurry from the river to the dam embankment; constructed four diversion tunnels comprised of 57,000 tons of steel and 600,000 yards of concrete; and erected a sixteen-gate, 830-foot-wide spillway three miles downriver from the dam. Still other people were employed in providing the services needed by the construction workers and their families—staffing stores that sold goods and supplies of all kinds as well as outlets for recreation, including saloons, brothels, and the 1,200-seat Fort Peck Theater.

To accommodate its personnel and others in "positions of responsibility," the Corps of Engineers built the well-planned and carefully designed Fort Peck townsite. Additionally, boomtowns—consisting largely of tar-paper shacks and bearing names like New Deal, Square Deal, Delano Heights, and Wheeler (honoring Montana Senator Burton K. Wheeler)—sprang up haphazardly to house the workers and their families who flooded into what had previously been a sparsely populated region.

Sixty men were killed during construction—six of them buried in a massive landslide in 1938. Despite the associated dangers, workers embraced the opportunity to earn a living during one of America's darkest periods, and today, according to Corps of Engineers archaeologist Rebecca J. Otto, "Fort Peck Dam stands as the symbol of the New Deal in Montana." *—KL*

Left: Fort Peck's first powerhouse (right)—with its ten-story-tall surge tower designed to prevent damage to the turbines by absorbing the surge of water if flow is suddenly shut off at the turbines—was completed in 1943. A second powerhouse (left) was constructed in 1961.

Opposite page: This uncredited photograph from around the time of its completion shows the stark contrast in size between an unidentified man and the massive Fort Peck Dam.

F1-11, BOX 2, FORT PECK DAM COLLECTION, MTHS PHOTOGRAPH ARCHIVES

81. Washoe Theater

Anaconda | 46°07′41″N 112°57′11″W

Seattle architect B. Marcus Priteca designed approximately 150 theaters—including the Washoe—over the course of his notable career. He is best known as the designer of the Coliseum in Seattle, which opened in 1916 and gained renown as the first "movie palace." Theaters of such opulence brought luxury to the masses. They were, in the words of historian Maria A. Slowinska, places where "ladies from cold-water flats could drop in . . . after a tough day . . . and become queens to command." Movie palace decorator Harold Rambusch called these theaters "social safety valves," because they let the public "partake of the same luxuries as the rich."

Priteca designed the Washoe to replace Anaconda's premier theater, the Sundial, which had burned in 1929. Built for an extravagant $200,000 (approximately $3.7 million in 2020 dollars), the Washoe remains one of the best-preserved Art Deco theaters in the United States. Construction began in June 1930, and the Washoe Amusement Company promised a January 1931 opening for the "first picture house in the Northwest to be constructed solely for sound reproduction." Sound was a relatively new feature for theaters; the first "talkie," *The Jazz Singer*, was released in 1927.

The Great Depression delayed completion of the thousand-seat theater until 1936, which explains some of the design's old-fashioned elements. Priteca included space for an organ—necessary to accompany silent movies—that was never installed. He also included a stage and dressing rooms, a legacy of the silent film era, when theaters doubled as vaudeville houses (or vaudeville houses doubled as theaters). In other ways, though, the theater's design was thoroughly modern. It boasted the "latest projection machines," "Mirro-phonic sound" (a stereophonic sound system that debuted in 1935), and a heating plant that "in summer is transformed into a cooling plant."

While chevrons, diamonds, and other decorative brickwork ornament the relatively unassuming exterior, patrons leave ordinary life behind once they enter the building. Hollywood decorator Nat Smythe designed the interior. Local union painters completed most of the decorative wall and ceiling work while Smythe brought in specialists for the murals. A Persian fairy tale inspired the painting in the lobby; a large circular mirror integrated into the mural helps fulfill the theater's implicit promise of offering a magical escape from reality. While still magical, the allegorical mural on the auditorium's ceiling ostensibly depicts "the dependence of modern civilization on the copper Montana produces." Other decorative homages to Montana include bas-relief ram heads, the prolific use of both gold and copper leaf and paint, and the two stags that emblazon the plush velvet stage curtains. Large, Deco-style chandeliers and colorful geometric designs complete the décor.

Tickets to the opening show—*The Texas Rangers*, which was nominated for best sound recording in 1937—cost only thirty-five cents. The price enabled patrons not only to enjoy the film but also to partake of the Washoe's comfortable seats and climate-controlled opulence, made all the more remarkable by its Depression-era birth. *—MK*

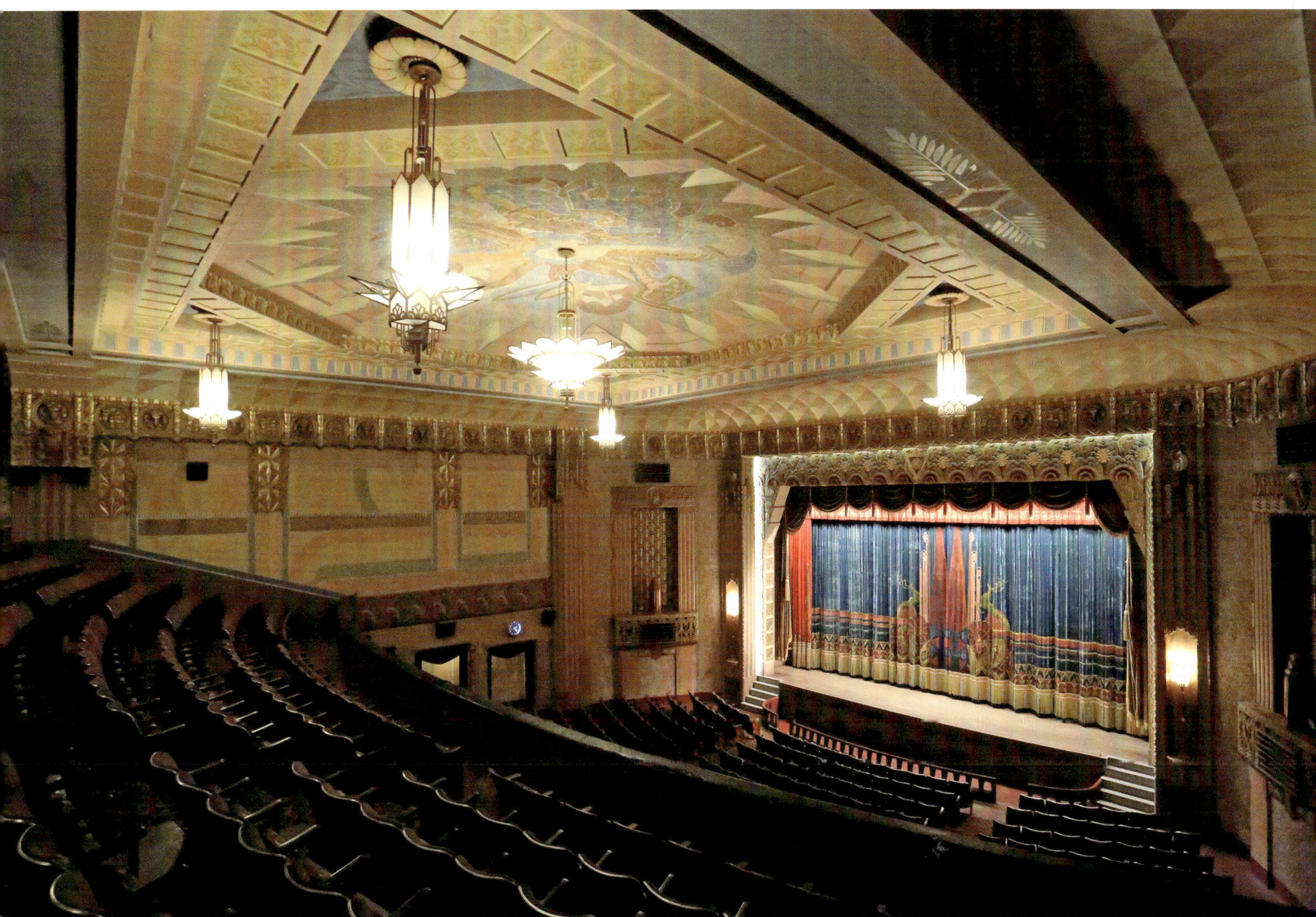

82. Lewis and Clark Caverns

Jefferson County | 45°50′21″N 111°53′12″W

Lewis and Clark Caverns is one of the largest and most remarkable caves in the Northern Rockies. Part of the 350-million-year-old Madison Limestone Formation, this remarkable geological spectacle became Montana's first state park in 1937.

Although it is likely that at least some of the region's Native peoples were aware of the caverns, no human presence was documented in the caves until the close of the nineteenth century when, according to local lore, either bats or steam escaping from a vent hole led to the subterranean discovery.

By 1901, local quarry owner Dan Morrison was working to make the site a tourist attraction, but he ran afoul of the Northern Pacific Railway, which claimed ownership of the land. Legal battles ensued. After the courts ruled in favor of the railroad in 1906, the Northern Pacific, surprisingly, transferred the title to the federal government. Two years later, President Theodore Roosevelt declared the caverns a national monument, naming it in honor of the intrepid explorers Meriwether Lewis and William Clark, who Thomas Jefferson had tapped to lead the Corps of Discovery from 1804 to 1806. In 1908, the centennial anniversary of their journey was still fresh on America's mind, and although Lewis and Clark were unaware of the wonders far below, their path had crossed above the caverns.

Morrison continued to conduct unauthorized tours of the caves, but due to the monument's remote location and a lack of resources, the caverns received little official attention for the next three decades. This changed with the advent of the Civilian Conservation Corps (CCC) during the Great Depression. In 1934, Montana officials asked the federal government to improve access to and develop facilities within the monument to better realize its potential as a tourist attraction. Consequently, between 1935 and 1941 the men of CCC Company 574 transformed the site into the park we know today.

Before electric lights were installed in 1940, visitors to Lewis and Clark Caverns relied on candles to light their way through the underground labyrinth. This N. A. Forsyth photograph from around 1908 shows a group of nuns during a visit to the caves.
108.01H ST 001 493A, MTHS PHOTOGRAPH ARCHIVES

Initial efforts involved removing tons of bat guano, packrat nests, and rock debris from the caves. Survey work followed, resulting in a complete mapping of the caverns, the discovery of new caves (triple the number that had originally been identified), and, ultimately, the blasting of a 538-foot exit tunnel so that visitors could avoid "the rather tedious climb" back up to the surface. CCC laborers also installed electric lighting, eliminating the need for hand-held candles or lamps.

Above ground, workers built a Rustic-style headquarters building, visitor center, and stone latrine. To provide access to these new facilities they also constructed a steep, 3.2-mile-long curving roadway that included a granite keystone bridge and an observation point with spectacular views of the Jefferson River valley below. Picnic and camping facilities rounded out the visitor experience.

In August 1937, while construction was ongoing, Congress transferred Lewis and Clark National Monument to the State of Montana. As historian Chere Jiusto observed, Montana's first state park was so well designed and built, "there has been little reason to . . . alter the original improvements in the park. [It continues to serve as] a wonderful example of the high-quality craftsmanship and design engineering executed by the Civilian Conservation Corps in this and thousands of other projects across the United States." *—KL*

83. Anselmo Mine

Butte | 46°01′02″N 112°30′37″W

The most intact mine yard left on the Butte Hill, the Anselmo embodies the complexity of extracting ore from deep underground. A small silver mine in 1887, it grew into a two-hundred-man operation focused on copper, zinc, and silver in the 1920s. The Anaconda Company acquired full control over the mine in 1926 and employed up to eight hundred people in the yard and underground workings, some as far down as 4,301 feet.

The 150-foot-tall headframe—known with Butte's typical dark humor as a gallus, or gallows, frame—looms over the mine yard. The frame's sheave wheels and cables lowered machinery and men into the mine and hoisted ore out. Ropemen cared for the headframe, installing new cables, untangling snags, and regularly recoating the existing cables with pine tar. Gallus frames were designed to be dismantled and moved after a vein played out; the Anselmo's came from the Black Rock Mine in 1936, replacing a 1906 wooden headframe that was half the size.

The mechanized hoisting of men and materials into the mine and ore from the mine was controlled from the hoist houses, which stand north of the headframe. Hoist engineers operated engines that turned the drums, winding and unwinding the cable that lowered and raised cages (elevators for workers) and skips (large buckets for ore). At the Anselmo, after building a larger hoist house for its main hoist engine, the company used the original hoist house (built circa 1920) to run the "chippy hoist." Connected to the smaller third wheel on the headframe, it transported men and equipment while the main hoist was busy bringing ore to the surface.

It took about an hour for a hoist engineer to bring a full crew into or out of the mine at shift change. Seven or eight men crowded in each cage, with three or four cages being lowered at a time. Responsible for regulating the cable speed to lower the cages to their specific level and deliver miners safely to their destination, the engineers communicated with station tenders underground through a complex system of rapidly firing bells. After all the miners were at their stations, ropemen swapped out the cages for skips, which traveled at over two thousand feet per minute to hoist the ore and dump their loads into the tipple, which in turn loaded ore into waiting railcars.

The Anselmo's adjacent timber yard (in operation between 1950 and 1980 and now demolished) served as the Anaconda Company's pickling plant, where the company treated mine timbers with arsenic to prevent them from rotting. Carpenters cut timbers into "square sets" to shore up underground workings to prevent collapse of unstable ground.

Also of significance is the "dry," where men changed in and out of their work clothes and showered after shifts. Since heat—sometimes over one hundred degrees—and high humidity characterized most underground mines, unions fought hard for a place for miners to clean up and dry off before braving the walk home during Butte's brutally cold winters.

Together, the Anselmo's structures reveal the surface workings of underground mining as well as its massive scale. They also reflect the skilled work of the men, from blacksmiths and carpenters to ironworkers and hoist engineers to the miners themselves, through whose labor Butte became known as the Richest Hill on Earth. *—MK*

Above: This photograph shows the north end of the AC-to-DC motor-generator set used at the Anselmo hoist house to convert alternating current to direct current. Direct current was better suited for powering the giant electric hoist engine mounted on the floor above.

Opposite page: An uncredited photographer captured this aboveground view of Butte's Anselmo Mine in 1935.
LOT 048 BUTT, MTHS PHOTOGRAPH ARCHIVES

84. McCart Fire Lookout

Bitterroot National Forest | 46°01′02″N 112°30′37″W

After the 1910 "Big Burn" destroyed huge swaths of forestland in Montana and Idaho, the US Forest Service increased its commitment to fire suppression. Fire lookouts were integral to the effort. Region 1—which managed national forests in northern Idaho, Montana, North Dakota, and part of South Dakota—had 127 lookout points by 1915. That number increased to around 800 by 1930, but most of these points did not have buildings.

Part of the problem was that building lookouts required carpentry and design skills that existing Forest Service staff members did not possess. Transporting building supplies to the remote sites posed an even greater problem. In 1927, forester Clyde Fickes—who served as Region 1's architect from 1929 to 1944—addressed both issues with his design for a twelve-by-twelve-foot lookout topped with a six-by-six-foot cupola made from precut lumber.

Orders for these inexpensive, easy-to-pack and assemble lookouts poured in. Carpenters cut the lumber and experienced packers assembled the material into mule-sized pack loads, which were then shipped to ranger stations. There, the bundles were loaded onto mules and packed up to the peak with "a couple of handymen who could read."

With input from Regional Forester Evan Kelley, Fickes redesigned the standardized lookout plan in 1929. Measuring fourteen-by-fourteen feet, L-4 lookouts were large enough to accommodate fire-finding equipment and living quarters. Fickes's detailed plans specified precut and labeled lumber, so employees with limited carpentry skills could assemble the structures "using only a hammer, screwdriver, and carpenter's level." Notable design elements included a catwalk and ribbons of nine-light windows on all four sides that provided a 360-degree view. A pyramidal hipped roof required shorter lengths of lumber than a gable roof, making it easier to transport material to the site by pack train.

The New Deal—especially public works programs like the Civilian Conservation Corps—was a boon to the Forest Service. In the 1930s, the CCC built thousands of miles of roads and trails, strung telephone lines, fought fires, planted trees, and constructed bridges and observation towers. By 1938, Forest Service Region 1 had 838 improved lookout points. Over half boasted hipped-roof L-4 lookout houses.

The McCart Lookout was a late addition. Built in 1939 and named for longtime district employee Bill McCart, it is a classic example of the L-4 series. Mules packed in the prefabricated wood-frame house, and native timber was cut on site to support it. Sliding glass windows and a two-foot catwalk surrounding the cab allowed the watchman to be on constant alert for forest fires.

Vintage equipment inside the lookout includes an Osburne fire finder, used to pinpoint fire locations, and a hand-cranked telephone. Lack of radio technology and isolation in this vast, roadless wilderness required a complex telephone communications network. Intact segments of phone line insulators are still visible in the trees between McCart and the East Fork Guard Station. By 1960, aerial surveillance had replaced lookouts for most fire detection. McCart provided a vital communication link, however, and remained in service until 1984. *—MK*

Bill McCart, the namesake of this fire lookout in the Bitterroot National Forest, stands on the far right in this photograph taken following renovations to the structure in 1992–1993. Also pictured here (from left to right) are Kirby Matthew, Gina Owens, Brian Pickell, Frances Acibo, Jerry Hinman, and Wilma McCart, all of whom helped with the restoration effort.

FS99.01054, UNITED STATES FOREST SERVICE REGION 1 ARCHIVES COLLECTION, MSS 889, ARCHIVES AND SPECIAL COLLECTIONS, MANSFIELD LIBRARY, UNIVERSITY OF MONTANA

DAVID RICHARDS PHOTOGRAPH

85. WPA Projects

Beginning in 1935, at the height of the Great Depression, Franklin Delano Roosevelt's New Deal government created the WPA to provide work for the millions of Americans who were unemployed. Initially called the Works Progress Administration but renamed the Work Projects Administration in 1939, the WPA employed men, women, and youth in endeavors ranging from theater and the arts to the recording of American history. By far the greatest number of WPA workers, however, built roads, improved parks, and constructed schools and other civic buildings. The efforts of the WPA touched every county in the United States, and the contributions of WPA workers—whom historian Nick Taylor extols as "extraordinary beyond all expectation . . . [the] golden threads woven in the national fabric"—continue to benefit us today.

View of a Works Progress Administration crew posing around a truck on the Dagmar Church Dam about a half-mile south of the Dagmar Lutheran Church in Sheridan County, Montana. LOT 045 V2P59.4, MTHS PHOTOGRAPH ARCHIVES

Culbertson Armory

Culbertson | 48°08′48″N 104°30′32″W

During the nineteenth century, states in the northeastern part of the country built armories where volunteer militias—most of which later became National Guard units—could train and store arms and munitions. States in the South and West, however, fell behind in erecting such facilities.

Consequently, when WPA monies became available for civil works projects, the construction of armories became a priority for the federal government. Compared to their eastern counterparts—especially those located in major cities that were often large, castellated structures—WPA-built armories like the one constructed in Culbertson in 1938 were smaller and simpler in design.

Woodland Park

Kalispell | 48°14′02″N 114°20′20″W

The WPA transformed the low-lying grounds that initially comprised Kalispell's Woodland Park from a "worthless mosquito breeding swamp" into an "iconic and cherished refuge." As the *Eureka Mirror* reported in October 1936, "The project is typical of the 81 [WPA] park and playground projects employing over 1,000 workers . . . which have been prosecuted throughout Montana." Improvements to the park completed during the 1930s included a lake created from a series of stagnant sloughs, a concrete swimming pool with a "spacious rustic change house," a log pavilion and gazebos, a large stone barbecue pit, improved landscaping, wooden bridges, and a five-acre "tourist camp" for travelers.

Madison County Fairgrounds

Twin Bridges | 45°32′31″N 112°20′08″W

The Madison County Fair had its origins in the 1880s, but with the onset of the Great Depression the annual tradition languished and the fairgrounds fell into disrepair. To revitalize the fairgrounds and employ local workers, the WPA began construction of six Rustic-style log buildings in 1936, including an octagonal pavilion known as the community building; an octagonal gazebo; a caretaker's house; and horse, cattle, and sheep barns. Additionally, workmen built a two-thousand-seat grandstand and replaced the siding on an 1894 structure known as the "Square Building" with a log veneer to mirror the new construction. Workers gathered lodgepole pine, fir logs, and other building materials and prepared them on site. On August 5, 1938, the *Madisonian* reported that the "largest strictly 4-H fair to be held in Montana this year . . . fittingly dedicated the new fair grounds buildings," with an estimated two thousand visitors enjoying the five hundred exhibits on display there.

Gehring Ranch Outhouse

Lewis and Clark County | 46°43′31″N 112°08′28″W

Although not among its most glamorous projects, the WPA's sanitation program was among its most consequential. At a time when indoor plumbing was far from universal, the WPA built 2.3 million outhouses nationwide, nearly ten thousand of them in Montana. Property owners were required to supply the building materials, but the WPA provided plans and labor to construct identical wooden structures that housed concrete-lined vaults and integrated molded concrete pots. This outhouse is one of approximately twenty structures that document the history of the Gehring Ranch in the Prickly Pear Valley northwest of Helena from its founding in the mid-1860s through the present.

Great Falls Civic Center

Great Falls | 47°29′30″N 111°17′21″W

Leading Great Falls architects George Shanley and Johannes Van Teylingen collaborated to design the Electric City's 1939 Civic Center. Funded in part by the WPA, the monumental Art Deco edifice is prominently situated on the west end of Central Avenue. Its east-facing, colonnaded façade is built of local sandstone, while interior finishes include terrazzo and travertine. The proposal to site the building in Gibson Circle, a beloved municipal park, upset many Great Falls residents, but the city prevailed in a lawsuit that was ultimately decided by the state supreme court. Today, the Civic Center still houses city offices and an 1,800-seat auditorium, but its original ice rink was converted into a convention center in the 1980s. *—KL*

This photograph of the entrance to the Great Falls Civic Center, at the intersection of Park Drive and Central Avenue, dates to 1944.
1990-026-0254, THE HISTORY MUSEUM, GREAT FALLS

86. MacDonald Pass Airway Beacon

Powell County | 46°33′16″N 112°18′32″W

The MacDonald Pass airway beacon was the last of eighteen beacons constructed across western Montana as part of the Northern Transcontinental Airway's airmail route connecting New York City to Seattle. Before the advent of aviation radio and radar navigation, airway beacons served as critical nighttime navigational aids, guiding pilots along routes between airports.

The US Army and the Postal Service began experimenting with nighttime flying in 1921. Seeing its potential, Congress passed the 1926 Air Commerce Act, which enabled construction of beacon towers every ten miles across flat terrain and every fifteen miles in rugged areas. By 1938, the US Bureau of Air Commerce had created 18,000 miles of airway corridors and installed 1,550 airway beacons to mark them for night flying. Establishing the corridors and beacons signaled a profound advance in the evolution of the nation's air transportation system.

Construction of the first towers in eastern Montana began in October 1934 between Miles City and Billings. In the spring and summer of 1935, work began on six beacons between Bozeman Pass and Helena and twelve beacons between MacDonald Pass just west of Helena and Lookout Pass on the Idaho border. The International Derrick and Equipment Company of Columbus, Ohio, fabricated the towers, which were paid for with funds from the federal Works Progress Administration. Engineer A. S. Watson supervised twenty-four-man construction crews, all hired through the US Reemployment Service. In western Montana's most remote areas, the National Forest Service also provided crews with pack mules to haul supplies to the sites.

The MacDonald Pass beacon, located on the Continental Divide, represents the standardized beacon design developed by the Bureau of Air Commerce. Its ninety-one-foot-tall steel structure held a revolving, one-million-candle-power beacon, which was originally encased in a glass dome. Red and green directional lights attached to the tower indicated the route, while flashing red lights identified the beacon in Morse code. Two gas-powered generators (a main and a backup generator) powered the beacon until 1942. Thereafter, it was connected to electrical lines. A light-sensitive astronomical clock or a photocell signaled the generator to start or stop running at dusk and dawn. To maintain the system, the Bureau of Air Commerce employed an army of "mechanicians." The men visited the beacons every two weeks to service the generators, grease the rotating beacons, replace burned-out bulbs, and adjust the directional lights.

When the Civil Air Administration lit the MacDonald Pass beacon in November 1935—completing Montana's system—over four thousand people braved frigid weather to attend a celebration at the Helena airport. By 1945, Montana's nighttime navigation network included seventy beacons strung across three air corridors, with an additional fourteen located at airports. Though radar systems replaced most of the country's beacons by the mid-1970s, Montana's private pilots successfully lobbied to keep seventeen beacons lit through 2017. As of 2025, several "adopted" beacons still light the night sky, recalling a vital component of Montana's aviation heritage. *—CWB*

87. Club Moderne

Anaconda | 46°7′40″N 112°56′38″W

Saloon owner John "Skinny" Francisco debuted his luxurious new Anaconda cocktail lounge and bar to an eager public during a gala event on October 9, 1937. He gave out souvenir roses and etched liquor glasses to commemorate the opening of the Club Moderne, Montana's most exuberant example of the Streamline Moderne style. The Streamline style was an offshoot of the more opulent and angular 1920s Art Deco style. Designers responded to the Great Depression with a sleek (and less expensive) aesthetic that suggested confidence in the machine age.

The Club Moderne represented a futuristic leap for downtown Anaconda, the streets of which were lined with Victorian-era red brick commercial buildings constructed at the Smelter City's zenith. Hoping to inspire a new and prosperous era, Francisco hired prolific Bozeman architect Fred Willson to design the bar. Willson had recently completed the Gallatin County Courthouse and an addition to the Gallatin County High School in the Streamline Moderne style.

Willson's reserved yet elegant designs for Bozeman's public buildings reflected government constraints imposed by Works Progress Administration funding. However, Francisco's $25,000 budget for the Club Moderne allowed Willson to fully realize a high-style building. He embellished the gently curved façade with glossy white, black, and grey Carrara glass panels and specified a profusion of boldly colored neon lights, a circular entrance window, and a lustrous aluminum band at the cornice. A more traditional saloon—featuring a mirrored back bar with diamond-patterned inlaid wood—comprised the front half of the building, while a trendy rear "lounge" offered chrome-framed leather chairs and booths with integrated chrome hall trees. Each tabletop boasted a colorful new machine-made coating—Formica—and a lavishly upholstered and mirrored back bar served lounge customers.

The Club Moderne quickly earned the label "The Northwest's Most Modern and Beautifully Appointed Bar and Cocktail Lounge." Subsequent owners and patrons respected and maintained the high-style design, so much so that it remained in near original condition well into the late twentieth century. It was listed in the National Register of Historic Places in 1986, before it had reached the statutory age of fifty years usually required for listing. Thirty years later, and still unchanged, the bar gained national recognition when voters elected it "America's Favorite Historic Bar" in the National Trust for Historic Preservation's 2016 Big Tap contest.

Just days after that honor and almost exactly seventy-nine years after it opened its doors, a major fire nearly destroyed the beloved watering hole. Flames and smoke consumed the roof and many interior features, but remarkably, signature portions of the building remained intact. Owners John and Stephanie Hekkel moved quickly to rebuild. Dale Harris, a skilled local craftsman, rebuilt the lighting and interior ceilings, restored the booths, and installed reproduction Carrara glass panels. Just a year after fire nearly reduced the architectural gem to ruin, the owners and community members celebrated its eightieth birthday with a grand reopening. —*CWB*

Both its exterior design and interior styling—as seen in this 1979 Jet Lowe photograph—contributed to the Club Moderne being hailed as "The Northwest's Most Modern and Beautifully Appointed Bar and Cocktail Lounge."
HABS MONT,12-ANAC,1-A—3, LIBRARY OF CONGRESS

Club
Moderne
BAR
LOUNGE
Budweiser
1224

These remnants of the Smith Mine Number 3 stand on a hillside near Bearcreek.

88. Bearcreek

Carbon County | 45°09′38″N 109°09′27″W

The town of Bearcreek sprang to life in 1905 with nearby coal discoveries. The Montana, Wyoming and Southern Railroad linked the Bearcreek mines to outside markets and prompted the Montana Coal and Iron Company (MCI) to further develop the Smith Mine. In 1907, the mine produced eight thousand tons of high-grade coal.

Miners from distant places like Croatia, Montenegro, Italy, Scotland, Germany, Finland, France, and England established local enclaves, and, by 1910, the main settlement of Bearcreek claimed a population of 302. Situated on either side of Bear Creek, the tough town boasted telephones, city water, electric streetlights, and some twenty-three businesses, including ten saloons, but no churches. The 1906 Romanesque-style Bearcreek Bank sported thick walls of locally quarried sandstone to visually assure its patrons that their investments were safe; its first president was copper king William A. Clark.

MCI electrified its mining operation by 1915 and completely mechanized it by 1929. Throughout the 1930s, the company continued to invest in new equipment, building a new crushing plant, elevator, cleaning plant, coal sheds and scales, electrical substation, and other aboveground structures to support the underground operation. By 1943, miners worked three shifts a day, six days a week at the Smith Mine, producing almost five hundred thousand tons of coal annually to meet the needs of a nation at war.

Safety measures, however, lagged. In the 1940s, many Smith miners still used open-flame carbide headlamps instead of safer electric lamps. Inadequate ventilation and a lack of rock-dusting equipment to control coal dust proved deadly. On February 27, 1943, methane gas exploded in the Smith Mine Number 3. Seventy-four miners (and later, one rescuer) died in Montana's worst coal mining disaster. Only three men working that day survived. MCI subsequently shuttered

Number 3 but continued to work its other mines, raking in record profits through 1945. Declining demand, lower-quality coal, competition from diesel and natural gas, and mismanagement eventually led to the mine's closure in 1953.

The United Mine Workers of America installed a red granite memorial in the Bearcreek Cemetery in 1947, commemorating the men who died in the Smith Mine disaster. Twenty-two of the casualties are among the 472 burials, but there are also 107 children whose graves suggest the harshness of mining camp life. Headstones marked with Cyrillic lettering and ethnic surnames reflect the diversity of many Bearcreek families. At the community's height, in 1920, a third of its residents were immigrants while another third were the children of immigrants.

After the disaster, Bearcreek became a near ghost town. Many of its buildings were demolished or moved elsewhere. The Bearcreek Bank is one of the few that remain. It closed twice during the depressed 1920s and became a restaurant from 1928 until it closed in 1943. Rehabilitated in 1967, the building now functions as Bearcreek's city hall.

The Smith Mine's dark past survives in thirty-nine ghostly, corrugated metal structures that mark the site. The Bearcreek Bank, Bearcreek Cemetery, and the Smith Mine Historic District are all listed in the National Register of Historic Places. Bearcreek today, with a lively population under one hundred, is famous for its fundraising pig races and annual gathering of falcon trainers. *—EB*

First introduced in the 1920s, loading machines—such as the one these workers in the Smith Mine lined up at in this undated photograph—made the underground mining of coal much quicker and easier on the miners, but not safer.

LOT 026 B6F04 01,
MTHS PHOTOGRAPH ARCHIVES

89. Lewistown Satellite Airfield

Lewistown | 47°02′57″N 109°28′00″W

In the dark days following Japan's December 7, 1941, attack on Pearl Harbor, Congress authorized massive defense appropriations. The US Army selected Great Falls as the site of a major air base. Concurrently with its construction, the army established satellite airfields at Cut Bank, Glasgow, and Lewistown.

On October 28, 1942, the first Boeing B-17 Flying Fortresses roared over Lewistown's Main Street with their bomb bays open. They buzzed the treetops and landed at the Lewistown Airfield. Crews trained day and night, combining navigation, bombing, and gunnery practice. The US Army Air Force prioritized the creation of united teams. For every hour in the air, the men spent eight hours on the ground, studying aircraft identification, learning first aid and emergency procedures, listening to veteran combat pilots' experiences, and viewing government training films. Each man had to learn his own job and that of his fellow crew members to ensure effective mass tactics. A corporal succinctly stated the mission of the airfield: "This is a place where we will learn to work together, play together, live together, fight together, and if necessary die together."

In addition to familiarizing themselves with all aspects of the B-17, the men trained with the top-secret Norden bombsight, a mechanical analog computer used to determine the exact moment a bomb should be released. The fifty-pound computerized aiming device contained two thousand precision parts, and its accuracy depended on the bombardier's ability to correctly calculate speed, altitude, temperature, barometric pressure, and the "bomb curve."

Since the bombsight was top secret, crews swore that they would destroy the device rather than allow it to be captured; at the airfield it was stored in a concrete bunker encircled in barbed wire and kept under constant guard. While Norden Company executives asserted that the bombsight could "put bombs in a pickle barrel," the reality was less impressive. Especially in combat situations, accuracy varied markedly depending on the bombardier. Setting the instrument required such precision that one reporter likened it to playing a violin. Wearing silk gloves so that his fingers wouldn't stick to the metal and breathing pure oxygen in temperatures reaching forty degrees below zero, the bombardier crouched in the Plexiglas nose of the aircraft, the worst seat in the house.

Nearly one thousand GIs trained at Lewistown Airfield before heading to Europe to join the air war. While in Lewistown—for training periods ranging from one to three months—the soldiers became a part of the community, married local girls, and won the hearts of the townspeople. Many never came home. B-17s carried four thousand pounds of bombs and served in every World War II combat zone, but casualties among bomber squadrons were horrific. A single mission over Germany in October 1942 claimed sixty B-17s and six hundred lives.

After eleven months of service, the Army Air Force deactivated the training program but, remarkably, evidence of the airfield's role still stands. Extant structures—most of which were built quickly, following standardized plans—include a water tower, a pump house, training and recreation buildings, offices, hangars, warehouses, and shops. In addition, the historic district includes one of the few Norden bombsight shelters remaining in the United States. —***MK***

To protect the top-secret Norden bombsight, barbed wire encircled this double-compartment storage building and a twenty-four-hour sentry kept guard.

90. Fort Missoula Alien Detention Center

Missoula | 46°50′34″N 114°03′29″W

Established in 1877, Fort Missoula already had a long history by the time the Japanese bombed Pearl Harbor in December 1941. Even before America's official entry into the war, however, the fort assumed a unique role in the worldwide conflict.

Fearing the possibility of espionage or sabotage, in March 1941 President Franklin D. Roosevelt ordered that Axis ships docked in American ports be seized and their crews detained at secure sites far removed from the nation's industrial centers. Fort Missoula offered such a location.

Consequently, the US Army transferred control of the fort to the Department of Justice, Immigration and Naturalization Service (INS). Over the next three years, the Fort Missoula Alien Detention Center housed 2,500 internees from two primary groups—Italian nationals and Issei (first-generation Japanese immigrant) resident aliens.

In anticipation of forthcoming internees, workers constructed additional barracks and erected a ten-foot, barbed-wire-topped fence guarded by forty-foot watchtowers. Then, beginning in spring 1941, the government relocated twelve hundred Italian civilians to Fort Missoula, which they named Bella Vista in recognition of the site's "Beautiful View." Most of these men had been employed on impounded merchant ships or a luxury cruise liner seized in the Panama Canal, but others included artists, musicians, and entertainers who had worked at the Italian pavilion at the 1939–1940 New York World's Fair. Most would remain at Fort Missoula until Italy surrendered to the Allies in September 1943.

As soon as the United States declared war on Japan on December 8, the FBI began arresting prominent Issei businessmen and community leaders. US law stated that anyone born in Asia could not apply for citizenship, so these men were legally resident aliens even though some had lived in America for decades. The government agents took the Issei without telling them or their families where they were going or what would happen to them. At the end of the war, most would not have homes or businesses to return to.

On December 18, the first Issei began arriving at Fort Missoula from Salt Lake City and the West Coast. Later Issei internees would come from Hawaii and Latin America. At Fort Missoula, they faced proceedings conducted by INS Alien Hearing Boards to determine their perceived "loyalty" to the United States. Depending on the board's findings, some Issei faced deportation or transfer to War Relocation Authority detention camps to join their families, but 70 percent were sentenced to continued internment and sent to army-run camps where they generally remained until war's end. None were ever convicted of disloyal conduct.

While at Fort Missoula, the two groups were segregated from each other, and Japanese detainees faced racial discrimination not experienced by their Italian counterparts. Both nationalities staffed their own laundry, mess halls, and other facilities, but, after a time, officials allowed the Italians to work for wages off-site. In their leisure time, Italian internees played soccer and bocce and staged musical performances for themselves and the local community. Japanese detainees favored baseball and golf, even building a nine-hole course they dubbed the "Beautiful Sky Golf Course." The Issei also succumbed to "stone fever," crafting distinctive artworks from colorful river pebbles that they carefully gathered and polished.

Fort Missoula's detention center closed in July 1944. After the war ended, the army dismantled or moved the simple frame barracks in which the men had lived. Today, the physical reminders of this little-known aspect of Montana's past include one barracks that has been returned to the fort's grounds, the rows of concrete pads where the barracks once stood, and, most notably, the restored courtroom where, in a lamentable breach of civil liberties, the Issei loyalty hearings were held. *—KL*

Left: This 1943 photograph shows an unidentified Japanese detainee at Fort Missoula holding a toddler.
2001.048.139, HISTORICAL MUSEUM AT FORT MISSOULA

Opposite page: Italian detainees held at Fort Missoula work in the garden in this uncredited 1943 photograph.
2001.048.199, HISTORICAL MUSEUM AT FORT MISSOULA

91. Graf Duplex

Bozeman | 45°40′38″N 111°02′36″W

While most Montana towns experienced steep population declines throughout the depressed 1920s and 1930s, a few towns, like Bozeman, increased in size. The well-watered Gallatin Valley provided agricultural jobs and Montana State College (now Montana State University) drew unemployed workers back to school. Energetic town boosters responding to the opportunity made the Sweet Pea City one of the few towns to see new, modern buildings rise during Montana's prolonged Depression.

Two important promoters responsible for the addition of Depression-era buildings on Bozeman's streetscape were German baker and entrepreneur Eugene Graf and respected Bozeman architect Fred F. Willson. By the time Willson designed this sleek white duplex for Graf in 1941, the two men were seasoned collaborators, committed to improving Bozeman's appeal and economy through modern architecture.

Willson, who attended Columbia University and the prestigious Ecole de Beaux Arts architecture school in Paris, enjoyed the distinction of designing nearly every major public building in Bozeman between 1910 and 1956. Ultimately, his firm created plans for more than three hundred Bozeman buildings. Graf, who owned the Bon Ton Bakery on Main Street and the Bon Ton Flour Mill on Wallace Street, appreciated high-style European architecture and worked to elevate the town's economic prospects through modern design. He first became Willson's client in 1927 while serving as chairman of the Bozeman Community Hotel Association—the town's ambitious effort to bring a first-class hotel to Bozeman.

Willson's Art Deco–style design for the seven-story Baxter Hotel made it the tallest building on Main Street and an attraction for residents and visitors alike. With the Baxter under construction in 1928, Graf commissioned Willson to remodel the exterior of his Bon Ton Bakery on Main to match the Baxter Hotel's Mediterranean Revival–style interior. Even with the Great Depression gripping the nation, Bozeman's economy remained robust enough for Graf to hire Willson for several more commissions.

In 1931, Graf engaged Willson to create the Bon Ton Flour Mill facility to supply flour for his own bakery. Willson used the stripped-down, smooth Streamline Moderne variant of the Art Deco style, which he would later employ on numerous 1930s public buildings across the state. With the mill complete and the latest machinery in place, Graf's Bon Ton Bakery became the first Montana bakery to deliver a novel innovation: sliced bread. Graf went on to hire Willson to design a 1934 Safeway store and the Graf family's eclectic 1936 Chateauesque/Moderne–style mansion on West Cleveland Street.

During World War II, demand for modern housing in Bozeman continued to escalate, and Willson created this minimalist duplex, likely his last design for Graf. The white stucco walls, circular windows, and decorative pipe railings reflect the Streamline aesthetic common on many of Willson's 1930s buildings, while the home's boxy massing, flat roof, and corner windows display the emerging International style. Although more modest in scale than some of Graf and Willson's other projects, the duplex remains an expression of their commitment to sustaining Bozeman's prosperity through modern design. —***CWB***

221
219

P&H
WIDE LOAD
GMC

CHAPTER EIGHT

MAKING MONTANA MODERN
1946–PRESENT

The federal government has shaped Montana's history since the Lewis and Clark Expedition. The dispossession of Native peoples, land grants to the Northern Pacific, homesteading, and the creation of national forests and national parks all required acts of Congress. Then, according to historian Mary Murphy, "during the 1930s, the hand of government was made glaringly obvious in government paychecks and government projects." The federal government—which directly controls about 30 percent of Montana's landmass—shaped the Treasure State throughout the postwar period and remains one of the largest employers in the state.

Mike Mansfield, the US Senate's longest-serving majority leader, was famous for bringing federal money to Montana, including funding to build the Hungry Horse, Canyon Ferry, Yellowtail, and Libby dams between 1953 and 1975. Even more significantly, the Cold War brought huge federal investments to central Montana as the state's northern latitude, high altitude, and sparse population made it a logical location for Minuteman Intercontinental Ballistic Missiles. The construction of Montana's missile silos—begun in 1961—ultimately spread across a 13,800-square-mile area. According to historian Troy Hallsell, the project injected "millions of dollars into the state's economy" and "made Montana dependent on defense dollars in the decades that followed."

A still larger federal investment, with more impact on daily life, was the construction of the interstate highway system. Initiated in 1956 and completed in 1988, interstates allowed people to live farther away from urban cores and routed traffic away from main streets. People who lived within fifty miles of one of Montana's regional trading centers no longer relied as heavily on local merchants; instead, they could easily drive to Billings, Great Falls, or Butte to do their shopping at the malls and box stores built on the outskirts of town. At the same time, travelers abandoned downtowns for the motels, restaurants, and gas stations that sprouted along the new interstates. No other postwar development, according to historian Jon Axline, has been more transformative for Montana. Interstates reshaped "the landscape, culture, and economy of the state itself."

Construction of Montana's Minuteman Intercontinental Ballistic Missile silos began in 1961. This photograph shows the construction of a launch control center and corresponding elevator shaft, probably in Cascade County.
PAC 84-91 MMINSTALL1, MTHS PHOTOGRAPH ARCHIVES

As cars and trucks diverted traffic from trains, over a dozen railroad towns in Montana suffered major employment losses. In 1977, the Milwaukee Road declared bankruptcy, and in the 1980s, crews tore up its tracks. The town of Harlowton lost seventy-four jobs and, between 1950 and 1999, 40 percent of its population. At the same time, completion of the interstate system bolstered both the trucking and tourism industries.

By the 1960s, tourism was Montana's third-largest revenue producer, and 85 percent of the state's visitors arrived by car. Commercial air travel also made Montana seem less remote. Although most tourists visited during the summer season, ski resorts like Big Mountain in Whitefish, which opened in 1947, and Big Sky, founded in 1974, began attracting winter visitors as well.

Travelers filled their tanks with inexpensive gas, some of which came from Montana. With the discovery and development of the Williston Basin Field in 1949, "the value of crude oil produced in Montana actually exceeded that of copper," according to geographer Joseph Ashley. Billings became a hub for energy companies and more than doubled its population between 1940 and 1960, becoming Montana's largest city.

Petroleum overtook copper not just because of increasing demands for oil and gas but also because most of Butte's high-grade ore had already been mined by the 1950s. In response, the Anaconda Company started open-pit mining in 1955, a process that required massive equipment but far fewer workers. The resulting pit ultimately consumed several neighborhoods in northeastern Butte. Despite this sacrifice, hard-rock mining continued to decline; the smelter in Anaconda and the refinery in Black Eagle both closed in 1980.

Coal mining, on the other hand, expanded markedly during the 1970s. Railroads had initially provided the largest market for Montana coal, but as diesel locomotives replaced steam engines in the 1950s, coal production declined. In the 1960s, however, Montana began providing coal for electric generating plants. In 1971, Montana produced seven million tons of coal; by 1980, it produced thirty million.

During the same period, anger over strip mining and the construction of coal-fired power plants fueled Montana's burgeoning environmental movement, which in turn bolstered efforts to create additional wilderness areas and re-

As was often the case when building roads through mountainous terrain, the construction of Interstate 90 near Tarkio in Mineral County required the effort of both men and machines.

MONTANA DEPARTMENT OF TRANSPORTATION, PHOTO SECTION UNIT, AUG. 3, 1959, PAC 86-15.119-D, MTHS PHOTOGRAPH ARCHIVES

Left: In the era before interstates diverted highway traffic, downtown business districts bustled with a mixture of local and long-distance travelers. This postcard printed by the Miles City Chamber of Commerce around 1946 shows the city's Main Street abuzz with activity. LOT 048 MICI, MTHS PHOTOGRAPH ARCHIVES

Right: "Urban removal"—as detractors dubbed urban renewal—resulted in the loss of many treasured buildings, including Helena's Marlow Theater. FROM THE COLLECTION OF HENRY W. JORGENSEN, COURTESY OF KENNON BAIRD

form forest management practices. Senator Lee Metcalf led the charge to protect wilderness, helping to create the Scapegoat, Great Bear, and Absaroka-Beartooth Wilderness Areas. At the same time, Montana's tribal nations led the fight to protect sacred places and important cultural landscapes, including the Sweet Grass Hills and the Badger-Two Medicine area.

Despite federal investment, a booming tourism industry, and increasing energy development, Montana's overall growth in the postwar period paled compared to that of other states. The only decade in which Montana grew faster than the rest of the United States was the 1970s, during the energy production boom. In the 1960s, by contrast, Montana's population grew by only 2.9 percent, far below the 13.3 percent national average. As a result, Montana saw relatively little new construction aside from government and university buildings, including at tribal colleges.

For many Montana communities, the second half of the twentieth century was mostly a story of stagnation or decline. Rural populations decreased as farms grew bigger, farming became more mechanized, and government programs encouraged farmers to take land labeled marginal out of production. In cities with failing downtowns, officials saw demolition and new construction as a catalyst for economic development. Butte and Helena tore down swaths of dilapidated nineteenth-century buildings as part of the 1960s "Model Cities" (urban renewal) program. In smaller towns with little economic pressure to expand or modernize, communities more often practiced "preservation by neglect."

In 1966, the historic preservation movement—a backlash to urban renewal—successfully lobbied Congress to pass the Historic Preservation Act. That legislation, which required federal agencies to consider impacts to historic places, coupled with the celebration of the 1976 US Bicentennial, renewed appreciation for—and investment in—historic buildings and landscapes. The closing decades of the twentieth century saw historic preservation begin to shape Montana's built environment, a sustainable trend that hopefully will continue through the twenty-first century. *—MK*

This ca. 1955 Harold Sanborn photograph shows the distinctive building that housed Livingston's KPRK radio station.
LOT 048 LIVI, MTHS PHOTOGRAPH ARCHIVES

92. KPRK Radio Station

Livingston | 45°40′22″N 110°32′24″W

World War II dampened the growth of radio broadcasting by prohibiting expansion of existing stations and disallowing the licensing of new stations. When the freeze finally lifted, KPRK Radio in Livingston became the fourth new station to sign on in postwar Montana. KPRK's streamlined presence on the highway welcomed visitors entering Livingston, a Northern Pacific Railway hub. At 8:00 pm January 9, 1947, more than twenty prominent residents representing a broad spectrum of interests christened the new station in an opening ceremony and premier broadcast. Station owner Paul McAdam and Walter Carle, his general manager, organized the event.

William J. Fox drew the plans for the futuristic Art Moderne–style station in 1946. Fox, a World War II navy veteran, had worked for the US Forest Service during the Great Depression. During his tenure, he drew the first architectural plans for Montana ranger stations. Working under Clyde Fickes, Fox drew the Rustic-style plans for the buildings at the Boy Scouts' Camp Paxson on Seeley Lake. After the war, Fox struck out on his own. The KPRK station was one of his first projects. Although Fox at the time had little experience in the Moderne style, his whimsical design has endured. Intended to contrast with Livingston's many turn-of-the-century brick buildings, the KPRK station affirmed the town's connection with the latest technology and the outside world.

The station's space-age appearance served as a sort of "billboard of progress," but it was also a conscious nod to the flamboyant radio and film media of the 1930s and 1940s. The stuccoed, wood-frame station features a rectangular plan with horizontal banding and an asymmetrical, semicircular vestibule. Glass blocks fill in the horizontal spaces flanking and above the doorway. A four-tiered, futuristic, round roof structure topped by a miniature radio tower crowns the vestibule. KPRK's stylized call letters prominently accent the front façade. Originally, lightning bolts punctuated the call letters, which repeated in neon on the roof.

The KPRK station is a tribute to its architect and the harbinger of a stellar career. William J. Fox rose to prominence, and his firm of Fox, Ballas, and Barrow went on to design many mid- to late twentieth-century buildings in Missoula and throughout the state, including the 1955 Swedish Moderne–style Immanuel Lutheran Church in Missoula and the 1969 University Center on the University of Montana campus.

KPRK was a Livingston fixture for more than half a century. The voice of broadcaster Jack Hinman, who later owned the station, was a local mainstay until his death in 1977. Under several other later owners, KPRK broadcast daily from 5:30 AM to midnight. Programming included music, high school sports, fairs, rodeos, swap meets, and news. When the station changed hands in 2008, broadcasts from the station ceased and the building sat vacant for more than a decade. As of 2024, a new owner is planning to use historic preservation tax credits to restore the building as part of an outdoor entertainment venue. —*EB*

93. Greyhound Bus Stations

Billings | 45°46′50″N 108°30′15″W

Great Falls | 47°30′21″N 111°17′54″W

During the twentieth century, buses played a crucial role in the motorization of America by providing an option for long-distance travel for those who did not own a car or did not want to drive. Additionally, bus fares were generally cheaper than train fares, and buses served destinations not reachable by rail.

Although designed by different architects and located in different parts of the state, two Montana Greyhound terminals tell a remarkably similar story. They also illustrate the importance of one company's nationwide branding as the United States became increasingly homogenized throughout the twentieth century.

Greyhound traces its origins to Hibbing, Minnesota, where in 1914 two Swedish immigrants began selling rides to local miners in their seven-passenger Hupmobile. Highly successful on the local level, the company soon expanded by merging with or buying up other bus lines until—within just a couple of decades—it became the largest intercity bus carrier in the country. In 1930, the company adopted the name Greyhound Bus Corporation, and the "running dog" became its widely recognized trademark.

The Billings Greyhound station—now a live music venue known as the Pub Station—appears in this uncredited photograph likely taken around the time of its opening in 1944.
99-55-07, WESTERN HERITAGE CENTER

Beginning in 1937, Greyhound built a number of new stations in a style of Art Deco architecture known as Streamline Moderne or Art Moderne. Popular internationally, Streamline Moderne architecture featured long horizontal lines accentuated by curved forms, the use of modern materials like glass block and aluminum, and a lack of ornamentation to create a sleek, aerodynamic effect. Because it suggested speed and efficiency, the style was especially popular for transportation-related buildings like bus depots and train stations. Beyond architecture, the Streamline Moderne style also influenced the design of a great variety of items ranging from household appliances to locomotives and buses, including the "Super Coaches" operated by Greyhound beginning in the 1930s.

Greyhound employed Louisville, Kentucky, architect William Strudwick Arrasmith to design more than sixty of these new Streamline Moderne stations in the eastern part of the country. In places like Montana, local architects followed suit and adopted the style for their own buildings.

J. G. Link & Company designed the Billings Greyhound station, which was built in 1944—a rare wartime construction justified by the bus line's role in transporting troops—at a cost of $78,000. According to historian Kevin Kooistra, "The structure included a passenger waiting area, bus terminal, newsstand, and the Greyhound Café, where you could buy a hearty Sunday dinner for $1.00 in 1946." It continued to serve bus passengers for the next seventy years. In 2014, it was reimagined as a distinctive entertainment venue and taphouse. To herald the transformation, the iconic "BUS" sign was switched to one that now reads "PUB," and the image of the running greyhound was replaced with a marquee announcing upcoming acts.

Greyhound constructed its Great Falls terminal in 1947. The prominent firm of McIver and Cohagen designed the Streamline Moderne building, which, harkening back to an earlier form of transportation, sits on the site of a former livery stable. In 2002, taking advantage of its location in the city's central business district, the Great Falls Transit District rehabilitated the facility, continuing its use as a transfer center. *—KL*

The Great Falls Greyhound station features the curved shapes and modern materials that characterize the Streamline Moderne style.

94. Charles M. Bair Family Museum

Martinsdale | 46°27′30″N 110°18′48″W

The Bair Museum pays homage to a unique Montana family and their many contributions to the Treasure State. The museum's story also exemplifies the importance that history holds for Montana's citizens, whether they live in larger urban areas or small rural communities.

Charles Bair came to Montana Territory in 1883 with only—as his biographer Lee Rostad recorded—"fourteen cents and seven green apples." Working initially as a railroad conductor, he earned his first fortune through savvy business dealings during the Alaskan gold rush. In 1899, he returned to Montana where he engaged in a variety of pursuits, including banking, oil, and real estate. It is as a highly successful sheep rancher, however, that he is most often remembered. In 1910 alone, he reportedly shipped 1.5 million pounds of wool to eastern markets from his three hundred thousand head of sheep.

Bair and his wife Mary had two daughters, Marguerite and Alberta, born in 1889 and 1895, respectively. Beginning in 1910, the three women summered in Montana but lived primarily in Portland, Oregon, where they began collecting antiques. In 1934, they returned permanently to Montana, settling at their Martinsdale ranch house, which had been built around an earlier homestead building. In 1936, they completed a remodel of the house designed to modernize it and to showcase the antiques they had amassed, as well as the family's collection of Western art and American Indian artifacts. Marguerite married ranch foreman Dave Lamb in 1939; Alberta remained single.

Following the death of their parents—Charlie in 1943 and Mary in 1950—the sisters remained in the family home. Loving to travel, they also made numerous trips to Europe where they continued their pursuit of art and antiques: especially silver by noted English silversmith Paul Storr, Georgian period furniture, English and French porcelain, and paintings.

While the Bairs showcased their extensive collections of art and antiques in other rooms, the kitchen served as the heart of the family's private life as well as Alberta's office.

Back in Montana, as their collections grew, so did the house, until the Colonial Revival–style mansion ultimately included twenty-six rooms and eleven thousand square feet. Dave died in 1973 and Marguerite followed three years later. Before her death in 1993, Alberta established the Charles M. Bair Family Trust to ensure that the family's legacy would continue as a museum, a plan agreed upon by both sisters years earlier.

The Bair Family Museum opened to the public in 1996, but in 2003 trustees of the estate—more attuned to financial management than running a museum—closed it. Knowing the long-held wishes of the Bair sisters as well as the importance of the new institution to the community, local residents fought back. Ultimately, the Montana Supreme Court ruled that the trust had breached its fiduciary responsibility in closing the facility. As a result, a new board of trustees assumed oversight in 2008 and the museum was back on course.

Today, visitors can still enjoy a tour through the rambling house filled with the eclectic collections cherished by the Bairs. In addition, in 2011, the museum opened a complementary state-of-the-art facility to better exhibit and preserve the most fragile items in its care. *—KL*

95. Mann Gulch

Lewis and Clark County | 46°53′7″N 111°53′56″W

The Gates of the Mountains area of the Missouri River, northeast of Helena, has been celebrated for its scenic beauty since it was so named by Captain Meriwether Lewis in 1805. Nearly 150 years later, it was also the site of one of Montana's most tragic events, when a seemingly routine firefighting mission led to the horrific deaths of thirteen young men and changed the course of wildfire management history.

Around noon on August 5, 1949, a small wildfire was reported at the head of Mann Gulch in a remote area of the Big Belt Mountains. By 4:10 that afternoon, fifteen Forest Service smokejumpers—firefighters who parachute into remote areas to fight wildfires—were on the ground near the fire. While they completed their jump without incident, growing turbulence forced the C-47/DC-3 that delivered them from Missoula to climb higher than normal for the cargo drop, resulting in widely scattered equipment. One parachute's failure to open resulted in a broken radio and the loss of any way to contact the outside world. Recreation Guard James O. Harrison—who had earlier in the day walked over from nearby Meriwether Canyon to begin fighting the fire alone—also joined the smokejumpers.

Initially, the heavily laden firefighters headed down Mann Gulch toward the Missouri River and a safer spot from which to attack the fire. Soon, however, erratic winds started new spot fires that blew up, blocking the smokejumpers' route to the river. By 5:45 pm, growing flames driven by high winds—gusting to forty miles per hour—had forced the sixteen men to drop their equipment and attempt a retreat up the extremely steep, rocky hillside.

Estimates indicate that the fire spread to three thousand acres in just ten minutes. Foreman R. Wagner Dodge stopped his ascent of the gulch and lit a small "escape fire," ordering his men to join him. Since the small burned-over area was now free of fuel, Dodge remained safe. But tragically, none of the other crew members heeded (or perhaps even heard) his order. Instead, they attempted to outrun the flames. Only two of the smokejumpers, Walter B. Rumsey and Robert W. Sallee, reached the safety of the ridgetop. By 5:56 pm, the other thirteen firefighters—primarily college students and World War II veterans, all between the ages of nineteen and twenty-eight—had perished in the inferno.

Recovering the remains of the young men who died in the inferno was a gruesome and arduous task. US Forest Service photographer Dick Wilson caught this photograph of responders recovering a body from the charred mountainside.
WIKIMEDIA COMMONS

The impacts of the tragedy were long-lasting and far-reaching. The Mann Gulch deaths were the first experienced by the Forest Service's nine-year-old smokejumper program. Many people blamed Dodge for what, at the time, was an unprecedented tactic. Subsequent investigations vindicated his actions and led the agency to adopt the use of escape fires, increase training for all firefighters, implement improved safety practices and equipment, and conduct scientific fire behavior studies as an essential component of wildfire management. The calamity also captured the nation's attention, resulting in widespread media coverage, the 1952 motion picture *Red Skies of Montana*, and *Young Men and Fire*, author Norman Maclean's epic study of the tragedy, published posthumously in 1992.

In memory of those who died: Robert J. Bennett, Paris, TN; Eldon E. Diettert, Moscow, ID; James O. Harrison, Missoula; William J. Hellman, Kalispell; Philip R. McVey, Babb; David R. Navon, Modesto, CA; Leonard L. Piper, Blairsville, PA; Stanley J. Reba, Brooklyn, NY; Marvin L. Sherman, Missoula; Joseph B. Sylvia, Plymouth, MA; Henry J. Thol Jr., Kalispell; Newton R. Thompson, Alhambra, CA; and Silas R. Thompson, Charlotte, NC. *—KL*

96. Glacier County Public Library

Cut Bank | 48°37′45″N 112°19′46″W

Franklin Roosevelt's New Deal programs brought many new or updated public buildings to Montana towns during the 1930s, but Montana's prolonged depression left communities with antiquated or inadequate public buildings following World War II. As Montana's economy recovered in the 1950s, architects and their clients shunned "the old," favoring thoroughly modern architectural styles devoid of historical references.

The rich oil fields nearby bolstered Cut Bank's local economy during the Great Depression, but the town still lacked a dedicated public library in 1950. The Cut Bank Woman's Club had organized a free library in 1922, which they moved into the basement of City Hall in 1937. A major flood in 1940 destroyed the library, but the Woman's Club rallied to raise funds to restore the book collection by the following year. The county assumed ownership of the collection in 1944. Ten years later, Cut Bank citizens voted for a bond issue to fund a new building.

Designed by young Great Falls architects George C. Page and Vincent S. Werner and completed in 1957, the library demonstrates the mid-twentieth-century architectural preference for modern designs and materials. Page and Werner's plans eschewed the stately, symmetrical Neoclassical style that defined turn-of-the-century libraries and instead specified a one-story asymmetrical design employing curtain-wall construction, a then-new method of prefabricating entire walls using non-structural glass and aluminum.

This innovation—so named because the exterior wall hangs curtain-like from a structural support above—had been around for decades, but advances in aluminum and glass manufacturing during World War II perfected the production process. Not only did these glass walls let ample natural light into interior spaces, the large, prefabricated units cost less and required less labor to install than traditional windows.

Further elevating the library's modern aesthetic is the three-panel ceramic tile mural on its west wall. The mural, sculpted by preeminent Montana ceramic artist Rudy Autio, is a memorial to local lumberman, town booster, and horseman Bill Linder, who died in 1950. It is one of Autio's earliest public art commissions and represents his fifty-year career creating modern art. Autio helped establish the renowned Archie Bray Foundation for Ceramic Arts in Helena in 1952, created and led the ceramics department at the University of Montana from 1957 to 1985, and became internationally recognized for his large-scale "ladies and horses" pieces. His art is housed in museum collections worldwide.

An article in the *Cut Bank Pioneer Press* lauded Page and Werner's modern design: "Those of us accustomed to the ponderous, memorial-type library structures of the early 1900s era are apt to feel library buildings have to be that way. They don't, and nothing illustrates the point better than the plan for the new Glacier county library." The piece went on to praise the library as a "modern building, attractive, fresh in its openness, crisp-lined, a definite contribution to the city's beauty—yet more functional and better able to provide community service than the monuments of a quarter century ago." —***CWB***

OUNTY LIBRARY
·THIS·RELIEF·PRESENTED·
·IN MEMORY·OF·BILL LINDER·
·BY THE·OILFIELD·LUMBER CO.

97. University of Providence

Great Falls | 47°29′30″N 111°17′21″W

The College of Great Falls (now known as the University of Providence) already had a long history when the Sisters of Providence announced plans to build a campus in 1957. The project was the culmination of many years and especially remarkable since it came at a time when Catholic institutions were being reappraised. Funding for the $3 million project came from a joint effort by the Catholic and civic communities. The eleven-building Modern-style campus, a unified whole of simplicity and utility, opened in September 1960.

The Sisters of Providence and Ursuline Sisters of Great Falls planted the seeds of the college in 1932, when the two orders collaborated to found Great Falls Junior College, then the only Catholic college for women between St. Paul and Spokane. By the late 1930s, the college offered a coeducational four-year degree program with classes at the Ursuline Academy and Columbus Hospital. The Ursulines withdrew in 1942, and the Sisters of Providence dreamed of building a campus. World War II delayed their plans, but the sisters purchased land south of Great Falls in 1944.

Finally, in the late 1950s, Great Falls architects George C. Page and Vincent S. Werner designed the campus master plan. As with their design for the Glacier County Public Library, their Modern-style plan employed curtain-wall and lift-slab construction methods, hallmarks of midcentury architecture. The process of lift-slab construction allowed on-site concrete slabs for roofs and floors to be poured, cured, and then lifted in place.

Consistent throughout the campus, materials included painted metal panels, glass in aluminum frames, concrete foundations, load-bearing steel walls, and multicolored brick. Precast materials and on-site assembly cut both production and delivery costs while allowing designs and features that made each building distinctive. For example, the three-story Emilie Hall—named for Sisters of Providence founder Emilie Gamelin—features dramatic cantilevers and a glass-pavilioned social center. An angular, multicolored brick campanile (free-standing bell tower) distinguishes the concrete-and-frame chapel. The science building—which originally served as the sisters' convent—is appropriately a simple rectangle. The architects used changes in the landscape to add visual interest to the designs.

As campus plans came together, Sister Henry Alphonse Lippens took a year of architectural courses at the University of Washington to oversee construction. Sister Mary Trinitas Morin, a 1940 college alum and longtime art professor, planned and created the art that ornaments the campus and chapel. During the 1960s under Sister Rita Mudd, the school's only female president, the College of Great Falls transformed into a liberal arts university. In 1965, Sister Rita secured funds from the McLaughlin family to build the physical education center, the final piece of the campus master plan.

The University of Providence, as it was renamed in 2017, retains its distinctive Modernist aesthetic as well as its catholic identity in the universal sense of welcoming all. Although no Sisters of Providence physically remain at the college, Emilie Hall, Rita Mudd Hall, and Trinitas Chapel recognize some of the women whose vision and persistence continue to inspire its students. *—EB*

This thirty-six-foot-long frieze depicting the history of the Sisters of Providence was designed by Sister Trinitas and crafted by her students in in the State of Washington in 1962. It is composed of balsa wood and tooled and lacquered brass.

98. Logan Pass and St. Mary Visitor Centers

Glacier National Park | 48°41′47.72″N 113°43′5.91″W | 48°41′43″N 113°43′4″W

As the National Park Service (NPS) approached its fiftieth anniversary in 1966, park administrators launched Mission 66, a multiyear effort to upgrade national parks to meet escalating visitor demands in the post–World War II era. Construction of headquarters buildings, employee housing, maintenance areas, entrance stations, bathrooms, exhibits, roads, parking lots, campgrounds, concession buildings, and stand-alone visitor centers (a new concept for national parks) resulted in massive improvements for both visitors and employees. It also meant a break from the Park Service's half-century tradition of constructing Rustic-style log buildings in our national parks. In Montana, the St. Mary and Logan Pass visitor centers in Glacier National Park exemplify this significant shift to Modernism in park facilities.

Across the country, national park improvements halted and visitation slowed dramatically during World War II. By the 1950s, with the return of economic prosperity, however, national parks were struggling to accommodate a new flood of visitors. NPS Director Conrad L. Wirth developed the idea of modernizing the parks in 1954 through a massive, multiyear redevelopment program. The visitor center, a key feature of Wirth's new Mission 66 program, created a "one-stop" service building, equipped with an information desk, lobby exhibits, museum, library, restrooms, and administrative offices. This type of design represented a major departure from the earlier NPS concept of a "park village," where different functions were spread out in individual, Rustic-style buildings.

The Kalispell firm of Brinkman and Lenon oversaw the design, engineering, and construction of the St. Mary and Logan Pass visitor centers. Architect Cecil Doty of the NPS Western Office of Design and Construction provided preliminary designs for Logan Pass in 1960 but not for St. Mary; Brinkman and Lenon architect Burt L. Gewalt began planning the latter in 1963. Gewalt, who previously worked as the project supervisor on the park administration building at West Glacier, felt he had a "free hand" to design St. Mary, later noting that he provided 100 percent of the building's design. He drew inspiration from his previous work designing Modernist churches in Minnesota and North Dakota, and integrated design elements found in Yellowstone's Modernist-style Canyon Village Visitor Center created by Welton-Beckett and Associates in 1958. Both Logan Pass and St. Mary feature several hallmarks of mid-twentieth-century architectural design: dramatic, asymmetrical gabled roof lines; exposed glue-laminated wood beams (glulam); stone embedded in concrete walls; and expansive curtain-wall windows.

The billion-dollar, multiyear Mission 66 program, which continued as the Parkscape program through 1972 (the hundredth anniversary of Yellowstone National Park), produced about 110 new visitor centers and modernized the nation's national parks. The St. Mary and Logan Pass visitor centers, completed in 1966, remain outstanding examples of the Mission 66 concept and the Modernist style in Montana. —*CWB*

Left: This photograph postcard, which likely dates to the late 1960s or early 1970s, offers an early glimpse of the Logan Pass visitor center, completed in 1966.
IMAGE COURTESY OF GLACIER NATIONAL PARK ARCHIVES

The NPS Western Office of Design and Construction provided plans for the Logan Pass visitor center, but Burt Gewalt of Kalispell's Brinkman and Kennon firm designed the St. Mary's visitor center, pictured here.

99. Heritage Museum

Libby | 48°22′47″N 115°33′17″W

The Heritage Museum is a tribute to Libby's community spirit. This unusual, twelve-sided building features a 130-foot-diameter first floor and a 30-foot-diameter cupola. The Rustic-style log museum celebrates the region's forests and logging roots and the town's commitment to preserving its history.

Community members began imagining a museum in 1971 to display the paintings and extensive artifact collection of Libby landscape artist and collector Roy Porter. Porter had made his home an informal museum, displaying his own art and his large collection of historical artifacts. After Roy died in 1971, his son Doug, faced with the task of sorting through his father's collection, decided to pursue his father's lifelong dream of building a public museum.

Doug Porter became president of the museum's volunteer board, which incorporated in 1973. John Davidson, who worked for the US Army Corps of Engineers at Libby Dam, was named vice president, and Lincoln County librarian Inez Herrig served as secretary. The board's vision grew beyond creating a home for the Porter collection to building a repository for other local history collections as well as a community archive.

The nation's upcoming bicentennial provided additional motivation. Following the national themes of "Heritage," "Festival," and "Horizons," the Montana Bicentennial Commission encouraged communities across the state to recognize the anniversary with a wide variety of projects. These included activities that preserved the state's history (heritage), celebratory events (festivals), and new improvements designed to guarantee a better future (horizons). The Lincoln County Bicentennial Committee made construction of the Heritage Museum its primary contribution to the commemoration. In its application for funding from the state commission, the museum board noted that "the whole community is together working toward one project" and that the "feasibility of completing" the project was "high" because "we're stubborn."

The museum was designed and constructed almost entirely by volunteers. Floyd Lucas, a structural engineer who worked for the US Army Corps of Engineers at the Libby Dam, designed the Neotraditional Rustic–style building. National Forest landscape architect Wayne Tlusty created a site plan. Other community members dug the well and excavated the basement while John Davidson designed and completed the museum's electrical system. Local loggers felled

and skidded up to nine hundred larch and lodgepole pines that the Kootenai National Forest donated to the county for the project. Truckers delivered the logs to the site at no charge. Then, volunteers at the construction site hand-peeled and notched the logs to prepare them for assembly. Libby High School students built the museum's large front doors in their shop class.

The community finished the museum's shell as planned by the July 4, 1976, bicentennial celebration. Its forty-one interior exhibits opened to the public two years later. Normally, buildings included in the National Register of Historic Places must be at least fifty years old. However, an exception was made in this case; because of the building's "exceptional importance" to the community, it was listed in the National Register in 2020, only forty-two years after its completion. *—MK*

100. Montana Veterans and Pioneers Memorial Building

Helena | 46°35′11″N 112°0′55″W

As soon as the First Territorial Legislature founded the Montana Historical Society (MTHS) in 1865, facilities suitable for the storage, preservation, and display of its irreplaceable collections documenting the region's past became an overriding concern. Initially, individual members housed the society's holdings as best they could, but in 1887, MTHS joined Montana's territorial government, moving temporarily into the new Lewis and Clark County Courthouse and opening its first "public rooms."

The completion of the state capitol building in 1902 provided the society with a much-sought-after, long-term home, but by the early 1920s MTHS librarian David Hilger was already decrying a critical lack of space. Soon, two organizations—the Society of Montana Pioneers and the Sons and Daughters of Montana Pioneers—joined Hilger in calling for the construction of a dedicated MTHS building that would be "modern, impressive, dignified and attractive inside and out."

By 1941, veterans' groups—including the American Legion, Disabled American Veterans, Veterans of Foreign Wars, and the 163rd Infantry of the Montana National Guard—had joined the call for a new building. That year, spurred by funds offered by the veterans and land offered by the pioneers, the legislature authorized bonds to construct a building to house not only MTHS but the partner organizations as well. World War II intervened before construction could begin, but following the war, building proponents called on the legislature for additional funds in 1945 and 1949. An official groundbreaking ceremony was finally held in 1950.

In reviewing potential designs garnered through a statewide call for proposals, the pioneer and veteran groups independently but unanimously selected a plan submitted by Angus V. McIver. A native of Great Falls, McIver studied architecture at the University of Michigan before returning to the Electric City to open an architectural firm in 1915. McIver, whose resume included courthouses for Pondera, Toole, and Glacier Counties, as well as numerous schools, hospitals, and other public buildings across the state, was well-suited for the commission.

From the beginning, the involved parties had agreed that they wanted a building that was "modern, yet respectful of the past." Accordingly, McIver's design adhered to the tenets of International-style architecture, an extension of the German Bauhaus movement, which in the United States came to symbolize capitalism and dominated midcentury office-building design. Accordingly, when the building opened to the public in January 1953, Montana's new "perpetual memorial to the war veterans and the pioneers" was asymmetrical, featured sleek lines and non-load-bearing "curtain walls" constructed of steel and glass, and eschewed almost all external ornamentation. As noted by architectural historian Kate Hampton, "The serene limestone walls, ribbons and curtains of glass, bronze details and solid concrete foundation testify to the appropriateness of the International Style of architecture for a building designed to keep the history and legacy of Montana safe and relevant through the twentieth century."

In spite of the building's suitability, the society's need for additional space periodically resurfaced as collections and services continued to increase. Consequently, architecturally sympathetic additions were constructed in 1970 and 1986, and a major building expansion—almost doubling the size of the existing Veterans and Pioneers Memorial Building—opened in 2025. Designed by Cushing Terrell Architects, this newest addition marks the latest chapter in the society's ongoing quest to preserve the Treasure State's past and display it in a modern, up-to-date home. —***KL***

101. Indigenous Nations: Challenges and Resilience

Since the beginning of the Republic, federal Indian policy has swung wildly between recognizing and respecting tribal sovereignty and actively working to destroy Native cultures and communities. During the treaty-making period (1778–1871) the federal government acknowledged, if sometimes begrudgingly, tribes as sovereign nations, but assimilation was the watchword of the boarding school era (1887–1934). The 1930s saw a renewed albeit limited respect for sovereignty, but assimilationist policies once again gained traction in the 1950s.

The 1960s and 1970s saw the rise of the American Indian Movement and a new era of activism, with Indian activists and tribal governments pressuring the federal government to repair past wrongs and empower tribal members. The work continues to this day. Tribal nations have established colleges on all seven Montana reservations; asserted off-reservation hunting, fishing, and water rights; demanded voting rights; expanded economic development programs; lobbied for legislation protecting religious freedom; worked to solve problems caused by past federal policies; and challenged the Bureau of Indian Affairs' misuse of funds. Every Indigenous nation in Montana has examples of successfully asserting sovereignty and enabling cultural preservation in the twenty-first century.

Dancers perform while wearing brightly colored regalia during North American Indian Days in Browning.
DONNIE SEXTON PHOTOGRAPH

Little Shell Tribe Administrative Office

Great Falls | 47°30′07″N 111°16′26″W

In 1882, Chief Little Shell of the Pembina Band of Ojibwe (Chippewa) Indians refused to sign away his people's land for ten cents on the dollar. As a result, Little Shell's band and those associated with them were removed from the rolls of what would eventually become the Turtle Mountain Reservation in North Dakota. The federal government refused to recognize members of the Little Shell Chippewa Tribe for over 130 years. Tribal members, who lived in communities across Montana, created a formal organization in 1921 to advocate for reservation land and federal recognition. It was a long fight. In 2003, the State of Montana formally recognized the Little Shell as an independent tribal nation; the federal government followed suit in 2019. In 2014, the Little Shell purchased this property in Great Falls to house their tribal program offices and meeting rooms, renovating it in 2021. Program initiatives include tribal health, housing, food security, language instruction, and cultural preservation. *—MK*

KIRBY LAMBERT PHOTOGRAPH

CSKT Bison Range

Flathead Reservation | 47°19′30″N 114°13′33″W

Members of the Confederated Salish and Kootenai Tribes (CSKT) were central to preserving the buffalo, bringing six orphaned calves across the Continental Divide and onto the Flathead Reservation in the 1870s. The herd grew to around eight hundred head, but in 1908, the federal government allotted the reservation over the tribes' strong objections. The resultant loss of grazing land led to the bison being rounded up and sold. Around the same time, in violation of the 1855 Hellgate Treaty, the federal government withheld 18,766 acres of the Flathead Reservation to create the National Bison Range. It purchased some of the buffalo that had roamed the reservation to populate the preserve.

CSKT never stopped wanting both to regain control of their treaty land and to care for the bison they had worked to save. In 1994, they began navigating the federal bureaucracy with the goal of partnering with US Fish and Wildlife to manage the herd. In 2020, Congress passed legislation transferring the Bison Range to CSKT. —***MK***

James E. Shanley Tribal Library

Fort Peck Reservation | 48°21′40″N 105°32′18″W

The creation of Fort Peck Community College (FPCC) mirrored that of tribal colleges across the United States. The Diné (Navaho) founded the first tribal college in 1968; soon, many other Indigenous nations saw the wisdom of creating pathways to formal education that perpetuated tribal values, cultures, and languages while also providing students with academic and vocational training. By 2024, there were thirty-five accredited tribal colleges in the United States and seven in Montana, one on each Indian reservation. The Tribal Executive Board of the Assiniboine and Sioux Tribes of the Fort Peck Indian Reservation chartered FPCC in 1978. By 1994, it had become an accredited land grant college. FPCC's library, named in honor of retired college president Dr. James E. Shanley, opened in 2012. In addition to serving the college, the library is both the tribal library and an affiliate of the Roosevelt County Library. *—MK*

SCOTT SMOKER PHOTOGRAPH

A procession of three Piikuni women in blanket robes walking among tipis and lodges in a field during a Sun Dance ceremony held near Little Badger Creek in 1941. ROLAND H. WILCOMB PHOTOGRAPH. 955-581 MTHS PHOTOGRAPH ARCHIVES

Badger-Two Medicine Area

Glacier County | 48°17′26″N 112°50′11″W

Some of the most significant places in Montana history are traditional cultural properties—landscapes that encompass Indigenous people's beliefs, customs, and religious practices. One such Montana locale is the Badger-Two Medicine area, a wild, mountainous area on the Rocky Mountain Front where Glacier National Park and the Blackfeet Reservation meet. This pristine area is where the Piikuni believe that their people were created.

In 1895, after federal Indian policy had pushed many Piikuni families into abject poverty, the tribe sold a strip of land on the western portion of its reservation—the landmass of which had already been much diminished. This area, known as the "ceded strip," included the Badger-Two Medicine area. When the US government purchased the land, the sale agreement expressly provided that the Piikuni reserved their existing rights to access the land for cultural and religious purposes, hunting, fishing, and gathering timber. Even when Congress created Glacier National Park out of a portion of the ceded strip in 1910 and the remainder became part of the Lewis and Clark National Forest, the Piikuni continued to use the Badger-Two Medicine as set out in the 1895 agreement.

Threats to the Badger-Two Medicine area arose in the early 1980s when the US Department of the Interior (DOI) expanded its oil and gas leasing policy, resulting in forty-seven leases authorized by the DOI without an environmental impact statement and without tribal consultation. Drilling in the Badger-Two Medicine area would industrialize the landscape with roads, traffic, and heavy equipment, effectively severing Piikuni spiritual connections with the land.

In the following decades, the Piikuni were forced to fight for their right to share the land. They formed coalitions with conservation groups and made significant gains, including designation of the area as a Traditional Cultural District and the banning of all future leases and motorized vehicles. The Piikuni won the battle to stop development in the Badger-Two Medicine area in September 2023, when, after forty-one long years of litigation, a final settlement retired the last drilling lease. —***CWB***

OPPOSITE PAGE: TONY BYNUM PHOTOGRAPH

ABOUT THE AUTHORS AND PHOTOGRAPHER

As interpretive historian at the Montana Historical Society from 1992 to 2018, **Ellen Baumler, PhD** (1949–2023), developed Montana's National Register sign program, writing hundreds of sign texts for historic sites across the Treasure State. Her contributions to Montana history have been widely celebrated. She received the Governor's Award for the Humanities in 2011, the Peter Yegen Jr. Award from the Montana Association of Museums (2017), the Award for Outstanding Service to Historic Preservation in Montana (2023), and the Montana Historical Society's Board of Trustees Heritage Keepers Award (2023). An indefatigable and popular presenter, she spoke in every corner of the state and was a frequent contributor to *Montana The Magazine of Western History*, *Montana Magazine*, and *Distinctly Montana*. Ellen also authored a dozen books on Montana history, and coauthored and contributed to several more. Even as she was fighting cancer, she managed to finish twenty-five essays for this, her last book.

Christine Brown has been an interpretive historian at the Montana Historical Society since 2019. She researches and writes about the Treasure State's notable properties for MTHS's National Register of Historic Places sign program, organizes the annual Montana History Conference, and promotes a love of Montana history through social media, lectures, tours, articles, and books. From 2005 to 2019 she

was Outreach and Education director at the nonprofit Preserve Montana. She received a BA in English from DePaul University in 1996 and a MS in historic preservation from Ball State University in 2001. She is the co-author, with Chere Jiusto, of *Hand Raised: The Barns of Montana* (2011) and a contributing author to *A History of Montana in 101 Objects: Artifacts and Essays from the Montana Historical Society* (2021).

Martha Kohl has worked at the Montana Historical Society since 1995, most recently as Outreach and Education program manager. She received both her BA and MA in history from Washington University in St. Louis and began her career in public history at the Missouri Historical Society, where she served as editor for the quarterly magazine *Gateway Heritage*. She has written hundreds of National Register signs for Montana's historic places. Her award-winning public history projects include Montana and the Great War and Montana Women's History, both findable online. She has written dozens of lesson plans and articles is the author of two books—*Montana: A History of Our Home* and *I Do: A Cultural History of Montana Weddings*—and the editor of *Beyond Schoolmarms and Madams: Montana Women's Lives*, all published by the Montana Historical Society Press.

Now retired, **Kirby Lambert** worked for almost thirty-seven years at the Montana Historical Society where he served in a variety of capacities—as museum registrar, curator, and Outreach and Interpretation program manager. Lambert graduated from Texas Tech University with a BA in history and MA in museum studies and received the Peter Yegen Jr. Award from the Montana Association of Museums in 2014 and the Governor's Award for the Humanities in 2015. He is a co-author of *A History of Montana in 101 Objects*, *Montana's Charlie Russell: Art in the Collection of the Montana Historical Society*, and *Montana's State Capitol: The People's House*. He is also a regular contributor to *Montana The Magazine of Western History*.

Tom Ferris grew up in New York City and after high school studied art at City University. A work/study job in Yellowstone National Park lured him west in 1980, and he later earned a BA in photography from Montana State University. From 1995 to 2024, Tom worked as the archival photographer at the Montana Historical Society while also operating a professional photography studio. His photographs have appeared in numerous magazines and books, including *Hand Raised: The Barns of Montana*, *A History of Montana in 101 Objects*, and *The Best Gift: Montana's Carnegie Libraries*. Tom's work is in many private collections in the United States and overseas, including the Ministry of Culture in France and the Shimada Museum in Japan.

HISTORIC MONTANA PLACES CHECKLIST

We hope that everyone who reads this book will want to visit all the historic Montana places profiled within. While there are several that can't be visited (and remain unlisted here), we provide this checklist to help you tally the historic Montana places that you have seen. We have first organized the sites regionally, using regions of the state as defined by the Montana Office of Tourism. Then, we have listed the sites alphabetically; when the location of a given place is not apparent based on name alone, we have included geographical information in parentheses. Luckily, a large majority of the sites are open to the public, on public land, or managed as state or national parks. Some of the sites are only open at certain times of the year or for special events. Sites marked with an asterisk are not generally open to the public and are viewable from the exterior only. Ownership and accessibility are subject to change, so search for visitor information before you go.

CENTRAL MONTANA

- ☐ Bear Paw Battlefield/Place of Many Manure Fires National Historic Landmark (Chinook)
- ☐ The Castle Museum (White Sulphur Springs)
- ☐ Charles M. Bair Family Museum (Martinsdale)
- ☐ Charlie Russell Home and Studio National Historic Landmark (Great Falls)
- ☐ Dave's Texaco* (Chinook vicinity)
- ☐ First People's Buffalo Jump National Historic Landmark (Ulm)
- ☐ Flatwillow/Howard Lepper Memorial Hall* (Winnett vicinity)
- ☐ Fort Assinniboine (Havre vicinity)
- ☐ Fort Benton National Historic Landmark
- ☐ Fort Shaw
- ☐ Great Falls Civic Center
- ☐ Great Northern Railway Depot (Kevin)
- ☐ Greyhound Bus Depot (Great Falls)
- ☐ Havre Masonic Temple*
- ☐ Judith Landing Historic District (Winifred vicinity)
- ☐ Judith River Ranger Station (Utica vicinity)
- ☐ Little Shell Tribal Programs Building* (Great Falls)
- ☐ Power Mercantile Block* (Lewistown)
- ☐ Reed and Bowles Trading Post* (Lewistown)
- ☐ Sacred Heart Catholic Church* (Harlem)
- ☐ Shelby Town Hall
- ☐ St. Peter's Mission (please close the gate) (Cascade vicinity)
- ☐ St. Wenceslaus Church* (Danvers)
- ☐ Tenth Street Bridge (Great Falls)
- ☐ Union Bethel African Methodist Episcopal Church (Great Falls)
- ☐ University of Providence (Great Falls)

GLACIER COUNTRY

- ☐ Badger Two Medicine (Bob Marshall Wilderness Area and vicinity)
- ☐ C. E. Conrad Memorial Cemetery (Kalispell)
- ☐ CSKT Bison Range (Moeise)
- ☐ Daly Mansion (Riverside) (Hamilton vicinity)
- ☐ Evaro School*
- ☐ Farmers and Merchants State Bank (Eureka)
- ☐ Fort Connah (St. Ignatius)
- ☐ Fort Missoula
- ☐ Glacier County Library (Cut Bank)
- ☐ Gleim Buildings* (Missoula)
- ☐ Going-to-the-Sun Road National Historic Landmark (West Glacier)
- ☐ Heritage Museum (Libby)
- ☐ Kootenai Falls (Troy)
- ☐ Lake McDonald Lodge National Historic Landmark (West Glacier)
- ☐ Lincoln Community Hall*
- ☐ Logan Pass Visitor Center (Glacier National Park)
- ☐ McCart Lookout (Bitterroot National Forest)
- ☐ Milwaukee Railroad Depot (Missoula)
- ☐ Savenac Nursery (Haugan)
- ☐ St. Mary's Mission (Stevensville)
- ☐ St. Mary's Visitor Center (Glacier National Park)

- [ ] Travelers' Rest National Historic Landmark (Lolo)
- [ ] Troy Jail*
- [ ] University of Montana Main Hall (Missoula)
- [ ] Woodland Park (Kalispell)

MISSOURI RIVER COUNTRY

- [ ] Culbertson Armory*
- [ ] Daniels County Courthouse (Scobey)
- [ ] Fort Peck Dam
- [ ] First National Bank of Glasgow
- [ ] James E. Shanley Tribal Library (Fort Peck)
- [ ] Lewis and Clark Bridge (Wolf Point)

SOUTHEAST MONTANA

- [ ] Armour Cold Storage* (Billings)
- [ ] Bell Street Bridge (Glendive)
- [ ] Billings Mausoleum, Mountview Cemetery
- [ ] Chief Plenty Coups Home National Historic Landmark (Pryor)
- [ ] Dion Brothers Buildings (Glendive)
- [ ] Grandey School* (Terry)
- [ ] Greyhound Bus Depot (Billings)
- [ ] Holy Rosary Hospital* (Miles City)
- [ ] Little Bighorn Battlefield National Monument (Garryowen)
- [ ] Medicine Rocks State Park (Ekalaka)
- [ ] Miles City Waterworks
- [ ] Pictograph Cave National Historic Landmark (Billings)
- [ ] Pompeys Pillar National Historic Landmark (Billings vicinity)
- [ ] Rosebud County Courthouse (Forsyth)
- [ ] Rosebud Battlefield/Where the Girl Saved Her Brother National Historic Landmark (Busby)
- [ ] Slayton Mercantile* (Lavina)
- [ ] Yucca Theater (Hysham)
- [ ] Jersey Lilly Bar & Cafè (Ingomar)

SOUTHWEST MONTANA

- [ ] Anaconda Smoke Stack State Park
- [ ] Anselmo Mine* (Butte)
- [ ] Bannack National Historic Landmark
- [ ] Big Hole Battlefield (Wisdom)
- [ ] Canyon Creek Charcoal Kilns (Melrose)
- [ ] Carpenters' Union Hall* (Butte)
- [ ] Club Moderne (Anaconda)
- [ ] Deer Lodge Woman's League Chapter House*
- [ ] Elkhorn Fraternity Hall
- [ ] Grant-Kohrs Ranch National Historic Landmark (Deer Lodge)
- [ ] Lewis and Clark Caverns State Park (Whitehall vicinity)
- [ ] Madison County Fairgrounds (Twin Bridges)
- [ ] Mann Gulch (Helena National Forest)
- [ ] MacDonald Pass Airway Beacon
- [ ] Metals Bank Building (Butte)
- [ ] Montana Veterans and Pioneers Memorial Building (Helena)
- [ ] Montana State Capitol (Helena)
- [ ] Old Montana Prison (Deer Lodge)
- [ ] Oregon Shortline Railroad Depot (Dillon)
- [ ] St. Helena's Cathedral (Helena)
- [ ] Sayrs Building (Hyde Block) (Philipsburg)
- [ ] Temple Emanu-El (Helena)
- [ ] U.S. Assay Office* (Helena)
- [ ] Virginia City National Historic Landmark
- [ ] Wah Chong Tai/Mai Wah Noodle (Butte)
- [ ] Washoe Theater (Anaconda)
- [ ] William A. Clark Mansion (Butte)

YELLOWSTONE COUNTRY

- [ ] Atlas Block (Columbus)
- [ ] Bearcreek
- [ ] Big Timber Carnegie Library
- [ ] Hotel Bozeman*
- [ ] KPRK Radio* (Livingston)
- [ ] Melville Lutheran Church
- [ ] Northern Pacific Railroad Depot (Livingston)
- [ ] Red Lodge Brewery/Cannery*
- [ ] Romney Gymnasium (Bozeman)
- [ ] Teslow Grain Elevator* (Livingston)
- [ ] Three Forks of the Missouri National Historic Landmark (Willow Creek)
- [ ] Union Pacific Dining Hall (West Yellowstone)

RELEVANT NATIONAL REGISTER AND NATIONAL HISTORIC LANDMARK NOMINATION SOURCES

Authorized by the National Historic Preservation Act of 1966, the National Park Service's National Register of Historic Places—the official list of historic places in the United States deemed worthy of preservation—is part of a program to coordinate and support public and private efforts to identify, evaluate, and protect America's historic and archaeological resources.

In addition to the many helpful people listed on our Acknowledgments page, the authors of this book are indebted to the numerous historians and writers who documented, researched, and wrote about Montana's historic places in the process of listing them in the National Register of Historic Places. Their research and writing provided much of the information needed to write most of the essays in this book.

Links to many of these National Register nominations are available at Historic Montana (https://historicmt.org/), which offers curated tours as well as more information about individual sites and properties. Digitized versions of the nomination forms listed below can also be found on the National Park Service's digital archives: https://npgallery.nps.gov/nrhp.

Aaberg, Steve. First People's Buffalo Jump National Historic Landmark, 2015.

Abraham, Stephanie, Nate Boyd, Rod Boyer, Carl M. Davis, Dana Deininger, Greg Dorrington, Ashley Finnegan, Jenny Gambill, Allyson Hamill, Lee Holmes, Tanner Jackson, Martin Kuhl, Kurt Michels, Mac Mullette, Heather Paulson, Valerie Platts, Monty Schindler, Kim Tallent, Karolina Topolski, David L. Turner, Nate Warner, and Chrystal Warinski. Mann Gulch Wildfire Historic District (Lewis and Clark County), 1999.

Allison, Amorette. Holy Rosary Hospital (Miles City), 2007.

Amos, Christine, and Alan S. Newell. Going-to-the-Sun Road (Glacier National Park), 1983.

Ashley, Joseph M. Dave's Texaco (Chinook), 1993.

Axline, Jon. Havre Residential Historic District (Masonic Temple), 1989.

Axline, Jon. Helena Historic District (Boundary Increase) (U.S. Assay Office), 1993.

Axline, Jon. Milwaukee Road Railroad Substation #10 (Primrose Station, Missoula), 2014.

Axline, Jon, Ramie Bidegaray, George Budak, Carl Fourstar, Larry Mires, Greg Rauschendorfer, and Boone Whitmer. Wolf Point Bridge; Lewis and Clark Bridge, 1997.

Axline, Jon, and Joan L. Brownell. Atlas Block (Atlas Bar, Columbus), 2011.

Axline, Jon, and Joan L. Brownell. Smith Mine Historic District (Carbon County), 2009.

Axline, Jon, and Kate Hampton. MacDonald Pass Airway Beacon (Powell County), 2013.

Babcock, William A., Jr. Bell Street Bridge (Glendive), 1987.

Babcock, William A., Jr. Gleim Building (Missoula), 1989.

Babcock, William A., Jr. Gleim Building II (Missoula), 1994.

Babcock, William A., Jr. Historic Resources of Glendive (Dion Brothers Building, Glendive), 1987.

Baumler, Ellen. C. E. Conrad Memorial Cemetery (Kalispell), 2012.

Baumler, Ellen. C. E. St. Mary's Mission Historic District Boundary
Increase (Stevensville), 2010.

Baumler, Ellen. C. E. Temple Emanu-el (Helena), 2001.

Bearss, Edwin C. Chief Joseph Battleground of the Bear's Paw (Blaine County), 1988.

Begley, Susan, and Ethan Carr. Going-to-the-Sun Road (Glacier National Park), 1996.

Behan, Barbara, Ken Robison, and Ellen Sievert. Union Bethel African Methodist Episcopal Church (Great Falls), 2003.

Bik, Patricia, Matthew Cohen, and James R. McDonald. Graf Building (Bozeman), 1983–1987.

Bik, Patricia, David G. Conklin, Susan W. Curtis, Kingston Heath, and Frederic L. Quivik. Fort Connah Site (Lake County), 1981.

Bik, Patricia, and Genevieve Hostetter. Deer Lodge American Women's League Chapter House, 1982.

Bik, Patricia, and James R. McDonald. Fort Missoula Historic District, 1986.

Boughton, John, Peter Brown, and Kate Hampton. Helena Historic District (US Assay Office), 2013.

Boughton, John, Kate Hampton, Becki Miller, and Candi Zion. Fort Assinniboine (Boundary Increase/Additional Documentation) (Hill County), 2017.

Bradley, Besty H. Howard Lepper Memorial Hall (Petroleum County), 2020.

Brewster, Elizabeth, Linda Frey, James R. McDonal, Patrick McCleary, and John Westenburg. University of Montana Historic District (Main Hall/University Hall, Missoula), 1984/1991.

Brown, Christine, Kate Hampton, Jim Jenks, and Chere Jiusto. Alvin Young Barn and Cabin Historic District (Big Horn County), 2010.

Brown, Christine, and Chere Jiusto. Reed and Bowles Trading Post (Lewistown), 2010.

Brown, Johanna, and Chere Jiusto. Farmers and Merchants State Bank (Eureka), 1995.

Brownell, Joan L. Bones Brother Ranch (Rosebud County), 2003.

Brownell, Joan L. Kero Farmstead Historic District (Carbon County), 2007.

Brownell, Joan L. Red Lodge Brewing Company/Red Lodge Canning Company, 2007.

Brownell, Joan L. Sacred Heart Church: Owacegiya Sá'imna ba' ééí'biibíthiiníiin'ć (Harlem), 2019.

Bunyak, Dawn, Ann Hubber, and Christine Whitacre. Grant-Kohrs Ranch/Warren Ranch (Deer Lodge), 2001–2002.

Carter, Lorette. Shelby Town Hall, 2005.

Cederberg, Leon, Nellie Cederberg. Anna Scherlie Homestead Shack (Blaine County), 1998.

Chamberlain, Chelsea D. Montana State Training School Historic District (Old Administration Building, Boulder), 2014.

Conklin, David G. Fraternity Hall (Elkhorn), 1974.

Conklin, David G., and John DeHaas, Jr. Montana Territorial and State Prison (Deer Lodge), 1976.

Cook, Kathleen, and Lon Johnson. Riverside (Daly Mansion, Hamilton), 1987.

Corbyn, Ronald C. Pictograph Cave (24-Y1-1) (Yellowstone County), 1979.

Crain, Ellen C., Chere Jiusto, and Derek Strahn. Butte-Anaconda Historic District (Revised Document) (409 Alaska Street, Anaconda Smoke Stack, Anselmo Mine, Carpenter's Union Hall, Metals Bank Building, and Wah Chong Tai/Mai Wah Noodle Parlor), 2006.

Curtis, Susan W., John N. DeHaas Jr., and Frederic L. Quivik. The Castle (White Sulphur Springs), 1976.

DeHaas, John N., Jr. St. Mary's Mission Church and Pharmacy (Stevensville), 1969

DeHaas, John N., Jr. Washoe Theater (Anaconda), 1981.

DeHaas, John N., Jr., and William J. Ottem Jr. Grandey Elementary School (Terry), 1977.

DeHaas, John N., Jr., and Gregory H. Warner. St. Peter's Mission Church and Cemetery (Cascade County), 1983.

DeVitt, John M., and Samuel M. Thomas. Historic Resources of Billings Montana (Greyhound Bus Depot), 1977.

Doeden, Kathy. Miles City Water Works Building and Pumping Plant Park, 1979.

Eklund, Margaret. Grace Lutheran Church of Barber (Golden Valley County), 1980.

Fulbright, Zane L. Canyon Creek Charcoal Kilns (Beaverhead County), 2005.

Fulbright, Zane L. Lewistown Satellite Airfield Boundary Increase IV, 2017.

Fulbright, Zane L., and Benjamin Miller. Lewistown Satellite Airfield Historic District (Boundary Increase III), 2009.

Ganskop, Jeana. St. Wenceslaus Catholic Church (Fergus County), 2012.

Garfield, Mrs. Russell M., and Eldon Rice. Rosebud County Courthouse (Forsyth), 1984.

Guyaz, Norman, and John G. Lepley. Fort Benton Historic District (Power Mercantile Block), 1972.

Guyaz, Norman. Battle of the Rosebud (Big Horn County), 1972.

Hafer, W. Randall, Chere Jiusto, and Rolene Schliesman. Armor Cold Storage (Billings), 2003.

Hagener, Toni, and Gary Wilson. Fort Assinniboine (Hill County), 1989.

Hall, Daniel S., Susan L. Knudsen, and Allan J. Mathews. Travelers' Rest (Revised Documentation) (Lolo), 2004.

Hampton, Kate. Judith Landing Historic District (Boundary Increase) (Fergus County), 2013.

Hampton, Kate. Montana Veterans and Pioneers Memorial Building (Montana Historical Society, Helena), 2003.

Hampton, Kate, and Jeannie Boggess. Evaro School, 2000–2001.

Hampton, Kate, and Jerry L. Jacobson. First National Bank of Glasgow, 2002.

Hampton, Kate, and Lon Johnson. Lewistown Satellite Airfield Historic District (Boundary Increase), 1999, 2003.

Hampton, Kate, and Laura MacMillan. Carnegie Public Library (Big Timber), 2001–2002.

Hampton, Kate, and Wheelhouse Consulting. Troy Jail, 2006.

Harrison, Laura Soulliere. Lewis Glacier Hotel (Lake McDonald Lodge, Glacier National Park), 1985.

Hedron, Paul, Alfred W. Schulmeyer, and Susan A. Tenney. Big Hole National Battlefield (Beaverhead County), 1977, 1984.

Higgins, Blanche. Pompeys Pillar (Yellowstone County), 1976.

Hoskinson, Paige. Slayton Mercantile Co. (Lavina), 2000.

Howard, Elaine. Judith Landing Historic District (Fergus County), 1977.

Hufstetler, Mark, Ellen Sievert and Ken Sievert. Wiley, Clark & Greening Bank (Jersey Lilly, (Ingomar), 1994.

Jiusto, Chere. Lewis and Clark Caverns Historic District (Jefferson County), 2017.

Jiusto, Chere. Sleeping Buffalo Rock (Saco), 1996.

Jiusto, Chere. Helena Historic District (Amendment) (U.S. Assay Office), 1989.

Jiusto, Chere, and Tande C. William. Daniels County Courthouse (Scobey), 1995.

Jiusto, Chere, and The Teslow Group, LLC. Billy Miles & Bros. Grain Elevator (Teslow Grain Elevator, Livingston), 2019.

Johnson, Lon. Lewistown Satellite Airfield Historic District (Norden Bombsite), 1999.

Keim, Kelly, and Ken Sievert. Judith River Ranger Station (Judith Basin County), 1990–1991.

Kooistra-Manning, Ann. Billings Communal Mausoleum, 2019–2021.

Koop, Michael. Lincoln Community Hall, 1986.

Koop, Michael. Philipsburg Historic District (Sayrs Building), 1986.

Leavengood, David. Historic Resources of Livingston (KPRK-Radio, Northern Pacific Depot), 1979.

Light, Timothy, and Charles "CD" Schroeder. Savenac Nursery Historic District (Mineral County), 1998.

Loehr, Scott W., and Bruce Westerhoff. Custer Battlefield National Monument (Multiple Resource Nomination) (Little Bighorn Battlefield National Monument, Big Horn County), 1985.

Mattison, Ray H. Fort Benton, 1960.

Mattison, Ray H. Three Forks (Gallatin County), 1958.

Mattison, Ray H., and Blanche Higgins Schroer. Bannack Historic District (Beaverhead County), 1958/1975.

Mattison, Ray H., and Blanche Higgins Schroer. Charles M. Russell House and Studio (Great Falls), 1963, 1976.

Mattison, Ray H., and Blanche Higgins Schroer. Virginia City, Montana, 1958, 1976.

McCahon, Dennis H. Cathedral of St. Helena (Roman Catholic), 1980.

McDonald, James R., Kirk Michels, and Billie L. Nelson. Milwaukee Depot (Missoula), 1980/1982.

McKay, Kathy. Historic and Architectural Properties of Kalispell, Montana (511 4th Avenue East, Woodland Park), 1993.

Morrison, Kimberly Currie. Goosetown Historic District (Club Moderne, Anaconda), 1996.

Nunn, Jessie. Montana State Capitol Campus Historic District (Helena), 2015.

Nunn, Jessie. Montana State University Historic District (Romney Gymnasium, Bozeman), 2013.

Otto, Rebecca J. Fort Peck Dam, 1984.

Otto, Rebecca J. Fort Peck Townsite and Dam, 1984.

Porter, Pam. Kevin Depot, 1979.

Preston, Garry L. Madison County Fairgrounds (Twin Bridges), 1984.

Putz, Paul M. Gehring Ranch (Outhouse, Lewis and Clark County), 2017.

Reed, Brenda Lynn. Oregon Short Line Passenger Depot (Dillon), 1989.

Rennie, Patrick. Lewistown Satellite Airfield Historic District (Boundary Increase II), 2005.

Rick Mayfield Associates, Inc. West Yellowstone, MRA (Union Pacific Dining Lodge), 1981.

Sanford, Dena. Great Falls Railroad Historic District (Civic Center), 1992.

Sievert, Ellen, and Ken Sievert. Tenth Street Bridge (Great Falls), 1996.

Sievert, Ellen, and Candi Zion. Great Falls Central Business Historic District (Bus Depot and Garage), 2003–2004.

Simmons, R. Laurie, and Thomas H. Simmons. Chief Plenty Coups (Alek-Chea-Ahoosh) Home (Pryor), 1998.

Urbaniak, Timothy. Medicine Rocks State Park (Carter County), 2016.

Varnum, Vicki. McCart Fire Lookout (Ravalli County), 1996.

Westenburg, John. Montana State Capitol Building (Helena), 1980.

Wheaton, Rod L. Logan Pass Visitor Center (Glacier National Park), 2006.

Wheaton, Rod L. Saint Mary Visitor Center, Entrance Station, and Checking Stations (Glacier National Park), 2006.

Zottnick, Carol J. Yucca Theater (Hysham), 1993.

INDEX

Page numbers in *italics* refer to illustrations.